MORAL RESISTANCE AND
SPIRITUAL AUTHORITY

Terry + Phyllis,

To our study
+ action!

w/ des

Karen R. Perlman

MORAL RESISTANCE

AND

SPIRITUAL AUTHORITY

*Our Jewish Obligation
to Social Justice*

Edited by

RABBI SETH M. LIMMER, DHL
AND RABBI JONAH DOV PESNER

Foreword by Reverend Cornell William Brooks

Introduction by Rabbi David Saperstein

Central Conference of American Rabbis

Library of Congress Cataloging-in-Publication Data

Names: Limmer, Seth M., editor. | Pesner, Jonah Dov, editor.
Title: Moral resistance and spiritual authority : our Jewish obligation to
    social justice / edited by Rabbi Seth M. Limmer, DHL and Rabbi Jonah Dov
    Pesner ; foreword by Reverend Cornell William Brooks ; introduction by
    Rabbi David Saperstein.
Description: New York : Central Conference of American Rabbis, [2019] |
    Includes bibliographical references and index.
Identifiers: LCCN 2018047183 (print) | LCCN 2018047928 (ebook) | ISBN
    9780881233193 | ISBN 9780881233186 (pbk. : alk. paper)
Subjects: LCSH: Social justice--Religious aspects--Judaism. | Jewish ethics.
    | Reform Judaism.
Classification: LCC BM645.J8 (ebook) | LCC BM645.J8 M67 2019 (print) | DDC
    296.3/8--dc 3
LC record available at https://lccn.loc.gov/2018047183

CCAR Press, 355 Lexington Avenue, New York, NY 10017
(212) 972-3636
www.ccarpress.org
Printed in the U.S.A.

10 9 8 7 6 5 4 3 2 1

Contents

Acknowledgments

This book is of a moment and of a generation.

The moment was April 2017, when an unprecedented concentration of Reform Jewish justice leaders descended on Washington, DC, for the biennial Consultation on Conscience of the Religious Action Center. Among the seven hundred participants were over one hundred rabbis: these colleagues, committed to justice, felt summoned, in the face of overwhelming obstacles, to mount a resistance to language, policies, and practices of hate. For months, we had been mobilizing on our pulpits, in airports, and on the National Mall. We were determined to confront "the fierce urgency of now," in the words of Reverend Martin Luther King Jr., as we saw immigrants, refugees, Muslims, Jews, people of color, LGBTQ folk, women, and poor people threatened by an onslaught of injustice that represented an assault on our most cherished enduring Jewish values and American ideals. We were called by the Torah's repeated injunction to protect the widow, the orphan, and the stranger: the most vulnerable among us. We knew our generation was being tested, and we would need each other, our Reform Jewish movement, and a broad array of allies across lines of difference to repair the catastrophic breach. Being together, we realized we also needed new resources for such an unprecedented moment. Within months, we began taking our assignments and drafting the essays that comprise this book.

And our generation had already been preparing for this moment. A decade ago saw a touchstone when, in 2006, Rabbi Jonah Dov Pesner founded Just Congregations with the full support of Rabbi David Saperstein. In addition to its energy and commitment to community organizing, two key aspects of the work of Just Congregations are central to this generation of colleagues: a focus on training Hebrew Union College–Jewish Institute of Religion students, and a program to regularly convene members of the Central Conference of American Rabbis (CCAR). The "Rabbinic Gatherings" began to overlap with the rabbinic delegation to the Commission on Social Action of Reform Judaism, on which Rabbi Seth Limmer served. In 2010, when Seth became chair of the CCAR's Justice, Peace, and Civil Liberties Committee, the growing group of rabbis who were outspoken about their commitment to the work of social justice were more formally brought together. In what seemed like moments, but required years of planning, this group launched Rabbis Organizing Rabbis, created Reform CA under the leadership of Rabbi Stephanie Kolin, and celebrated the ultimate unification of our many efforts as Jonah became the new director of the Religious Action Center (RAC). Within months of that appointment, over two hundred Reform rabbis—nearly 10 percent of the entire CCAR—made their way on the road from Selma to DC to march on the NAACP's America's Journey for Justice. The lessons learned in trainings, gatherings, conference rooms, and the RAC basement translated to a beautiful statement of a new generation stepping up to carry the Torah of our Jewish commitment to *tikkun olam* forward in our time.

Our Jewish tradition reminds us we are rooted in the past even as we grow toward the future. We are indebted to countless teachers and mentors who are our forebears, most notably Rabbi Maurice E. Eisendrath, Rabbi David Saperstein, Al Vorspan, Arnie Graf, and Mike Gecan. Likewise we have served with, fought alongside, and learned from some incredible partners whose titles are *not* "Rabbi": Joy Friedman, Barb Weinstein, Lila Foldes, and Julie Weill, to name the few in it with us from the beginning.

It might be most appropriate to dedicate this book to the generation represented within its pages, this group who have spent the past decade focused on moving justice to the center of the American rabbinate, to make social justice again synonymous with Reform Judaism. Indeed these remarkable, courageous rabbis are our teachers and our friends. However, the articles and passion of the following pages already serve as a testament and a marker—Isaiah's *yad vashem*—to this incredible, ever-growing group of rabbis.

Instead, we dedicate this book to two women who have been to both of us lifelong friends, and who happen to be each of our wives, Dana Gershon and Molly Limmer. Every bit as passionate and even more articulate than are we, Molly and Dana have marched and strategized alongside us every step of the way. They are the loves of each of our lives, and it is not only due to our Jewish heritage that we continue to try and improve the world, but also to leave it a better place for our children: Juliet, Noa, Bobbie, and Acadia Pesner, and Rosey and Lily Limmer. May our six daughters inspire their own generation, and may they and their generation—in due time—rewrite the book on Judaism and social justice. And may they bring us all to that day when every human being can sit under their vine and fig tree and never be afraid.

Special thanks to Rabbi David Saperstein for his close reading of the manuscript, Nathan Bennett and Graham Roth at the RAC, and everyone at CCAR Press: Rabbi Hara Person, Ortal Bensky, Debbie Smilow, Sasha Smith, Carly Linden, Rabbi Beth Lieberman, Rabbi Dan Medwin, and (then) rabbinic interns Vanessa Harper, Rabbi Jesse Paiken, and Rabbi Andrue Kahn. Thanks also to copyeditor Debra Corman and to the Press Council, headed up by Rabbi Don Goor.

Foreword

Reverend Cornell William Brooks

Generations of Americans are familiar with a black-and-white photograph taken in a long-ago time, a sepia-toned picture of several American prophets: Rabbi Abraham Joshua Heschel and the Reverend Martin Luther King Jr. walking arm and arm, beside a Torah, on the blood-stained road from Selma to Montgomery, as well Rabbi Maurice Eisendrath. On that day shortly after Bloody Sunday, when marchers were beaten nearly to death, Heschel, as scholar and rabbi, joined Dr. King—representing not only Judaism's spiritual authority but its moral resistance at the height of the civil rights movement. Amid what may be described as a Twitter-age civil rights movement, there is yet today an anguishing hunger for both spiritual resistance and moral authority. This spiritual resistance and moral authority is suggested in multi-colored digital pictures of our time, multi-hued pixelated photographs of a multi-racial group people walking in a prophetic tradition—*today*.

As a fourth-generation African Methodist minister, raised in and around the birthplace of the American Reform Movement, Charleston, South Carolina, I witnessed the spiritual resistance and moral authority of the Reform Jewish community a mere two years ago. As the then-president and CEO of the NAACP, I called for a march from Selma, Alabama, to Washington, DC, to oppose widespread voter suppression and restore a Voting Rights Act, gutted by a constitutionally wrong-headed and morally wrong-hearted Supreme Court decision, *Shelby v. Holder*. Rabbis, their adult congregants, and even grade-schoolers and Jewish summer campers responded with a prophetic courage, moral exuberance, and organizational speed that was frankly stunning.

Even today, neither the magnitude nor moral profundity of that response can be fully measured. One out of every ten Reform rabbis in the United Stated marched on America's Journey for Justice, a historic 1,002-mile march from Selma to DC. Not only did these rabbis march from Selma to DC, but they carried the Torah, and not only did they carry the Torah, but so did Baptists and Methodists, the faithful and the cynical, gentiles and Jews, African Americans and Latinos, seniors and their grandbabies, and many for whom the Torah was both an unexplained mystery and as yet unread tome. Beautiful digital images of these marchers circulated online, around the globe, and into the hearts of those seeking justice in this time.

As a Christian carrying the Torah, I discovered then and understand far better now the need for the modest but morally ambitious book you, dear reader, now hold. I and hundreds of non-Jews discovered that when you march carrying the Torah, with your right or left hand and the sacred scroll laying upon the opposite shoulder, the Scripture literally crosses and lays upon your heart. As I walked with the Torah, I came to understand that to truly "pray with your feet,"[1] as Rabbi Heschel said of marching for justice, one must have God's word pressing upon your heart.

Even and especially with the words of Scripture pressing upon our hearts and our time, many Jews—and their kinfolk in a larger family of faith—are seeking to learn about the moral authority that inspires and informs as well as critiques and holds accountable our moral resistance to the injustices of *our* time. Congregational leaders, rabbinate and lay, are yet asking how we can be better agents of social change. As Reform youth are recommitting to social justice, in ways that truly inspire and yet challenge—through NFTY's Gun Violence and Racial Justice campaigns—they too are asking for guidance. There is an urgent need to hear the Reform Jewish voice on the *social* injustices of and the prophetic call in our generation. These are the voices that reverberate through the pages and pixels of this book, that speak to this anguishing hour of our democracy.

In communities uneasily straddling a chasm of distrust between the police and those most heavily policed, protesters have shouted, tweeted, and declared, "Black lives matter." This anthem cry of a Twitter-age civil rights movement reflects the empirical and experiential reality that black men are twenty-one times more likely to die at the hands of the police than are their white brethren. And yet the moral declaration "Black lives matter," disguised as a hashtag, echoes a moral legacy far older than the current age of mass incarceration or the era of the new Jim Crow as described by Michelle Alexander.

Judaism asserted for the first time in human history the likeness of every human being to God and that it is this very bodily likeness to God that gives human beings innate worth—so much so that in the moral vocabulary of Rabbinic sources "dignity of God" and "human dignity" are used interchangeably.[2] Exodus makes clear that humanity is both unable to and proscribed from reducing God to a person-made image. We as human beings are divinely crafted mirrors of the handi-work of our Creator and as such are endowed with an innate value of that reflected image—in all the refracted and racially diverse beauty.

To assert that black lives matter—or trans lives, immigrant lives, Muslim lives, Jewish lives, amid rising hate crimes—means that we believe every human being has inherent value through the *imago dei* as a matter of theology, ethics, policy, and moral practice.

The Enlightenment produced two modern moral pillars of the West: every person deserves both moral consideration and equal con-sideration without regard to economic condition, color, or creed.[3] These Enlightenment ideals animate the Declaration of Independence and the Constitution—and yet they ring hollow for so many who see so many devalued under law and in spirit. The radicality of the *imago dei* and so much more must be reinterpreted for our time. We need the voices of the Reform tradition reverberating from these pages into the pulpits and well beyond to speak to the radical implications of the *imago dei* for the pseudo moral equivalence attributed to neo-Nazis shouting, "The Jews will not replace us," and counter-protesters in Charlottesville; the racist post-Reconstruction reincarnation of voter suppression that disempowers black and brown voters as well as young voters; policing that reduces black bodies to objects of suspicion rather than subjects of protection; the demonization of immigrants exorcised of their humanity, leaving them as empty vessels for xenophobic anger; and a rising hate-crime rate exacerbated by divisiveness online as well as in the neighborhoods in which we live.

More than anything, Jews (and this gentile with so many others) yet hunger for hope—a hope that may be found among the pages of this book. While hope may lack an empirical basis, it surely has a moral foundation in the Torah and its timeless teachings as they are interpreted for this generation in this moment by these writers. It is a hope greater than dry poll-tested probabilities of the prospects for uninspired reform. It is a hope that gives us an often tested determination that compels us to co-labor with God for a "justice that rolls down like waters and righteousness like a mighty stream" (Amos 5:24). It is a hope that inspires us to "dream dreams" and "see visions" (Joel 3:1) as well as to "write the vision . . . plain" (Habakkuk 2:2). It is a hope that compels us to pray—and to plan, strategize, study, mentor, teach, and partner as well as learn.

Rabbi Heschel and Reverend King were compelled by spiritual authority and practiced moral resistance in their journey together. This book offers insight into the spiritual authority and moral resistance for the journeys ahead in our time. With so many of my Reform brethren, I once had the sacred task of carrying the Torah on a journey. For the journeys ahead, I will carry this little book as well.

NOTES

1. Susannah Heschel, "Following in My Father's Footsteps: Selma 40 Years Later," *Vox*, April 4, 2005, http:// www.dartmouth.edu/~vox/0405/0404/heschel .html.

2. Y. Michael Barilan, "From Imago Dei in the Jewish-Christian Traditions to Human Dignity in Contemporary Jewish Law," *Kennedy Institute of Ethics Journal* 19, no. 3 (2009): 233, doi:10.1353/ken.0.0291.

3. Ibid., 231.

Introduction

Rabbi David Saperstein

In the ebb and flow of history, there come moments when we arrive at a crossroads. The future of generations to come will be shaped by the path we choose to follow. Sometimes the implications of the choices to be made are obvious; for others, only in hindsight do we see the implications of those diverging roads with stunning clarity.

In so many ways, we sense today that we are at such a crossroads.

The United States[1] is at a crossroads facing the most fundamental decisions about the role of government in securing the economic and social well-being of its people,[2] in rebuffing those forces that threaten our religious tolerance, racial comity, and our most fundamental commitment to equality without regard to religion, race, national origin, disability, gender, sexual orientation, or gender identity.[3] As opposed to the open and welcoming spirit for immigrants that has marked some eras of American history, and which has meant so much to the rescue, safety, and flourishing of millions of Jews, we seem to be diverging onto a path leading back toward our most xenophobic eras. As of this writing, President Obama's projected refugee target of 110,000 people for 2018 has been cut to 45,000 by the Trump administration, with announced plans to drop the number to 25,000 or fewer refugees permitted entry in 2019—all this in the face of the largest numbers of global refugees and displaced peoples in recorded history.[4] We are facing the prospect of such severe disparities between the rich and the poor, arguably inherent in the capitalist system, that even the most developed economics and democratic governments will be unable to achieve an equitable society. We have not deviated from the path of rampant gun violence that so devastates our schools, increases the number of completed suicides, and brings deadly violence into every corner of American life—our businesses, houses of worship, playgrounds, and homes.[5] We are witnessing the reshaping of our court system with the appointment and confirmation of younger, more conservative judges who seem willing to undo the Warner and Burger Courts' expansion of civil rights, civil liberties, and reproductive rights, as well as the strong separation of church and state that together have given Jews more rights, more freedoms, and more opportunities than we have ever known in our people's history.[6]

The world is at a crossroads in navigating the clash of civilizations, confronting the pervasive threat of terrorism, and resolving, in the face of global poverty and global climate change, whether we are committed to making reasonable sacrifices to ensure that future generations will enjoy the fruits of God's creation.[7] Will we go down a path toward nuclear war or away from it? Over two billion people in this world live in abject poverty, making less than $3.10 per day.[8] With over sixty-seven million displaced people—more than at the end of World War II—we face a migrant crisis across the globe, which threatens world stability and puts many millions at risk. Ethnic and religious minorities find themselves particularly at risk of genocide, ethnic cleansing, starvation, and disease and of becoming victims of human traffickers or of drowning in attempts to find a friendly shore. America is withdrawing from its historic leadership of multilateral institutions originally created to implement the lessons learned from World War II, leaving a vacuum that, as we write this book, is increasingly being filled by China, Russia, and the destabilizing forces of non-state actors and authoritarian regimes. The growth of democracy that spread so rapidly and encouragingly in the aftermath of World War II is now falling victim to escalating numbers of authoritarian rulers who are cracking down on civil society, stifling human rights, dismantling the rule of law, and eroding the most basic structures of democratic rule in their nations.

On all these issues and so many more, decisions must be made.

So, what is the right image to bear in mind as you read this book: that of the normal ebb and flow of social justice, in which the midpoint moves, as in Dr. King's long arc of history, toward justice; or of an actual crossroads in which we are veering ever further from the path of social justice gains of the past century? I suggest the correct image is yet to be determined by the choices America makes in these coming years and what role the Jewish community can and will play in shaping those choices.

I imagine that every generation has believed that the problems they faced were more dangerous, more perilous, more urgent than those of any generation before them. The only difference between theirs and ours is that they were wrong and we are right. The state of our technologies makes this an extraordinary moment in history, in which the consequences of bad decisions are more dangerous and perilous than humanity has ever known.

Compounding the urgent choices, discussed so well by my distinguished colleagues in this book, is the recognition—perhaps the fear—that we may be living in, and producing this book, at the first moment in all of human history in which we can no longer afford to make the mistakes we have made since time immemorial—and still learn from them.

We have always known the ravages of warfare and the moral challenges of deciding when the use of force may be justified, but never have we faced military technologies that if misused, could destroy the world as we know it.

We have always faced the threat of pollution to our water and air and the concomitant responsibility to protect the creation God has entrusted to our stewardship and care, but not when matched with the prospects of climate change, ravaged rainforests, rising sea levels, escalating eradication of whole species of life, and overpopulation—which together threaten to irrevocably alter the climate of the entire earth.

We have always experienced intrusions into our privacy, repression of our free speech, and persecution of our religious lives, but not when matched with the technology that can make Orwell's nightmare of 1984 the reality of the world.

We have always lived with the reality of economic injustice—some of the Bible's most common laws deal with protecting the poor, the stranger, the vulnerable—but never when globalization and technological disruptions to almost every sector of the economy portend moral tragedy and societal destabilization on a global scale.

We have always had the challenge of applying new technologies in an ethical and moral manner, but not when matched with genetic engineering and artificial intelligence that allow us to create entire new forms of life and alter human life itself.

In the next few years, we may indeed decide the path that humanity will follow in addressing these momentous issues and so many more.

Will we use our wisdom, wealth, and technology:

To help nations resolve their differences peacefully, or to destroy the world in a nuclear holocaust?

To clean up the damage to our environment and protect it for generations yet unborn, or to despoil and devastatingly contaminate it?

To enhance those freedoms so essential to democracy and to allowing people to find spiritual fulfillment, or to degrade and diminish them?

To share God's wealth equitably and fairly with all God's children, or to deny justice to the billions living in severe poverty and to ignore the warning of the Talmud two thousand years ago that the sword enters the world because of justice delayed and justice denied?

To use genetic engineering to cure birth defects, or to create Hitler's master race?

In the lifetimes of many of our readers, we have smashed the atom, cracked the genetic code, pierced the veil of outer space, and placed the corpus of human knowledge at the fingertips of billions. And in a world in which you *can* do anything, what you should do—the moral question—is the fundamental challenge facing humanity. And on that question, the religious communities of the world, including the Jewish community, have urgent, profound, and indispensable wisdom to offer.

It is in such a spirit that this book is compiled, a collection of policy prescriptions, prophetic warnings, moral insights, strategic and tactical guidance drawn from the wisdom of Jewish text and Jewish law, the lessons gleaned from the history of the Jewish people, and the hands-on experiences of the authors—an array of distinguished scholars, influential Reform Jewish leaders, and some of the outstanding practitioners of social justice work in contemporary Jewish life.

As we read these chapters drawn from our Jewish law, moral values, and history, we must keep in mind that the tradition does *not* suggest that the halachic (legal) answer to how a Jewish society should resolve social issues under Jewish law should be binding upon a non-Jewish society.[9] The binding character of Jewish law derives from the covenant at Mount Sinai, a contract between God and the Jewish people. The covenant at Sinai is binding only upon Jews. Non-Jews who have not chosen to enter into the covenant are free of these obligations. This understanding is shared by Jews from all streams of Jewish life.[10]

While halachah is not binding on a non-Jewish society, the moral model of how rabbis applied God's law and the fundamental moral values of the tradition to the political, economic, and social challenges of their society may offer invaluable insights that will speak across the centuries to the decisions Americans must make today. Many of the essays in this book draw precisely from the Jewish halachic tradition in such a manner.

At the same time, there are sources of our tradition that do convey universal principles; that is, they apply to all nations and all people, Jews and non-Jews alike, for all time: the extralegal principles, assumptions, and values underlying the halachic system; the Noachide covenant between God and all of humanity; the universal message of the prophets; our history; the aggadic interpretations of our texts; and the moral writings of our rabbis and philosophers.

Three of these I will highlight.

First, the Noachide covenant, as understood in the Rabbinic tradition, is considered binding on all humankind, asserting the proposition that there are certain fundamental moral laws that are basic to any civilized society. The seven Noachide Laws include prohibitions against murder, robbery, blasphemy, idolatry, sexual crimes, and the eating of living flesh, as well as the requirement that every community establish courts of justice (Babylonian Talmud, *Sanhedrin* 56a–60b; *Tosefta, Avodah Zarah* 8:4–8; *Mishneh Torah, Hilchot M'lachim* 8:10–10:12).[11]

Second, from the prophets comes a universal vision: Jonah's lesson of God's concern for the morality of all nations and the well-being of all peoples, and the prophecies of Isaiah, Jeremiah, Amos, and Micah. "Thus God will judge among the nations and arbitrate for the many peoples" (Isaiah 2:4). On this foundation of a universalist ethic and vision of the world, and of God's dominion over all, emerges the biblical and postbiblical ethic of peace and justice for all the nations of the world.

Third, the lessons of our history are a key aspect of the Jewish tradition, capable of illuminating our own challenges today. We who have been among the quintessential victims of group prejudice, discrimination, and ethnic cleansing know all too well the costs of good people standing idly by as the vulnerable and weak are victimized. We have much to offer the world regarding the need for justice and equality for others today. The lessons of our past, from the Exodus through the Holocaust, continue to warn and to inspire and shape political dynamics in the world today. Consider just a few obvious examples: the influence of the Exodus story and use of Exodus imagery in the U.S.

civil rights movement and the South African anti-apartheid movement; the use of the biblical charge to love and respect the stranger in the contemporary American and European controversies over immigration policy; and the use of the "never again" mandate derived from the Holocaust in confronting ethnic cleansing and genocidal activity from the crises of Darfur in the 2000s, the Yezidis, Christians, and Shia Muslims in Iraq and Syria over the past few years, and the desperate plight of the Rohingya today.

Underlying these sources are a number of core values, among them:

1. The infinite value of every human being, rooted in the belief that we are all created in the divine image; that all of us have the spark of the Divine within.[12]
2. The fundamental equality of all people (connected with the concept of the value and dignity of all humanity).[13]
3. The rule of law to which all citizens and even the highest human ruler are held accountable.[14]
4. The requirement that every moral society should create courts of justice.
5. The protection of the environment, God's creation, affirmed by the assertion that *l'Adonai haaretz um'loah*, "the earth is the Eternal's and the fullness thereof" (Psalm 24:1).[15]
6. Distributive justice, with care for the poor, the orphan and widow, the hungry, the elderly and the ill, understood by many authorities as a moral obligation for all societies.[16]
7. Freedom of choice, perhaps Judaism's most significant contribution to Western thought.[17]

These assumptions and principles are eternal. Jews who would live up to the aspirations expressed in the Jewish tradition will insist that all human actions and societal/government policies be measured by these principles. Many of them, in fact, have been absorbed into the mainstream of Western civilization. Through their acceptance, the Jewish people has altered the way the human race looks at itself and its world.[18]

So too, today, these universal values, as well as the halachic answers the Rabbis gave to moral challenges analogous to our own, can offer powerful moral guidance to our nation. This book compellingly lifts up such insights to help us navigate today's challenges.

As daunting as the challenges this book addresses are, we live at a time of hope of which our ancestors, our prophets, and our sages throughout the ages could only have dreamed. We may indeed face perilous and unprecedented problems, but paradoxically, we may well be the first generation of Jews living in a world capable of creating the kind of just, peaceful, and compassionate society our history and our values charge us to build.

For we are the first generation that can produce enough food to feed every human being on earth. A failure to do so now is a failure of moral vision and political will.

We are the first generation that can conquer malaria and an array of diseases that have plagued humanity from time immemorial. The failure to do so is a failure of moral vision and political will.

We are the first generation that can educate every child on earth, lift every person out of poverty, undo damage to our environment, and spread freedom across the globe. For all of these, our failure to do so is a failure of moral vision and political will.

We know what we must do to succeed: enhance the spiritual fulfillment that can transform people for the better, empower individuals and communities to organize to meet their own needs,[19] and act assertively on our own and in coalition with like-minded communities to change government policies to embody our vision of justice. Any one of these without the others will lead to failure.

On all these issues, what I have learned so clearly in my forty-five years of religious and moral advocacy to government and society is that someone *will* decide. Our only choice is whether we will be the audience, watching others make those decisions, or if we will be the authors of those decisions. And if we remain silent, in the vacuum of our silence will come voices that do not share our values, our dreams, our aspirations.

As Dr. King said in his remarkable Riverside Church speech on Vietnam:

> We are now faced with the fact, my friends, that tomorrow is today. We are confronted with the fierce urgency of now. . . . Over the bleached bones and jumbled residues of numerous civilizations are written the pathetic words, "Too late."

For the past two years, this call of "the urgency of now" has been the leitmotif for the Reform Movement and its Religious Action Center, under the gifted aegis of the RAC's director Rabbi Jonah Dov Pesner, working closely with Rabbi Seth M. Limmer during his tenure as a visionary chair of the CCAR Justice and Peace Committee. It is fitting that they serve as editors of this timely volume, for it is this very sense of urgency that animates this endeavor.

For God's sake and for the sake of our children, we must not be too late.

The twenty-first century offers vivid dangers and boundless opportunities for those who are *rodfei tzedek* and *rodfei shalom* (pursuers of justice and peace). Our duty is not merely to await the future patiently or to endure it stoically or even to welcome it actively. Our duty is to forcefully and wisely advocate for a more just, compassionate, and peaceful world with renewed vigor, to shape the future we will give to our children. Our task—our privilege—is to seize that future and to shape it according to the best traditions of the past, including those keenest insights we ourselves have added. That is our ethical will, our immortality. There can be no guarantees in such an explosive and volatile world, but there are some truths we do know. We know that Judaism—the religious civilization of the Jew—provides the most powerful answer to the mystery of Jewish survival—the answer to why we Jews survive to be a light to the nations, a holy people, God's partners in making real the world of justice and peace for all humankind. The faith of the Jew—God, Torah, Israel—has preserved a people, a God-intoxicated people, whose moral vision has graced the world—a people that has sought relentlessly to keep humanity human.

Long ago, we stood at the foot of Sinai. From our encounter with the Divine, we brought forth a message of ethical monotheism, of justice and hope—transforming all of human history. From that time on, the need for such a transforming vision has never been more urgent than it is now. At this vital crossroads for America, the world, and the Jewish people, we must acknowledge that it is a sin—not less—to do nothing when moral decisions must be made. Our task is to heal this battered and weary world. This volume is the manifestation of that mandate.

NOTES

1. The Union for Reform Judaism (URJ) and the Central Conference of American Rabbis (CCAR) are bodies that include synagogues and rabbis from both the United States and Canada. Canada, too, faces choices in responding to the global crises described in this book, and the Jewish community there has an important moral voice to contribute in the choices Canada will make. This book, does however, focus primarily on U.S. policy choices. The moral insights the authors of this book draw from Jewish text and tradition, as well as much of the policy analysis, are applicable to both countries and both Jewish communities.

2. See Sperling, Grant, Feldman, Miller, and Kaufman and Stern in this volume.

3. See Brooks, Landsberg, Langowitz, Timoner, Zamore, and Haber in this volume.

4. See Panken, Linder, and Chasen in this volume.

5. See Yoffie in this volume.

6. See Langowitz and Maderer in this volume.

7. See Greengrass and Messinger and Jacobs in this volume.

8. It is worth noting that this number—both in absolute and percentage terms—has declined dramatically. In percentage terms, the number in extreme poverty (those living on less than $1.90 a day) declined from 42 percent of the world population in 1981 to 9.1 percent in 2016 (see "The World Has Made Great Progress in Eradicating Extreme Poverty," *Economist*, March 30, 2017, https://www.economist.com/international/2017/03/30/the-world-has-made-great-progress-in-eradicating-extreme-poverty).

9. For fuller expositions of these issues, see David Saperstein, "The Use and Abuse of Jewish Tradition in Political Debate," *CCAR Journal*, (Spring 2008); 13–33; and David Saperstein, "Economic Justice and the Jewish Community," *CCAR Yearbook* 96 (1986): 667–76, from which pieces of this article were drawn.

10. For an analysis of how different American Jewish streams use halachah and the tradition in similar ways in their public policy pronouncements, see Saperstein, "The Use and Abuse of Jewish Tradition in Political Debate."

11. To what extent this conveys the existence of a broader "natural law" tradition in Jewish thought is debatable. Robert Gordis finds Jewish natural law in the ethics of Job and the Noachide Laws; Leo Strauss in Yehudah Halevi's writings and in the law of reason. Medievalists like Bachya ibn Pakuda and Saadyah Gaon articulate a natural law view linked to the Noachide Laws and the law of reason (see Saadyah Gaon, *Book of Beliefs and Opinions*, treatise 2, chap. 11). All argue that Judaism embodies a system of ethics applicable to all peoples and all nations (see Robert Gordis, *The Root and the Branch: Judaism and the Free Society* [Chicago: University of Chicago Press, 1970]). For a more in-depth examination on natural law issues in Judaism and the application of the Noachide Laws to non-Jewish societies and the problems that arise with idolatrous societies, see David Novak, *Natural Law in Judaism* (Cambridge: Cambridge University Press, 1998); and David Novak, *The Image of the Non-Jew in Judaism: An Historical and Constructive Study of the Noahide Laws* (New York: Edwin Mellen Press, 1983).

12. See Conover in this volume.

13. These are rooted in the midrashic stories that ask: Why we were all descended from one couple in the stories of the Bible? Why was Adam made from the dust of the four corners of the earth? (Rashi, Genesis 2:7). So none of us can claim that the merit of our ancestors was greater than anyone else's (*Mishnah Sanhedrin* 4:5). We are all equal before God; we are all truly brothers and sisters. "Have we not all one parent?" asks Malachi. "Has not one God created us?" (Malachi 2:10). Or as the midrash observes elsewhere: "I call heaven and earth to witness that whether one be gentile or Jew, man or woman, slave or free man, the divine spirit rests on each in accordance with his deeds" (*Yalkut Shimoni*, Judges, sec. 42). As the thirteenth-century French halachic scholar Menachem Meiri noted, "Those among the heathens of our ancient days who observe the seven Noachide precepts . . . enjoy the same rights as Jews" (Bezalel Ashkenazi, *Shitah Mekubetzet* [1761], 28A).

14. When Nathan the prophet confronts David over the incident with Bathsheba and says, "That man is you!" (II Samuel 12:7), and when Elijah confronts Ahab over Naboth's vineyard (I Kings 21), the principle of the Rule of Law over nations and kings is set forth unmistakably. And when Jonah brings God's message of righteousness to Nineveh, even the king of Nineveh feels bound by God's call (Jonah 3:6).

15. God's hegemony of creation and humanity's obligation to be *shomrei adamah* are set. One of the first commands of the Bible, long predating the Sinai covenant with the Jewish people, is the command to Adam, as the progenitor of all humanity, asserting our obligation "to work it and keep it" (Genesis 2:15). Noah too is a progenitor of humankind, and God's command to him to preserve the varied species of life is itself reflective of God's universal covenant, one made with all humanity and "with every living being with you" (Genesis 9:10, 9:12, 9:15).

16. In contrast to charity (from the Latin *caritas*, "love") or philanthropy (from the Greek *philo*, "love," and *anthropos*, "man"), *tzedakah* is doing what is required of us because it is just and it is right. We have a responsibility for the poor, the weak, the vulnerable whether we love them or not. This determines not only the obligations of individuals, but the obligations (and therefore the institutions) of societies as well.

These rules were binding upon Jews; but the moral requirement of providing for the poor is a universal norm. Abravanel, picking up on the theme that we are the trustees of God's creation entrusted to us, argues that we are like brokers handling the money of the king in accordance with the owner's instructions (Abravanel's commentary on Deuteronomy 15:8). Relegating people to their own resources without help (the impact of which would most affect the poor) was, according to Mishnah, the sin of Sodom (*Mishnah Avot* 5:10). In a debate in the Gemara on the responsibilities of non-Jews (Noachides), we read that *tzedakah* (i.e., the obligation to help the vulnerable) applies to the Noachide as well as the Jews (Babylonian Talmud, *Sanhedrin* 57b).

17. Jewish thought embraced none of the limitations of the Greek fates or Calvinist predestination, but rather, "I have put before you life and death, blessing and curse. Choose life—if you and your offspring would live" (Deuteronomy 30:19). As Maimonides wrote, "Free will is granted to every man. . . . The human species has become unique in the world in that it can know of itself . . . what is good and what is evil, and in that it can do whatever it wishes . . . so did the Creator desire that a man should be possessed of free will. . . . For this reason is a man judged according to his own actions" (*Mishneh Torah, T'shuvah* 5:1–4).

18. Quite obviously, there are other, non-Jewish sources for the values relating to human rights described below. As Milton Konvitz has noted in his book *Judaism and the American Idea* (Ithaca, NY: Cornell University Press, 1978, p. 38):

> But other streams of thought have also made contributions to the development of the theory of human rights: the teachings of the Stoic philosophers regarding the inviolability of human dignity; the natural law philosophy that has had a continuous life from the time of the late Roman Empire, through Thomas Aquinas and Richard Hooker, to the present time; the teachings of the Roman lawyers concerning a common law of nations and peoples, the *jus gentium*; the international law principles of Hugo Grocius and Samuel von Pufendorf; the writings of the French Enlightenment; the emphasis on the right of the individual conscience associated with the Protestant and Puritan Reformations; the stress on the inherent dignity of man that can be found in the great Renaissance writers like Erasmus and Pico della Mirandola.

19. See Kolin, Perolman, Asch, Stanton, Kleinbaum, and Namath in this volume.

· Part One ·

Spiritual Authority

JUDAISM AND THE POLITICAL WORLD

Rabbi Seth M. Limmer, DHL

"Rabbi, why does Judaism care so much about politics?"

It's a very good question. A question I've been asked countless times. And, as I've learned through the years, in order to address it fully we need to talk first about politics and then about Judaism.

"Politics" is famously the title of the Aristotle's treatise concerning *politica*, literally, "the matters concerning the city." Aristotle taught that humanity "is a political animal," meaning that we by nature form relationships, connections, and alliances with our neighbors. To be political, according to Aristotle, who essentially coined the term, is to be *social*; that is, to be engaged with the human beings who form one's surrounding society. Our need to connect, Aristotle posits, is not exclusively emotional, but also moral:

> Why man is a political animal in a greater measure than any bee or any gregarious animal is clear. For nature, as we declare, does nothing without purpose; and man alone of the animals possesses speech. The mere voice, it is true, can indicate pain and pleasure, and therefore is possessed by the other animals as well, but speech is designed to indicate the advantageous and the harmful, and therefore also the right and the wrong; for it is the special property of man in distinction from the other animals that he alone has perception of good and bad and right and wrong and the other

moral qualities, and it is partnership in these things that makes a household and a city-state.[1]

Our sense of right and wrong leads us to connect with human beings and to form partnerships for moral ends: in a household, a city, a nation, or—in modern times—a state. We are social beings who understand ourselves as interwoven with others, as part of society. Politics is the path, the art, or at least the term for the art, of how we share our moral sensibilities with our neighbors, express our understanding of what is right, and participate in the process of shaping our society. Once we understand politics in this fashion, our original inquiry is better posited in the converse: "Rabbi, how could anyone think that Judaism does *not* care about the world in which we live?" After all, the preponderance of our rituals and ethics serve to connect us constructively to the human beings who surround us; most of our commandments instruct us on how to structure society. Through this essay, as we encounter texts from Torah through Talmud, we will see the intricate connections linking Judaism and the political world.

The commandments of our Torah direct us to construct a community and instruct us on how to live with our neighbors (including neighboring nations). The Torah sees Jews as a political entity named *B'nei Yisrael*, "the Children of Israel": originally twelve sons, then a kinship circle, next a system of interconnected tribes, and ultimately a sovereign nation. How this political group relates to others becomes a theme from the moment Israel escapes Egypt and is commanded to be a nation that ministers, as a priest would to their congregation, to other nations: "You [all] shall be to Me a kingdom of priests and a holy nation" (Exodus 19:6).

This chapter of Exodus explicitly acknowledges that we are one people among the many peoples of the world. The job of the Jewish people, we learn moments after our own liberation, is to help other nations develop and fulfill their own holy potential. The priests of Leviticus have many tasks: they mediate individuals' attempts to draw near to God; maintain sacred objects, rituals, and texts; and see to the purity of each person (as well as to the purity of the people as a whole). Extending this analogy of the priests' role in Israel and Israel's role in the world, the biblical charge to the Children of Israel as a nation of priests is clearly political: we were called to aid other nations' attempts to be holy, maintain an international standard of the sacred, and try to see to the purity of everyone in wider society.

This metaphorical understanding of the international commitment of the Jewish people to play a political role in the wider world appears early on in the legal sections of the Torah. The specific instructions regarding how we are to structure and maintain society, however, appear throughout the entire Torah. Perhaps our most ancient legal collection can be found in Exodus, in a portion known simply as *Mishpatim*, "Laws." As we will see in a few paradigmatic examples, the laws of *Mishpatim* clearly govern societal relations. First, Torah teaches that we do not exist in a vacuum, but have responsibilities to our neighbors: "When a person opens a pit, or digs a pit and does not cover it, and an ox or an ass falls into it, the one responsible for the pit must make restitution—paying the price to the owner, but keeping the dead animal" (Exodus 21:33–34). Further governing our relationships with those who surround us are the commandments detailing our financial interactions: "If you lend money to My people, to the poor among you, do not act toward them as a creditor; exact no interest from them. If you take your neighbor's garment in pledge, you must return it to him before the sun sets" (Exodus 22:24–25). From early on in Exodus, Jewish law is concerned with the very political subjects of private property and the financial system.

The laws of Leviticus, whose chapters comprise the particulars of the priestly system, likewise speak to the structure of society. The Holiness Code, known in Hebrew as *K'doshim*, is famed for teaching, "You shall love your neighbor as yourself" (Leviticus 19:18). The scope of this loyalty and affection for neighbors is extended even further, not just in terms of the objects of our love, but our overtly political connection to them as well:

> When strangers reside with you in your land, you shall not wrong
> them. The strangers who reside with you shall be to you as your
> citizens; you shall love each one as yourself, for you were strang-
> ers in the land of Egypt: I the Eternal am your God. (Leviticus
> 19:33–34)

Setting equal standards for stranger and citizen is clearly a concern
of state. This commitment to social equity perhaps received its fullest
treatment in Leviticus 25, which describes the Sabbatical and Jubilee
years. These seven- and fifty-year cycles are intended for the physical
restoration of the land as well as communal revitalization. All who had
fallen into poverty and were separated from their land are restored to
their family holdings, as liberty is proclaimed "throughout the land to
all its inhabitants" (Leviticus 25:10). The general mores of a political
structure that seeks fairness and equality are put into place through a
detailed series of rules affecting life and trade before, during, and after
these sabbatical cycles.

The Torah continues to focus on the political. The end of the Book
of Numbers speaks to political alliances among tribes, treaties in times
of conquest, as well as systems of acceptable testimony (chapters 32
and 30, respectively). The Book of Deuteronomy perhaps most fully
addresses notions of statehood, as its laws set standards for taxation,
kings, and wars (chapters 14, 17, and 20, respectively). Most importantly, Deuteronomy establishes a formal judiciary: "You shall appoint
magistrates and officials for your tribes, in all the settlements that
the Eternal your God is giving you, and they shall govern the people
with due justice" (Deuteronomy 16:18). Even if we read this verse's
last clause more literally as "you shall judge the people with just judgments," Deuteronomy is legislating governance—establishing a network of local magistrates in order to ensure the proper mediation of
disputes in society. Laws governing politics and polity are a major focus
of Mosaic legislation.

Our prophets are also keenly political; they lead by example in the
age-old occupation of speaking moral truth to power, as they hold
kings and queens accountable to considerations of right and wrong.

The early prophets Nathan and Elijah rely on rhetoric to chastise Kings David and Ahab for selfishly asserting their prerogative over their subjects, Uriah and Naboth, respectively.[2] Later prophets are far more straightforward with their speech and direct their invective at the powerful. In the time of King Hezekiah, the prophet Micah promised political punishment for those who perverted the engine of state:

> Hear this, you rulers of the House of Jacob, you chiefs of the
>   House of Israel,
> Who detest justice and make crooked all that is straight,
> Who build Zion with crime, Jerusalem with iniquity!
> Her rulers judge for gifts, her priests give rulings for a fee,
> And her prophets divine for pay; yet they rely upon the
>   Eternal, saying,
> "The Eternal is in our midst; no calamity shall overtake us."
> Assuredly, because of you, Zion shall be plowed as a field,
> Jerusalem shall become heaps of ruins, and the Temple
>   Mount a shrine in the woods.
>
> (Micah 3:9–12)

Micah sets the standard for prophetic politics. His engagement with the leaders of state was so well-known that nearly a century after his career, leaders of later days listened to the likes of Jeremiah because they revered the role of the prophet:

> The officials and all the people said to the priests and prophets, "This man does not deserve the death penalty, for he spoke to us in the name of the Eternal our God." And some of the elders of the land arose and said to the entire assemblage of the people, "Micah the Morashtite, who prophesied in the days of King Hezekiah of Judah, said to all the people of Judah: 'Thus said *Adonai* of Hosts: Zion shall be plowed as a field, Jerusalem shall become heaps of ruins, and the Temple Mount a shrine in the woods.' Did King Hezekiah of Judah, and all Judah, put him to death? Did he not rather fear the Eternal and implore the Eternal, so that the Eternal

renounced the punishment decreed against them? We are about to do great injury to ourselves!" (Jeremiah 26:16–19)

The prophets understand their role as political, and so do the leaders of their day. While it is the role of the official, the judge, or the king to administer society, Judaism has long understood social criticism—which finds its greatest fulfillment in prophecy—to be a necessary religious addition to the political system. This critique of state starts during the dawning of prophecy in Israel and continues through to the end and rebirth of Judea. Amos railed against an unfair system of taxation: "Assuredly, Because you impose a tax on the poor and exact from him a levy of grain, you have built houses of hewn stone, but you shall not live in them; you have planted delightful vineyards, but shall not drink their wine" (Amos 5:11). Isaiah is unafraid to challenge the elders and officers of God's people (Isaiah 3:14); likewise he decries those who pervert their power: "Those who write out evil writs and compose iniquitous documents, to subvert the cause of the poor, to rob of their rights of the needy of My people" (Isaiah 10:1–2). Habakkuk's protests even addressed foreign policy: "Because you plundered many nations, all surviving peoples shall plunder you—for crimes against men and wrongs against lands, against cities and all their inhabitants" (Habakkuk 2:8). The invective of Malachi, the last of the prophets, blends scorn for ritual misdeeds with outrage at societal injustice:

> I will step forward to contend against you, and I will act as a relentless accuser against those who have no fear of Me: who practice sorcery, who commit adultery, who swear falsely, who cheat laborers of their hire, and who subvert [the cause of] the widow, orphan, and stranger, said *Adonai* of Hosts. (Malachi 3:5)

Our Rabbis of antiquity pick up the political mantle passed down to them by the prophets. Much of our Mishnah and Talmuds speak to societal administration and define our obligations in the public domain. No single organizational "order" of Rabbinic teaching does this more than *N'zikin*, literally the corpus regarding how "damages" are accounted in civil law. A cursory overview of the subjects covered in *N'zikin* demonstrates how Jewish law summarily addresses the questions of legal structures that keep society together: damages and compensation; torts; property law; land ownership, entitlements and restrictions; criminal procedures (including capital punishment); collusive witnesses; cities of refuge; oaths and their consequences; legal disputations; interactions between Jews and their non-Jewish neighbors; and reckoning for error in the rulings of the highest court, the Sanhedrin. We will examine a few excerpts from the pages of *N'zikin* in order to see how committed Rabbinic law is to shaping the standards of society.

Part of politics is settling disputes among neighbors. When human beings live in organized communities like cities and states, they wind up with shared property, from the walls of apartment buildings to public streets. The collection of supplemental discussions that parallels the Mishnah, the *Tosefta*, teaches that neighbors who live in close proximity can exercise certain rights on behalf of the majority, whether those neighbors share a courtyard or public water systems:

> One who owns a house in another courtyard can be bound by the residents of that courtyard in making a door, a lock, and a key for the courtyard; regarding all other things, they cannot compel him. If he resides with them in the courtyard, they can bind him to everything. One who has a house in another town can be bound by the townspeople to participate with them in digging cisterns, hollows, and caverns and in fixing the ritual baths as well as the aqueduct. Regarding all other things, they cannot compel him. If he resides with them in the town, they can bind him to everything. (*Tosefta, Bava M'tzia* 11:17)

Part and parcel of living together with other people entails subjugating personal privileges for the common good. If the majority of the residents surrounding a courtyard want a door with a lock and a key, they can compel a minority of dissenters to pay their fair share *even against their will*; if the majority of the residents of a town want funds for public projects, they can tax their residents, and—in certain instances—even those who merely own property within city limits. Balancing private interests with public needs is the subject matter of this passage; setting limits on individual rights while expanding public powers is precisely the negotiations of politics. This legislation of *N'zikin* is all about governance. In Aristotelian terms, the laws establish partnerships in city-states to make moral judgments that are enforceable on all: politics is the subject.

One might purport that while the Rabbis obviously create a legal system for a coherent Jewish society, they are silent on how Jews should act as residents (or citizens) of foreign nations. While many Rabbinic texts would contradict such a position, nowhere is the commitment of the Rabbis to participating in the (even non-Jewish) political world seen more clearly than in this Talmudic teaching, attributed to first-generation amoraic sage Sh'muel: *Dina d'malchuta dina*, "The law of the kingdom is the law." This principle, cited in Sh'muel's name in numerous Talmudic pages, proposes that Jewish statutes can be superseded by the laws of secular society.[3] We encounter this dictum in addressing the issue of how dealing with non-Jews, whose standards of obtaining ownership differ from Jews, might affect Jewish practices surrounding property acquisition:

> Rav Y'hudah says that Sh'muel says: With regard to the property of a gentile that was sold to a Jew for money, it is ownerless like a desert until the purchaser performs an act of acquisition; anyone who takes possession of it in the interim has acquired it. What is the reason for this? The gentile relinquishes ownership of it from the moment when the money reaches his hand, while the Jew who purchased it does not acquire it until the deed reaches his hand. Therefore, in the period of time between the giving of the money and the receiving of the deed, the property is like a desert, and anyone who takes possession of it has acquired it.
>
> Abayei said to Rav Yoseif: Did Sh'muel actually say this? *But doesn't Sh'muel say that the law of the kingdom is the law,* that is, the law obligates Jews to observe the laws of the locale in which they reside, and the king said that land may not be acquired without a document? Therefore, taking possession should not be effective for acquisition. Rav Yoseif said to him: I do not know how to reconcile

this contradiction, but there was an incident in the village of Dura that was founded by shepherds, where there was a Jew who purchased land from a gentile by giving money, and in the interim another Jew came and plowed it a bit. The two Jews came before Rav Y'hudah for a ruling, and he established the property in the possession of the second individual. This accords with the ruling of Sh'muel that the property is ownerless until a Jew performs an act of acquisition. (Babylonian Talmud, *Bava Batra* 54b; emphasis added)[4]

The above passage offers multiple solutions to the problem of how to reconcile Jewish systems of acquisition with those of the non-Jewish sovereign nations in which Jews live. However, the very existence of the debate demonstrates that the Rabbis understood the intricate difficulties of Jewish engagement with the wider political world: we had to determine the extent to which we would willingly conform with society's rules and under what circumstances we would place ourselves outside the law. These negotiations over the risks and rewards of societal engagement show that simple solutions are scarcely found. However, the existence of the debate of *how* we engage with non-Jewish political powers clearly demonstrates that, for the Rabbis of antiquity, political engagement was certainly an option, and political estrangement was not the preferable path.

Beyond discussions of how to negotiate life under foreign rule, the Rabbis also teach that our obligations to our immediate neighbors should be expanded and applied to the wider world. An evaluation of our obligations to the widest social spheres might not be what we expect from a legal discussion of the Sages' disapproval of a cow walking about with a strap between its horns, which is a potential signal that the cow is doing some kind of work for its owner on Shabbat. In a stunning literary leap, Talmudic logic takes us from the case of a Sabbath-breaking cow and brings us to an understanding of individual responsibility for the entirety of human society. We will walk through a remarkable progression of three paragraphs and see how this connection from one cow to the whole world is forged:

The Mishnah relates that the cow of Rabbi Elazar ben Azaryah would go out on Shabbat with a strap between its horns, contrary to the will of the Sages. The Gemara asks: Did Rabbi Elazar ben Azaryah have only one cow? Didn't Rav say, and some say that Rav Y'hudah said that Rav said: Rabbi Elazar ben Azaryah would tithe from his herds 12,000 calves each and every year? There were 120,000 calves born in his herds annually. There is no way, then, to speak of the cow of Rabbi Elazar ben Azaryah. The Gemara answers: It was taught in the Tosefta: The cow was not his; rather, it was his neighbor's. And because he did not protest her conduct and tell her that doing so is prohibited the cow was called by his name to his discredit, as if it were his. (BT *Shabbat* 54b)

Our first teaching, specifically about Rabbi Elazar ben Azaryah and the cow, teaches that each of us is responsible for the behaviors of our neighbors. In keeping with the principle of Leviticus that we reprove our neighbors and thereby not incur sin on their behalf (Leviticus 19:17), Rabbi Elazar ben Azaryah is held responsible for the Sabbath violation of his neighbor, because he did not intervene and correct her conduct. Specifically, the Sages describe his sin: he did not *protest*. For failing to speak up when his neighbors violated the law in his presence, his lofty reputation was discredited. This is the first premise of the Talmudic logic that leads to a more global sense of responsibility:

It was related that Rav, and Rabbi Chanina, and Rabbi Yochanan, and Rav Chaviva taught the statement cited below. The Gemara comments: . . . In any event, they said: Anyone who had the capability effectively to protest the sinful conduct of the members of his household and did not protest, he himself is apprehended for the sins of the members of his household and punished. If he is in a position to protest the sinful conduct of the people of his town, and he fails to do so, he is apprehended for the sins of the people of his town. If he is in a position to protest the sinful conduct of the whole world, and he fails to do so, he is apprehended for the sins of the whole world. (BT *Shabbat* 54b)

From the injunction making us responsible to protest the actions of our near neighbors, the Talmud's editors expand the understanding of social responsibility ever wider. Rav, Rabbi Chanina, Rabbi Yochanan, and Rav Chaviva outline concentric circles of our political responsibility: each of us is responsible first for our household, next for our neighbors, then for our townsfolk, and ultimately for every person in the world. They teach that we are as responsible for strangers on the far side of our planet as we are for the livestock of the elderly people who live next door. This expansive principle is next illustrated by an important real-life example:

> Rav Pappa said: And the members of the household of the exilarch [the Babylonian Jewish community's political leader] were apprehended and punished for the sins of the whole world. Because their authority extends across the entire Jewish world, it is in their hands to ensure that nobody commit a transgression. As indicated by that which Rabbi Chanina said: What is the meaning of that which is written: *Adonai* will enter into judgment with the Elders of the people and its princes, saying [Isaiah 3:14]: *It is you who have eaten up the vineyard; the robbery of the poor is in your houses?* The question arises: If the princes sinned by committing robbery, what did the Elders, that is, the Sages of that generation, do that was considered a sin? Rather, say: God will enter into judgment with the Elders because they did not protest the sinful conduct of the princes. (BT *Shabbat* 54b–55a)

Here we see that the exilarch, leader of the Jewish community throughout the Persian Empire, was punished for the misdeeds of the many; furthermore, we see that Rabbi Chanina taught that the Sages themselves should be held to account for failing to protest the sins of the princes, namely the non-Jewish governors and rulers who established the law of the land. Failure to eradicate the sins of society is itself a sin. Speaking truth, whether it be to our neighbors or to people with political power, is our inheritance from the prophets who maintained a formidable position in the Rabbinic era as well. In sum, these three paragraphs are a vivid and powerful affirmation of the responsibility of Jewish leaders to engage in the political world.

From the Torah through the Talmud we see that Judaism has a consistent vision of how a family, a neighborhood, a city, and a nation should behave; Jewish tradition expects us to make that vision a reality. Our English word for this society-regulating activity, courtesy of the Greeks, is "politics." Why does Judaism care about politics? Because the Torah teaches us that holiness is meant to enter the world through our interactions with others. Because the prophets protested injustice, whether sins in the sanctuary or abuse of power in the political realm. Because the Talmud sets forth an intricate system of law that binds us to our neighbors, whether we seek that societal connection or not. Because, for over three thousand years, our tradition has taught us that every human being is personally responsible for the moral standing of the entire world.

NOTES

1. Aristotle, *Politics* 1.1253a.
2. Nathan's chastisement of David is found at II Samuel 12; Elijah's admonishment of Ahab is detailed in I Kings 21.
3. Babylonian Talmud, *N'darim* 28a; *Gittin* 10b; *Bava Kama* 113a (three times), 113b (twice); *Bava Batra* 54b, 55a.
4. Talmudic translations are from the Koren Talmud Bavli Noé Edition, which prints the literal translation of the Talmud together with the expository illustrations of Rabbi Adin Even-Israel Steinsaltz to make fuller sense of its passages.

B'TZELEM ELOHIM

A Divine Mandate to Humanity

RABBI SHOSHANAH CONOVER

For Reform Jews, *b'tzelem Elohim*, "in the image of God," has become synonymous with the notion that each person has inherent dignity. We have grown up on this message from the Talmud: "The first human being was created alone to teach that whoever destroys one soul is regarded by the Torah as if they destroyed a whole world, and whoever saves one soul is regarded as if they saved a whole world" (Babylonian Talmud, *Sanhedrin* 37a).

This theme has been perpetuated at URJ summer camps and NFTY *kallot* for over a decade with the lyrics of "B'tzelem Elohim" by Dan Nichols:

> We've all got a life to live
> We've all got a gift to give
> Just open your heart and let it out. . . .
> When I reach out to you and you to me
> We become *b'tzelem Elohim.*

A close examination of this concept in Torah and its commentaries will yield manifold and diverse lessons about humanity and justice.

The exact phrase *b'tzelem Elohim* occurs in two chapters of Genesis. In Genesis 1:26–27:

> God now said, "Let us make human beings [*adam*][1] in our image, after our likeness. . . ." So God created the human beings in [the divine] image, creating [them] in the image of God [*b'tzelem Elohim*], creating them male and female.

In Genesis 9:6:

> The shedder of human blood, that person's blood shall be shed by [another] human; for human beings were made in the image of God [*b'tzelem Elohim*].

In Genesis 5:1–2, the Torah uses the phrase *bidmut Elohim* instead of *b'tzelem Elohim*, yet its context remains the same:

> This is the written record of the human line from the day God created human beings, making [them] in the likeness of God [*bidmut Elohim*], creating them male and female, blessing them, and naming them "Humans" on the day they were created.

From these examples, rabbis of old and Jews of today have sought to glean lessons about what it means for humanity to be made in the image of God—how that informs and, at times, mandates our behavior. We ask: What is the nature of God? What is the nature of humanity? If we are made in the image of God, does that image remain static? Do our human actions affect this divine image? The Torah and its commentaries help us answer these questions. The concept of *b'tzelem Elohim* conveys varied messages as it relates to the subjects of our intellectual capacity and free will, equality and gender identity. Yet, its most potent lessons for humanity lie in what this term teaches us about establishing power through relationships and the role humility plays.

Medieval philosopher Maimonides (1135–1204) took great pains to explain that being made in the image of God does not mean that human beings are made in God's physical form. God is incorporeal, therefore, the term "image" (*tzelem*) must represent a nonphysical quality. As he explains in *The Guide of the Perplexed*:

> Because of the divine intellect conjoined with man . . . it is said of the latter that he is *in the image of God and in His likeness*, not that God, may He be exalted, is a body and possesses a shape. . . . That which was meant in the scriptural dictum, *let us make man in our image*, was the specific form, which is intellectual apprehension, not the shape and configuration.[2]

A few centuries later, Italian biblical commentator Ovadiah ben Jacob S'forno (1475–1550) added another component beyond intellectual apprehension: like God, human beings have free will. In his commentary on Genesis 1:26, he writes that human beings "act intelligently like the angels, though from free choice, not like the angels who act under divine compulsion." Rabbi Abraham Isaac Kook claims that this interpretation of *b'tzelem Elohim* is the intellectual foundation of the entire Torah.[3]

Our intellect and free will give us the opportunity to choose between doing right or doing evil at every turn. With this perception, we may recognize not only the inherent dignity, but the equal value of each person. The Talmud teaches, "The first human being was created alone, for the sake of peace between humankind, so that no one could say to their fellow human being: My father was greater than yours" (Babylonian Talmud, *Sanhedrin* 88b). Ben Azzai puts a fine point on this notion as quoted in the midrashic text *B'reishit Rabbah*. While Rabbi Akiva taught that "Love your neighbor as yourself" (Leviticus 19:18) is the most important rule in the Torah, Ben Azzai says instead that the understanding that human beings are made in the image of God "is an even greater principle so that one should not say, 'Because I have been humiliated, let my friend be humiliated with me, because I have been cursed, let my friend be cursed with me'" (*B'reishit Rabbah* 24:7). Humanity, created in the image of God, shares a common origin and human experience.

As has already been shown, various translations of *b'tzelem Elohim* teach us a great deal about the myriad and varied interpretations of what it means to be made in the divine image. It remains difficult then to abide by static tropes about Creation, especially when they have implications for gender equality. Many of us have grown up with the understanding that Eve was created from the rib of Adam because of the following translation:

> And the LORD GOD caused a deep sleep to fall upon the man, and he slept; and He took one of his ribs, and closed up the place with flesh instead thereof. And the rib, which the LORD GOD had taken from the man, made He a woman, and brought her unto the man. (Genesis 2:21–22; 1917 JPS translation)

Man was created first. Woman was created afterward, as a "helpmate" for man. Yet, this second account of Creation does not seem to fit easily with the account that preceded it, in Genesis 1:

> God now said, "Let us make human beings in our image, after our likeness. . . ." So God created the human beings in [the divine] image, creating [them] in the image of God, creating them male and female. (Genesis 1:26–27)

Were man and woman created at the same time or was man created first? A midrash reconciles the account in the following way:

> Rabbi Yirm'yah ben Elazar said: In the hour when the Holy One created the first human, He created him [as] androgynous as it is said, "Male and female God created them." (*B'reishit Rabbah* 8:1)

The midrash continues with Rabbi Sh'muel bar Nachmani explaining that the first human being was double-faced, connected back to back, male and female. God then split the first being in half, down the back, creating separate human beings, Adam and Eve. Rabbi Sh'muel bar Nachmani explains that the word "rib" is a mistranslation of the word *tzela*. Eve was not created from Adam's rib. Rather, she was created from that splitting of the back side that they shared. As he cites, "It [*tzela*] means one of his sides, just as you would say, 'And for the side (*tzela*) of the Tabernacle' [Exodus 26:20], which bar Nachmani translates as 'for the side'" (*B'reishit Rabbah* 8:1).

Hence, a better translation of Genesis 2:21–22 may be:

> And *Adonai Elohim* caused a deep sleep to fall upon the human being as it slept, and God took its side and closed up the flesh on that spot, and *Adonai Elohim* built the side God had taken from the human being into a woman.[4]

This understanding of the creation of humanity in the image of God puts the formation and status of males and females on par with one another. The Reform Movement supports the implications of this reading in many ways, including in our siddur *Mishkan T'filah*, in which the editors have replaced a traditional prayer in the morning service. In a traditional siddur, men chant "Blessed are You . . . who has made me a man," and women chant, "Blessed are You . . . who has made me according to Your will." Reform Jews instead chant with one voice, "Blessed are You . . . who has made me in the image of God [*b'tzelem Elohim*]."[5]

Further, this notion of *b'tzelem Elohim* goes beyond gender equality. In a sense, the first human being—male and female—made in the image of God transcends gender. There is no need for binary divisions. Other creations were each made in its type—the fruit trees, the herbs, fish, birds, and land animals. The first human being (*ha-adam*) did not have a type—not a gender, not a race, no status other than human. Commenting on Genesis 1:27, thirteenth-century French rabbi Hezekiah ben Menoach, more commonly known as Chizkuni, points out, "The word *adam* includes males and females. Proof that this is so is found in Genesis 5:2, when both the males and the females of the species are described as having been 'created.'"[6]

Yet, it is understandable that the impulse of our Rabbis has been to define the first human being in narrow categories of gender. After all, the first account of Creation unfolds through order, separation, and sorting. It is no surprise then that many of the early Rabbis—made in the divine image—interpreted the account of Creation of humanity in an orderly, if ultimately shortsighted way.

Like God, human beings attempt to order our world through speech. God spoke the world into being: "When God was about to create heaven and earth . . . God said, 'Let there be light!'—and there was light" (Genesis 1:1–3). In this account of Creation, God orders the universe by calling each entity by its rightful category. In Genesis 2, God invites the first human being to do the same: "So God Eternal formed the wild animals and the birds of the sky out of the soil, and brought the man to see what he would call each one; and whatever the man called it, that became the creature's name" (Genesis 2:19).

Humanity, made in God's image, loves to name, categorize, and organize. What is the first toy many emerging toddlers receive? A shape sorter. They can sit playing with it for hours. When they get older, we delight as they learn colors and categories of animals. The iconic books of Eric Carle exemplify this truth: "Brown bear, brown bear, what do you see? I see a red bird looking at me."[7] We coax language from our children, urging them to order their world. In a sense, as it is for God, speech is a mode of creation for humanity.

In his book *This Is Real and You Are Completely Unprepared*, Rabbi Alan Lew shares an insight about the power of speech:

> In the account of creation we read every year in the Book of Genesis, God literally speaks the world into existence. And the Talmud affirms the creative potential of speech. Did you know that *abracadabra* is a Jewish word? The Aramaic words *Avra c'dabrah* mean "It came to pass as it was spoken," a popular talmudic dictum that expressed the widely held talmudic belief that things do indeed come to pass because they are spoken, that speech has the power to cause the world to come into being.[8]

While scholars have pointed out that this is probably a folk etymology,[9] the insight remains. Speech, both divine and human, has the power to cause the world to come into being.

Human beings are like God not only in our power of speech, but in our brute power over all of Creation:

> God now said, "Let us make human beings in our image, after our likeness; and let them hold sway over the fish of the sea and the birds of the sky, over the beasts, over all the earth, over all that creeps upon the earth."[10] (Genesis 1:26)

This aspect of being made in the divine image tantalized medieval sages—even as some today may find their commentaries cringe-worthy. In his commentary on this verse, thirteenth-century Spanish scholar Nachmanides wrote:

> The [meaning] of "and let them hold sway over" is that they should rule powerfully over the fish and the fowl and the beast and all that crawls. And the beasts [in this verse] includes the animals (which are not mentioned separately). And it states, "and over all the earth," [to mean] that they should rule over the earth itself: to uproot and to smash and to dig and to quarry copper and iron. And the expression "to hold sway over" (*r'diyah*) [is like the] rulership of a master over his slave.

Chizkuni perpetuated this teaching in his own commentary on this verse: "The common denominator between God and human beings on the one hand, and human beings and beast on the other, is that just as God is our ruler, so we rule over the other creatures in the universe."

Would those over whom human beings asserted power perceive humans as God? One midrash answers, "Of course." In its retelling of the creation of the first human being, *Pirkei D'Rabbi Eliezer* imagines the perspective of the rest of Creation:

> [The first human] looked upwards and downwards, and its stature extended from one end of the world to the other . . . and it saw all God's creatures. It began to glorify its Creator's name, saying, "How many are Your works, O God!" It stood on its legs and looked like one made in the image of God. The creatures saw it and were afraid, thinking that it had created them. So, they all came to worship it. (*Pirkei D'Rabbi Eliezer* 11:9)

If human beings are perceived as godlike, then humanity runs the risk of tarnishing God's image. If we are made in God's image, everything we do reflects on God, for good and for ill. In fact, as Genesis 6 attests, it is because of this blatant abuse of power, this tarnishing of God's image, that God brings the Flood:

> When the sons of God[11] [*b'nei ha-Elohim*] saw how fair were the human women, they took wives for themselves, as they chose. . . . The Nephilim were on the earth in those days; and afterward, too, when the sons of God mated with the human women, they bore for them those heroes who from of old enjoyed great renown. When the Eternal saw how great was the wickedness of human beings in the earth, that the direction of their thoughts was nothing but wicked all the time, the Eternal regretted having made human beings on earth and was heartsick. (Genesis 6:2, 6:5–6)

While some read this piece about *b'nei ha-Elohim* as a remnant from a mythological reference to half-human, half-divine beings, indispensable Jewish commentator Rashi (1040–1105) reads it more simply as referring to powerful people. He cites the interpretation of the classic-period collection of homiletical interpretations of Genesis, *B'reishit Rabbah*. According to a midrash in that collection, *b'nei elohim* means "the sons of princes and rulers—people in positions of power" (*B'reishit Rabbah* 26:15). Further, Rashi explains, wherever the word *Elohim* occurs in the Scriptures, it signifies authority and mastery. According to this reading, who are the Nephilim? Again, Rashi cites *B'reishit Rabbah*: they are people who abused their power. They were called Nephilim because they fell (*naflu*) and caused the downfall (*hipilu*) of the world (*B'reishit Rabbah* 26:7). Hence, humanity is made in the image of God's authority. If we don't use it for the betterment of Creation, we are subject to lose it. Like God, we must use our power for good. As the Talmud teaches, "Just as God is gracious and merciful, so too should you be gracious and merciful" (Babylonian Talmud, *Shabbat* 133b).

How do we do this? Just as God made space for us by creating the world, we must make space for one another through relationships. Like

God, the first human being is singular, without an equal among Creation. This singularity leads to loneliness. As Rabbi Joseph B. Soloveitchik laments:

> "To be" means to be the only one, singular and different, and consequently lonely. For what causes man [*sic*] to be lonely and feel insecure if not the awareness of his [*sic*] uniqueness and exclusiveness? The "I" is lonely, experiencing ontological incompleteness and casualness, because there is no one who exists like "I" and because the *modus existantae* of the "I" cannot be repeated, imitated, or experienced by others.[12]

Hence, like God, we crave relationship.

God created the first human as a sentient being, able not only to perceive God but to seek connection with the Divine. God wanted a partner in Creation. As the midrash teaches, "God said to Israel, all that I have created, I created in pairs: heaven and earth, the sun and the moon, Adam and Eve, this world and the next. But My glory is One and unmatched in the world" (*D'varim Rabbah* 2:22).

In his commentary on Genesis 2:22, Rashi shares a parallel midrash: "When God brought the animals to Adam, [God] brought each species in pairs, male and female. Adam said, 'They all have a partner. Only I have no partner.' Immediately, he fell asleep" (*B'reishit Rabbah* 17:4). This shows that, like God, the first human—before being separated into two beings—is lonely. The solution to humanity's loneliness intimated in this midrash is that we must not only reach out to God for the cure to our loneliness, but that we must reach for our fellow human being in relationship.

The first human being fell asleep, then awakened to a separate person ready to enter relationship. As Rabbi Norman J. Cohen comments:

> With a bit of imagination, we can picture the unity called Adam, made up of two distinct sides back to back, which could never see each other. . . . Only by standing over against and facing each other could they ever come to know one another and become truly one. The reunification of the two sides, the male and female in Adam,

would be far better than the original unity, for it would be based upon each other's knowledge and acceptance of the other.[13]

To be in relationship means to create space for the other. Ultimately, this is how we—human beings made in the image of God—act most powerfully. Our wedding liturgy implies as much. At the climax of the ceremony, during the *Sheva B'rachot* (seven wedding blessings), the officiant declares, "Blessed are You, *Adonai* our God, Ruler of the universe, who has fashioned human beings in Your image, according to Your likeness, and has fashioned from it a lasting mold."

We perpetuate humanity and holiness by humbling ourselves to one another in intimacy. We declare, "We cannot do this alone." We need intimate partners; not just lovers, but friends or family members—*ezrei k'negdo*—people who can help us most by challenging us to live up to our divine potential. Our intelligence and will must be employed in service of life, compassion, and righteousness. Our recognition of each other's equal value must compel us to act to ensure that this truth is represented in every society. We must use our power to amplify the power of others. This requires humility and the ability to make room for others to flourish. We commit to this under the chuppah. We celebrate this when we welcome new life into the world. We acknowledge this when our children teach us Torah as they become *b'nei mitzvah*. And we embrace this when we reach across chasms of difference in common cause. *B'tzelem Elohim* is our divine mandate—for blessing, for abundance, for life.

NOTES

1. As Robert Alter explains in *The Five Books of Moses*, "The term *'adam*, afterward consistently with a definite article, which is used both here and in the second account of the origins of humankind, is a generic term for human beings, not a proper noun. It also does not automatically suggest maleness, especially not without the prefix *ben*, 'son of,' and so the traditional rendering 'man' is misleading, and exclusively male

'adam would make nonsense of the last clause of verse 27." Robert Alter, *The Five Books of Moses* (New York: Norton, 2004), 19.

2. Moses Maimonides, *The Guide of the Perplexed, Part 1*, 1:2, trans. Shlomo Pines (Chicago: University of Chicago Press, 1963), 22–23.

3. Abraham Isaac Kook, *For the Perplexed of the Generation*, 1:1. (Tel Aviv: Yediot, 2014).

4. Author's translation.

5. Elyse D. Frishman, ed., *Mishkan T'filah: A Reform Siddur* (New York: CCAR Press, 2007), 40.

6. His commentary continues: "We also have a statement by Rav Huna, who asks the rhetorical question: How do we know that Chava was also called *adam*? Answer (Isaiah 44:13): *k'tiferet adam lashevet bayit*, which is translated by the *Targum* as 'like the beauty of a woman who resides in a house (or who transforms a house into a home).' Furthermore, we have a verse in Numbers 31:35: *v'nefesh adam min hanashim*, 'and human souls, of the women.'"

7. Bill Martin Jr. and Eric Carle, *Brown Bear, Brown Bear, What Do You See?* (New York: Henry Holt, 2004), 1–2.

8. Alan Lew, *This Is Real and You Are Completely Unprepared: The Days of Awe as a Journey of Transformation* (Boston: Little, Brown, 2003), 198.

9. As Daniel D. Stuhlman points out in his online article entitled "Abracadabra," "It [*abracadabra*] was first mentioned in a poem by Quintus Serenus Sammonicus in the second century. It is believed to have come into English via French from a Greek word *abrasadabra* (the change from s to c seems to have been through a confused transliteration of the Greek). It originated as a secret and mystical word with a Gnostic sect in Alexandria called the Basilidians (named after their founder Basilides of Egypt). The word was possibly based on Abrasax, the name of an Egyptian deity. It was used as charm to cure toothaches and infectious diseases. The word Abrasax was said to have magical powers. Using the gematria of the Greek letters the holy names Abraxas (Αβραξάς) and Mithras (Μίθρας) the Gnostics equated the numerical values of 365, the days of the year. Because of the relationship of Abraxas to the number of days, it was frequently used on amulets and precious stones" (Librarian's Lobby, December 2002, http://home.earthlink.net/~ddstuhlman/crc55.htm).

10. Gunther Plaut translates *b'nei ha-elohim* as "divine beings." Gunther Plaut, ed., *The Torah: A Modern Commentary*, rev. ed. (New York: URJ Press, 2005).

11. According to Gunther Plaut in *The Torah: A Modern Commentary*, this is a mythic fragment that nods to Hurrian, Phoenician, and Greek myths told of Titans, "supermen of great stature and strength, who were supposedly offspring of unions between gods and mortal women" (32).

12. Joseph B. Soloveitchik, *The Lonely Man of Faith* (New Milford, CT: Maggid Books, 1965, 2012), 29.

13. Norman J. Cohen, *Self, Struggle and Change: Family Conflict Stories in Genesis and Their Healing Insights for Our Lives* (Woodstock, VT: Jewish Lights, 1995), 24.

PEOPLE AT THE MARGINS

The Widow (*Almanah*), the Fatherless (*Yatom*), and the Sojourner (*Ger/Toshav*) in the Bible

Rabbi S. David Sperling, PhD

The Hebrew Bible calls for the proper treatment of classes of people who are typically disadvantaged: the widow (*almanah*), the fatherless (*yatom*),[1] and the sojourner (*ger/toshav*).[2] Widows and the fatherless are full Israelites, while the *ger* "sojourner" is not.[3] By examining the legal-literature (Torah), the prophets, the prose narratives (Joshua through Kings), Psalms, and wisdom literature (Job, Proverbs), we find a consistent picture of the biblical attitudes toward these groups. The picture we get is that Israelites are commanded to help those who have difficulty in helping themselves.

Readers of the Bible will be familiar with these words of God to Jeremiah:

> If you do not oppress the sojourner,[4] the fatherless, or the widow and do not shed innocent blood in this place, and if you do not follow other gods to your own harm, then I will let you live in this place, in the land I gave your ancestors, for ever and ever. (Jeremiah 7:6–7)

The above passage, in which the prophet lists God's conditions for the survival of the people of Judah in their own land, begins strikingly with the requirement not to oppress the sojourner, the fatherless, and the widow and only then proceeds to the shedding of innocent blood and the worship of other gods.[5]

Isaiah similarly exhorts his contemporaries: "Learn to be better, seek justice, support the oppressed, bring justice to the fatherless, argue the case of the widow" (Isaiah 1:17).[6]

The concern for the sojourner, the fatherless, and widow is found in all three sections of the Hebrew Bible.[7] Although embedded in a collection of laws, the following verses from the Book of Exodus might just as well have been delivered by an impassioned prophet calling for social justice:

> You shall not wrong or oppress a sojourner, for you were sojourn-ers in the land of Egypt. You shall not abuse[8] any widow or father-less child. If you do abuse them, when they cry out to me, I will surely heed their cry; You shall not abuse any widow or fatherless child. If you do abuse them, when they cry out to Me, I will surely heed their cry; My wrath will burn, and I will kill you with the sword, and your wives shall become widows and your children fatherless. (Exodus 22:20–23)

This is a blanket statement against abuse[9] of the sojourner, the father-less, and the widow.[10] More specific are the prohibitions against perverting justice due the sojourner or the fatherless, taking a widow's garment as a pledge,[11] and collecting forgotten grain sheaves or left-over olives that are required to be left available to the economically disadvantaged (Deuteronomy 24:17–19). Just like the poor Israelite day laborer, the non-Israelite sojourner must be paid by the end of the workday (Deuteronomy 24:14–15).

In assertions of his innocence and righteous character, Job swears:

> I have not withheld anything that the poor desired,
> nor have caused the eyes of the widow to fail,
> I have not eaten my morsel alone,
> so that the fatherless has not eaten from it—
> for from his youth like a father I reared the fatherless
> and from his mother's womb I guided him. (Job 1:16–18)

As for the sojourner:

> The sojourner did not spend the night in the street.
> I would open my doors to the wayfarer. (Job 31:32)

The notion that widows, fatherless children, and other disadvantaged groups need protection has a long history in the ancient Near East. A half-millennium before the rise of the people Israel, King Hammurabi of Babylon promulgated his famous laws. In the prologue to this legal collection, Hammurabi writes that his aim was "to make justice prevail in the land, to abolish the wicked and evil, to prevent the strong from oppressing the weak." In his epilogue he singles out the fatherless child and the widow as the beneficiaries of his laws and commends himself for being "King of Justice."[12]

His far less-known contemporary, King Zimri-Lim of Mari, is addressed by a prophet of the god Adad:

> Am I not Adad, lord of Aleppo, who raised you in my arms and returned you to the throne of your father? I do not request anything from you (but) when an oppressed man or an oppressed woman cries out to you stand up and render their judgment. This is what I request of you.[13]

A similar concern for the widow, the fatherless child, and the disadvantaged is found in the literature of Ugarit in Syria almost contemporary with the rise of Israel. We read of the righteous hero Danel,[14] "He judged the cause of the widow, tried the case of the fatherless."[15] Elsewhere in Ugaritic literature King Kirta is rebuked by his son, "You do not judge the cause of the widow, you do not try the case of the miserable."[16]

What appears to be an Israelite innovation is the concern for the sojourner. The biblical definition of *ger* (from the verb *gur*, "live where you are not a native"),[17] someone living in a land not his own,[18] is given by God to Abra(ha)m about the future of his descendants:

> God said to Abram, "Know this for certain, that your offspring shall be sojourners in a land that is not theirs, and will serve them [the natives of the land], and they shall be oppressed for four hundred years." (Genesis 15:13)

Similarly, we read of Moses who considers himself an Egyptian living in Midian:

> Moses agreed to stay with the man, and he gave Moses his daughter Zipporah in marriage. She bore a son, and he named him Gershom; for he said, "I have been a sojourner [*ger*] in a foreign land."[19] (Exodus 2:21–22)

According to Genesis 23:4, Abraham considers himself a *ger* in the Hittite territory of Hebron, where he pays an exorbitant price for a burial cave in which to bury Sarah and to belong to his descendants in perpetuity.

In Deuteronomy, God is described as the benefactor of the disadvantaged who "provides justice for the fatherless and the widow and who loves the sojourner, giving him food and clothing." The verse immediately following commands the native Israelites, "You [plural] shall love the sojourner, for you were sojourners in the land of Egypt" (Deuteronomy 10:18–19). Empathy for the sojourner is also nicely articulated in Exodus: "You [singular] shall not oppress the sojourner, for you [plural] know the inner being [*nefesh*] of the sojourner, for you were sojourners[20] in the land of Egypt" (Exodus 23:9).

The *ger* occupies an intermediate position between the native Israelite (*ezrach*) and the foreigner (*nochri/ben neichar*). According to Numbers 15:14–15, a *ger* may offer sacrifices to God as long as he performs them in accordance with standard Israelite practice.[21] As is the case with the native Israelite, if the *ger* wishes to eat the flesh of an ox, a lamb, or a goat, he must have it slaughtered at the sanctuary and offer it as a sacrifice of well-being (*sh'lamim*; Leviticus 17:1–9). Unlike the native Israelite, the *ger* is permitted to eat the flesh of an animal that has died of natural causes (*n'veilah*; Deuteronomy 14:21).[22]

The biblical writers disagree about the possibility of a *ger* changing his status. The speaker in Psalm 39:13 pleads with the Eternal:

> Hear my prayer, O Eternal,
> and give ear to my cry;
> do not hold your peace at my tears.
> For I am Your sojourner,
> just a resident like all my forebears.

The speaker in Psalm 119:19, who sings the virtues of Torah study, prays that God not hide the divine commandments from him just because he is a *ger*. The clear inference is that God might do just that.

In contrast, Exodus 12:43–49 appears to offer the possibility that a *ger* can change his status:

> The Eternal said to Moses and Aaron: This is the ordinance for the Passover: No foreigner [*ben neichar*] shall eat of it, but any slave [*eved*] who has been purchased may eat of it after he has been circumcised; no temporary resident or hired servant may eat of it. It shall be eaten in one house; you shall not take any of the animal outside the house, and you shall not break any of its bones. The whole assembly [*eidah*] of Israel shall celebrate it. If a sojourner [*ger*] who resides with you wants to celebrate the Passover to the Eternal, all his males shall be circumcised; then he may draw near to celebrate it; he shall be regarded as a native [*ezrach*] of the land. But no uncircumcised person[23] shall eat of it; there shall be one law for the native and for the sojourner [*ger*] who resides among you.

The Passover sacrifice serves as a marker of who is part of the assembly of Israel. Those who are not eligible to offer the Passover are less than full members (see Numbers 9:7). The foreigner is obviously not part of the community, nor are temporary residents or hirelings. The slaves are part of the household, just like the furniture. The only unclear status is that of the *ger*, who, as we have seen, is permitted and sometimes commanded (Leviticus 17) to offer sacrifices. The legislator of Exodus 12 regularizes his status. This may be the earliest ritual by which a gentile becomes part of the people Israel.[24] If so, it underscores the Israelite innovation in concern for the sojourner.

As Jews by either birth or choice, we are descendants of the biblical Israelites. The demands made on our ancestors continue to bind us. The biblical texts reminded our ancestors that they had been sojourners in Egypt and that therefore they should love the sojourners in their land. These same texts should remind us of the many centuries that we were sojourners in other peoples' lands and that that status found its natural culmination in the Holocaust.

We live at a time where the loss of memory is having serious consequences. Americans, including some Jews who were themselves sojourners or descendants of sojourners in other countries, have taken up the cause of nativism. We must never forget our past lest we destroy our future and the future of countless others.

NOTES

1. A *yatom* has a living mother. See Exodus 22:20–22; Lamentations 5:3.

2. Scholars differ over whether *toshav* describes a category separate from *ger* or whether it modifies *ger*. Leviticus 22:10, 25:6, 25:40, and 25:45 would point to separate categories. I understand a *ger* to be a long-term resident and a *toshav* to be a short-term resident.

3. For a rich widow, see II Kings 8. For a rich *ger*, see Leviticus 25:47.

4. Some Bibles translate *ger* by "foreigner," for whom the biblical term is *nochri*, a word that sometimes has the connotation "enemy."

5. These verses are in the context of Jeremiah's denunciation of his fellow Judahites who believe that any enormities committed by them will go unpunished as long as they participate in the ritual of the Jerusalem Temple. See Jeremiah 7:3–11.

6. Isaiah 1:23 shows that at issue here is access to the judicial system. The orphan and the widow cannot get their cases heard. Accordingly, God has to serve as "father of the fatherless, and judge for the widow" (Psalm 68:6). As is true of Jeremiah in the previous note, Isaiah 1:11–16 decries the reliance of the sinful people on Temple ritual.

7. See Deuteronomy 10:18, 14:29, 16:11–14, 24:17, 24:19–20, 27:10; Ezekiel 22:7; Zechariah 7:10; Malachi 3:5; Psalm 146:9; Job 22:9.

8. The verb *ayin-nun-hei* covers a wide range of abuses including political subjugation, forced labor, and rape.

9. Such abuse could be fatal, according to Psalm 94:6–7: "They [the wicked] kill the widow and the stranger, they murder the orphan, and they say, 'The Eternal does not see; the God of Jacob does not perceive.'"

10. It is worth quoting Rashi's comment on Exodus 22.21: "It is prohibited to abuse anybody, but Scripture spoke of the normal situation in which those who have no power are easily abused."

11. The author of Exodus 22:25–26 presumes that an Israelite borrower has only one garment and could get through the daytime without it, a presumption supported by ancient Egyptian depictions of bare-chested male workers. A woman with a living husband could pledge his garment, but a widow would lack that option. Job 24:1–3 characterizes the taking of a widow's ox in pledge as an act of the wicked.

12. For Hammurabi's laws in transliteration and English translation, see M. Roth, *Law Collections from Mesopotamia and Asia Minor* (Atlanta: Scholars Press, 1999), 71–142.

13. J. J. M. Roberts, *The Bible and the Ancient Near East* (Winona Lake, IN: Eisenbrauns, 2002), 175.

14. His story was known to the prophet Ezekiel. See Ezekiel 14:14, 14:20.

15. See J. Pritchard, ed., *Ancient Near Eastern Texts Relating to the Old Testament* (Princeton, NJ: Princeton University Press, 1959), 153. The Ugaritic words for "widow" and "fatherless," *almnt* and *ytm* respectively, are virtually identical to the Hebrew terms.

16. Ibid., 149.

17. See Judges 19:16.

18. In the figurative language of Jeremiah 14:8, the prophet complains the God is acting "like a sojourner in our land, like a wayfarer who turns off the road to spend the night." The sense is that the Divine Presence is no longer permanently to be found in Judah.

19. There is an unarticulated pun beneath the surface of the verse. The name "Gershom" is interpreted as comprising *ger*, "sojourner," and *sham*, "over there, in that place."

20. This appears to be distinct from the tradition that Israelites were slaves in Egypt (e.g., Deuteronomy 6:21), which is one big slave barracks. See Exodus 20:2; Deuteronomy 5:6.

21. The people from Mesopotamia who were resettled in Samaria by the king of Assyria quickly learned that it was in their best interest to serve the God of Israel in addition to their own gods. See II Kings 17:24–41.

22. In contrast, Leviticus 17:15 prohibits the *ger* as well from eating *n'veilah*.

23. Including an uncircumcised Israelite.

24. Note that *ger* later became the term for a male convert to Judaism and remains so. A female convert is a *giyoret* (from the same Hebrew root as *ger*).

LOVING YOUR NEIGHBOR
AS THE PATH TO JUSTICE

RABBI LISA D. GRANT, PhD

> You shall not take vengeance or bear a grudge against members of your people. Love your fellow [Israelite] as yourself: I am *Adonai*.
>
> —*Leviticus 19:18*

Not long ago, I was in Kiryat Shemona, a sleepy little city in the midst of Northern Israel's stunning natural beauty. On my way to the bus station, I passed by a modest shack with a Hebrew sign that read: Eliyahu's Hummus: *V'ahavta L'rei-acha Kamocha*. I still wonder to this day what, exactly, the eatery's owner meant by broadcasting the well-known biblical injunction to "love your neighbor as yourself." This injunction has been the subject of much discussion in our tradition.

Rabbi Akiva, an early Rabbinic sage from the latter part of the first and early second centuries, is quoted as saying *V'ahavta l'rei-acha kamocha* is the central instruction in the whole of Torah (Jerusalem Talmud, *N'darim* 9:4). If we get that right, then the world will be a far kinder and more just place. Indeed, loving our neighbor might be the ultimate form of justice, for if we can treat each other with love, then indeed the rest is commentary.

But, of course, understanding what it really means to love our neighbor isn't quite so simple. It certainly cannot be achieved through written or verbal exhortations to love one another. What does it really mean to "love your neighbor as yourself"? Which "neighbors" does the verse intend? What is love? Can we truly love someone in the same way as we love ourselves? And, how does this love motivate us in the pursuit of justice? Perhaps this simple injunction is not so simple after all.

Taking up Tikvah Frymer-Kensky's counsel on how to read a biblical text, we need to both zoom in for a close reading of the text and then zoom out for a better understanding of the text in its own context and then in ours.[1] Given Rabbi Akiva's bold claim that Leviticus 19:18 is the most important principle of the Torah, it is no surprise that a wide range of interpretation and commentary exists on the verse. As we will see, even from this brief exploration, there is certainly no clear consensus on its meaning. And that, of course, invites us in to explore and consider just how to live out this value that seems to be so key to caring for others and creating a more just world.

The verse appears in the large textual unit of Leviticus 17–26, which scholars label "the Holiness Code." The emphasis on holiness is particularly evident in chapter 19, given its opening line where God instructs Moses to speak to the entire Israelite community and say to them, "You shall be holy, for I, *Adonai* your God, am holy" (Leviticus 19:2). The chapter includes a curious assortment of ethical and ritual laws that defy categorization and are regularly punctuated by the phrase "I am *Adonai*." This absence of a clear logic to the chapter is even more apparent given that it is sandwiched by two chapters that do have a very clear focus. Chapter 18 concentrates on forbidden sexual relationships, and chapter 20 describes the dire consequences for those who engage in these various forbidden liaisons.

Scholars also point out that most of the laws of Leviticus 19 appear elsewhere in Torah. They suggest that the Holiness Code was composed by a group of religious reformers who were concerned more with everyday behavior than were their predecessors, who were focused more on ritual purity and sacrifice.[2] Indeed, interspersed throughout chapter 19 are commandments to care for others as a means of honoring and obeying God. The text powerfully reinforces the idea that holiness is as much, if not more, about acting justly toward one another than it is about ritual behavior. We are repeatedly instructed to care for those less fortunate: leave the corners of your field unharvested for the poor (19:9–10); don't put a stumbling block before the blind (19:14); don't degrade your daughter by turning her into a prostitute (19:29); stand up for and show deference to the aged (19:32); don't wrong the stranger who lives among you (19:33). The refrain "I am *Adonai*" reminds us that these acts are not just good to do, but are a reflection of the godliness within us. The more we care for others, the more we bring God into the world, and the more just the world becomes.

This idea is best summarized by the verse at the heart of our discussion here, which we most often quote as "Love your neighbor as yourself." Virtually all Christian sources and even a few Jewish ones translate the Hebrew word *rei-acha* as "your neighbor." Yet, almost all the Jewish bible commentaries translate the word as "fellow" rather than "neighbor." *The Torah: A Women's Commentary* translates the phrase as "your fellow [Israelite]."[3] The parenthetical addition of Israelite narrows the meaning considerably. Thus, these Jewish sources suggest we read *rei-a* as a kinsperson, someone within the Jewish family, so to speak.

The prevailing Christian understanding, as evidenced by the more universal choice of the word "neighbor," is that *rei-acha* applies to all human beings. Searching the Hebrew Bible for other examples of where the word *rei-a* appears shows it is used in different ways. For example, in the Tower of Babel narrative, *rei-a* seems to mean all human beings (Genesis 11:3). In other situations, it is used to refer to someone who is definitely not an Israelite (such as Job 2:11), or someone who definitely is (such as Exodus 2:13). *Rei-a* appears twice in the Decalogue: "You shall not bear false witness against your *rei-a*," nor shall you covet your *rei-a*'s wife (Exodus 20:13–14). In these instances, a strong argument can be made for a more universalist and expansive interpretation. Lying and coveting are prohibitions that apply across boundaries, not just within a clan or specific community. Indeed, midrash sees a close association between Leviticus 19 and the Ten Commandments, as we see in this text from *Vayikra Rabbah* 24:5:

> Rabbi Chiya taught: This *parashah* should be read publicly to the assembly because most of the body of Torah laws are derived from it. Rabbi Levi said: Because the Ten Commandments are embodied in it.

In contrast, many Rabbinic sources claim that a narrower interpretation suggested by the parenthetical "[Israelite]" is the only possible one. Examining Leviticus 19:18 in its entirety supports this more limited understanding. It begins: "You shall not take vengeance or bear a grudge against members of your people." Thus, we might logically infer that *rei-a* in the second half of the verse also applies to a fellow among "your people."

It seems that Rabbi Akiva also understands *rei-a* to be someone from within the people, as is reflected in a dispute between him and a colleague named Ben Azzai:

> Rabbi Akiva taught: *"Love your neighbor as yourself.* This is the most important rule in the Torah." Ben Azzai says: *"This is the written record of the human line* (Genesis 5:1). That is an even greater rule." (Jerusalem Talmud, *N'darim* 9:4)

Ben Azzai objects to Akiva's statement that Leviticus 19:18 is the most important principle of Torah. He offers an alternative verse from the Book of Genesis as the core: "This is the written record of the human line from the day God created human beings, making [them] in the likeness of God" (Genesis 5:1). Rather than trying to figure out just who is included in the word *rei-a*, Ben Azzai takes a different tack, reminding us of the universal principle that all of humanity is created in the image of God. Rabbi Lance Sussman notes that Ben Azzai's view is reinforced by the selection of Amos 9:7–15 as the Ashkenazic haftarah to *Parashat K'doshim*. The opening verse of the haftarah reminds the

Israelites that they are just like the Ethiopians—in other words, part of all humankind.[4]

Toward the end of Leviticus 19, similar language about love is applied to the stranger who resides among us as a citizen. We are instructed to "love each one as yourself, for you were strangers in the land of Egypt: I am *Adonai* your God" (Leviticus 19:34). The biblical commandment to treat the stranger fairly is repeated numerous times, more often than any other in Torah. However, other than in Leviticus 19, the commandment rarely says "to love" the stranger. We are enjoined to love both our *rei-a* and the stranger, so they must be two different categories of people. It thus makes sense to understand *rei-a* as the more intimate and proximate relationship and "stranger" as those more distant from us. Rabbi Lord Jonathan Sacks acknowledges that loving our fellow is the easier task. Someone more similar to ourselves may be naturally easier to care about, since we can more easily imagine ourselves in that person's place. Sacks writes, "Our neighbour is one we love because he is like ourselves. The stranger is one we are taught to love precisely because he is not like ourselves."[5] Both are deserving of justice. Bringing love into the mix teaches us that compassion is an essential element of justice, especially when it comes to judging people who are very different and distant from ourselves.

In addition to puzzling over the exact meaning of *rei-a*, we are also left with the question of what it means to love someone as oneself. Love in the Hebrew Bible is far more often connected to God than it is to love between people, romantic or otherwise. Loving God is actualized by fulfilling God's commandments. Tamara Eskenazi reminds us that "love in the Bible is about commitment, loyalty and action rather than feelings. To love others is to take responsibility for their well-being."[6] At the core, this biblical sense of love is all about building a just society where all feel a sense of responsibility for one another. Rabbi Akiva, the advocate of the central importance of the verse, notes that there are limits to taking responsibility for others, but only at the point of when one's life is threatened. In fact, we are commanded to do everything in our power to save someone else's life. However, if ours is threatened as well, we are permitted to save our own life before that of another (Babylonian Talmud, *Bava M'tzia* 62a).

The great majority of people feel a natural inclination to express love grounded in commitment and loyalty for family members and those within their most intimate communities. It is also naturally more difficult to make the same level of commitment to those more distant and different from ourselves. This is precisely Rabbi Sacks's point about loving both our "fellow" and the stranger. We must be more deliberate and intentional about caring for the stranger. This qualification may help to explain why many, though certainly not all, rabbinic sources interpret the verse more narrowly. They seem to say we can only do what is humanly possible. For some, this means focusing only on those qualities of one's fellow that are "lovable." For example, twelfth-century French tosafist (and grandson of Rashi) Sh'muel ben Meir says, "Love your *rei-a* only if he is virtuous, not if he is wicked."[7] Similarly, Ibn Ezra, a Spanish commentator from the same period, writes, "One must love the good that pertains to one's fellow as much as the good that pertains to oneself,"[8] meaning love only the good in someone else. Nachmanides, from the thirteenth century, agrees, saying, "The phrase is not meant literally, since one cannot be expected to love someone else as one's own self."[9]

And yet, there are those who take a more expansive view. Maimonides says we must love everyone without qualification. And he underscores this claim by boldly stating that one who gains honor by degrading one's fellow has no share in the world-to-come.[10] Similarly, a late midrash notes that the Torah obligates each person to love and desire for a friend all that a person loves and desires for oneself.[11] Imagine what the world would be if we were to truly live by these words.

We may never reach a definitive answer about how narrow or broadly to understand the precise meaning of *V'ahavta l'rei-acha kamocha*. Perhaps that is the point. We should struggle to consider the limits and potential for loving our fellow humans. It is no easy task to achieve. The significance of the verse is not diminished because we cannot arrive at a definitive understanding. It is an aspirational statement of what ought to be, but not always what is. The verse presents us with a great moral challenge to think carefully and deeply about our actions. It powerfully reminds us that how we treat others, both those closest to us and those more distant, is a test of our humanity, as well as a sign of spiritual health and well-being. And that is precisely why the verse has long inspired Jews to work ceaselessly for justice.

Sometime in the eighteenth century, the Chasidic masters established this teaching as a *kavanah*, an intention for readying oneself for prayer. Today, many congregations have integrated this into their own worship as well. May it be a constant reminder to us to strive to do the will of our Creator in bringing as much love as we can to each other, both in our closest circles of connection and throughout the world. For in acting with love, we do indeed create a more just and peaceful world. It is an awesome and holy task.

> I am ready to accept the commandment of the Creator: to love your neighbor as yourself.

NOTES

1. Tikva Frymer-Kensky, *Reading the Women of the Bible* (New York: Schocken Books, 2002).

2. S. Tamar Kamionkowski, Central Commentary to *K'doshim*, in *The Torah: A Women's Commentary* (New York: URJ Press and Women of Reform Judaism, 2008), 703.

3. Ibid, 707.

4. Lance Sussman, "It All Depends: Finding the Middle of the Torah," *d'var Torah* on *Parashat Tzav*, April 8, 2017, http://reformjudaism.org/learning/torah-study/tzav/it-all-depends-finding-middle-torah#sthash.wEg0pDwN.dpuf.

5. Jonathan Sacks, *Faith in the Future* (Macon, GA: Mercer University Press, 1997), 78.

6. Tamara Cohn Eskenazi, "Letter 26," American Values Religious Voices, February 14, 2017, http://www.valuesandvoices.com/letter26/.

7. Rashi, commentary on Leviticus 19:18.

8. Ibn Ezra, commentary on Leviticus 19:18.

9. Nachmanides, commentary on Leviticus 19:18.

10. "Jewish Concepts: Be Loving to Your Neighbor as You Would Yourself," Jewish Virtual Libary, http://www.jewishvirtuallibrary.org/be-loving-to-your-neighbor-as-you-would-yourself.

11. "L'Olam," *Otzar HaMidrashim*, 74.

N'VI-IM

Vision, Rage, Rhetoric

RABBI MONA ALFI

Vision

For many contemporary Jews, the teachings of our Torah, our prophets, and our other sacred texts feel distant and irrelevant to the world in which we live. Many dismiss them out of hand as archaic words meant for our ancestors, not for us. Familiarity with the prophets among contemporary Jews is often limited to looking at biblical names to give their children. But Micah, Jonah, Isaiah, Abigail, Deborah, and Miriam aren't simply the names of the children in our religious schools; they were the names of visionaries who offered us a glimpse into what the world can be. The stories, the teachings, and the legacy of moral outrage that the prophets left for us are just what we need today.

While our attention has been turned away from them, the prophets wait for us impatiently. They are waiting for us to stop and to listen: to pay attention to their warnings, those messages chanted in the haftarot on Shabbat morning by children who are taking their place in our community as soon-to-be young adults. Out of the mouths of babes we hear the warnings that were meant not only for the time that the prophets lived, but for our time as well. They are calling out to us to look up and out through the windows of our sanctuaries and pay attention to the world just beyond our temple doors.

Over and over, the prophets call us to care for the most vulnerable among us. Amos channels God's angry voice and warns us not to be too comfortable or callous and not to avert our eyes from those who have less. When he calls out to us decrying those "who trample the heads of the poor into the dust of the ground, and make the humble walk a twisted course" (Amos 2:7),[1] what he is really doing is asking us: What have we done to help the homeless family seeking shelter in their car just down the street? What have we done to help the elderly in our own congregations who need to visit the local communal food pantry just to get through the month? He is demanding that we look up from our prayer books and really see and pay attention to the world around us.

Throughout the Prophets we hear over and over again that God wants us to actively pursue the common good. But if doing what is good is not enough of a reward in and of itself, we are told that our very fate hangs on our enacting it. If we do good for others, good will come to all of us. If we ignore the needs of others, all will suffer:

> For I have noted how many are your crimes, and how countless your sins—you enemies of the righteous, you takers of bribes, you who subvert in the gate the cause of the needy! . . . Seek good and not evil, that you may live, and that the Eternal, the God of Hosts, may truly be with you, as you think. Hate evil and love good, and establish justice in the gate; perhaps the Eternal, the God of Hosts, will be gracious to the remnant of Joseph. (Amos 5:12, 5:14–15).

Central to Judaism is the understanding that our lives are interconnected, not just *dor l'dor*—generation to generation—but within each generation as well. We are responsible not just for ourselves, but for our brothers and sisters, our neighbors, and even the stranger in our midst.

The prophets build on the laws given to us in the Torah, which in painstaking detail lay out a blueprint for a society based on justice and equality for all people regardless of birthplace or social status. The

Torah's world is dependent on humanity working in partnership with God.

> Learn to do good. Devote yourselves to justice; aid the wronged. Uphold the rights of the orphan; defend the cause of the widow.
> "Come let us reach an understanding," says the Eternal. "Be your sins like crimson, they can turn snow-white; be they red as dyed wool, they can become like fleece." If, then, you agree and give heed, you will eat the good things of the earth; but if you refuse and disobey, you will be devoured [by] the sword. For it was the Eternal who spoke. (Isaiah 1:17–20)

We are called to implement the divine blueprint for a world redeemed. We must make this vision a reality.

We fail our *b'nei mitzvah* students, and those who celebrate with them, when we fail to comprehend that the words they are chanting from Zechariah and Micah are giving us a mandate to change the world. The prophets not only amplify the message of the Torah, but they often simplify it and remind us of the urgency of what needs to be done. By reiterating the ancient imperatives from Torah to the generation that stands before them, they also remind us that these truths endure generation to generation. "Thus said the God of heaven's hosts: Execute true justice; deal loyally and compassionately with one another. Do not defraud the widow, the orphan, the stranger, and the poor; and do not plot evil against one another" (Zechariah 7:9–10). While the Torah gives us a detailed list of what we have to do, Micah clarifies it, giving us the essence of the mitzvot: "He has told you, O man, what is good; and what the Eternal requires of you; only to do justice and to love goodness, and to walk modestly with your God; then will your name achieve wisdom" (Micah 6:8). Justice, mercy, humility—these elements are meant to guide all of our actions. During the *Yamim Noraim*,[2] the Ten Days of Repentance, when we sit in judgment on our individual and collective deeds over the last year, we are in essence being asked, "Did we act toward one another with justice, with mercy, and with humility?" It is when the answer is no to any one of those three values that we know we have gone astray.

Up until now I have spoken of the prophet only as "he"—and indeed, most of the writings that have been passed down to us are from the male prophets. But there were women prophets as well. Sarah, Miriam, Deborah, Hannah, Abigail, Esther, and Hulda are the prophetic women whose names have been remembered, whose wisdom and stories have survived through the ages. These women are notable not only for their teachings, but also for their style of prophecy, which was often different from that of their male counterparts. They are an important reminder that God speaks to us in different ways and through a variety of messengers and that the way we transmit a message can be as powerful as the vision itself.

It is God's words spoken through the mouth of a prophet that remind us to pay attention not only to the message, but also to the messengers who are sent to us. In Micah 6:4, God says, "In fact, I brought you up from the land of Egypt, I redeemed you from the house of bondage, and I sent before you Moses, Aaron, and Miriam." It is important to remember that even the greatest of all prophets did not work alone. Our redemption was possible because Moses worked in partnership with Miriam and Aaron. Each of them had their own unique style of leading, and each took responsibility for a different aspect of governance. Each of them was necessary for our redemption from Egypt to have occurred.

Rabbinic tradition goes further in solidifying the importance and interdependence of their roles by crediting each of them as establishing the three Israelite power structures: prophecy, priesthood, and monarchy. In *Sifrei B'midbar* 78 and *Sh'mot Rabbah* 48:3–4, we are taught that from Moses comes the tradition of the prophets; from Aaron, the priesthood; and from Miriam, the Davidic dynasty. Each one hears the word of God but transmits God's teachings in a different way. Moses, Aaron, and Miriam provide us with a model of leadership that is multivocal and shared. They are a reminder that even in a single generation God's voice can be heard and transmitted in many ways and through different types of leaders. Through the three of them, God's voice can be heard in preparing for battle, in making sacred offerings, being raised high in a song of thanksgiving, as well as when speaking truth to power.

Moses, Aaron, and Miriam's example of shared leadership continues to be a model for us today. One of the strengths of the Reform Movement's Commission on Social Action is that it seeks to unite the different visions and voices within our movement into a cohesive and actionable message for us to engage in social justice as a community. We know that rabbis, cantors, and educators do not have a monopoly on interpreting our sacred texts. We know that when we work together with our lay leadership to better understand how our sacred teachings are to be lived out in our day and age—in our summer camps and youth groups, in our synagogues and our seminary, through our collective voice at the Religious Action Center, and even simply in the way we live our lives—we come closer to fulfilling the vision of a world redeemed as articulated by the biblical prophets.

Deborah provides us with another model of the prophet. She teaches us that the words of the prophet can also provide courage and strength in difficult times. When Deborah instructs her general Barak that it is time to rally the troops and go to war, he responds that he will go on the condition that she join him (Judges 4:6–8). Barak needs the prophet by his side for courage and direction. In every generation we face battles, sometimes with weapons, sometimes with words and legislation. As we learn from Deborah and Barak, the prophetic voice can give us the necessary courage and inspiration to be able to move forward and to tackle the seemingly impossible task at hand.

When Rev. Dr. Martin Luther King Jr. was writing his "Letter from a Birmingham Jail," he was preparing for a battle that was being waged for the soul of our country. He looked to Amos for inspiration as Barak looked to Deborah. When Dr. King declared, "But let justice roll down like waters, and righteousness like a mighty stream" (Amos 5:24), it was an angry plea to his fellow clergy to stop being silent bystanders or, worse, obstructionists and to come and join him in fighting for the common good for all of our nation's children. In that moment, Amos's words became our battle cry for justice.

Abigail (I Samuel 25:23–35) and Nathan (II Samuel 12:1–13) provide yet a different understanding of the role of the prophet in society. They sit close to power, and each has the ear of the king; one becomes his wife, the other his advisor. They help us understand that sometimes the best way to convey a message to those in power is gently, allowing the person who needs to heed the lesson to learn it without shame, then to embolden them to do what is right. Just as Nathan uses a parable of a wealthy man who has stolen a sheep from a poor man to help King David come to understand the gravity of his sin against Uriah the Hittite, it is sometimes important not to directly point out someone's sins, but to give them a way to understand their mistakes without losing face. While it is important to speak truth to power, it is also true that sometimes it is important to do so in a way that the prophet might live to preach another sermon.

Rage

Throughout the Bible, God speaks more about what we label today as "politics" rather than what we think of as "religion." But the prophets are clear: God's passion is fueled not by ritual and prayer, but rather by how we treat each other. The prophet's voice is the conduit God uses to remind us what is demanded of us. The rage we hear belongs not to the prophet, but to God.

Because in generation after generation we continue to ignore God's enduring cry to bring justice into the world and to repair what is broken, the prophets raise their voices warning us that if we fail to heed God's admonishments and change our ways, we will continue to repeat the mistakes of previous generations. The prophets caution us that being a Jew demands much more than prayer and study. Our faith demands from us acts of justice and righteousness, sacrifice and moral courage.

The words of the prophets may be old, but they are always timely. Every generation must be reminded that the purpose of prayer and of study is to help us remember what God wants of us: that we must strive "to do justice, and to love goodness, and to walk modestly with [our] God" (Micah 6:8). Let us remain mindful of how to behave in both our personal and professional interactions, when we are at home and when on our way.

What happens when a prophet becomes weary and worn down from preaching the same message repeatedly to ears that are deaf to his or her plea? Sadly, it is Moses, the greatest and longest serving of all of our prophets, who allows his anger to become misdirected and unchecked. Weary from the task of constantly having to combat the complaints of his congregation, and mourning his sister Miriam's death (Numbers 20:1), Moses stands with Aaron against the people. A crisis arises in the camp when it becomes clear that there is no water. The Israelites are angry at Moses and begin complaining, wailing that it would have been better had they stayed in Egypt. God instructs Moses to simply speak to a rock and water will come forth. But Moses has had enough. Instead of doing as he has been instructed, he raises his voice in anger against the people. Then, rather than simply speaking to the rock, he strikes it twice, and the water gushes out (Numbers 20:7–12). But more than the rock is broken in that moment. It becomes clear to God that Moses is no longer fit to be the messenger. Moses's rage is now hindering his ability to lead and to transmit God's message.

Righteous anger in response to acts of injustice, callousness, indifference, and needless suffering is an understandable reaction. But when a prophet sees the people, and not their deeds, as the enemy, then the prophet loses the ability to transmit God's message, which is ultimately one of *t'shuvah* and redemption. As we are reminded each year during the High Holy Days, while at times God may become angry at our deeds, we believe that the gates of forgiveness are always open. The prophet's words are an articulation of the shofar's blast, a reminder not only of the fact that we need to do better, but also how we can.

Rhetoric

There is no single style of rhetoric that can be identified as the prophet's voice. Rage and inspiration, blessings and curses, these are the prophet's tools. God chooses different messengers to convey what needs to be said, to whom, and how.

Today we live in a world of sound bites and slogans. A prophet's moral tirade does not fit easily into 140 characters or less. There is no emoji or meme that can adequately express the need to engage in *tikkun olam*. So where can we turn to hear the voices of the prophets today, with their insistent demands? How does God make known the eternal commandments that the needs of the poor, the weak, and the stranger should not be ignored?

When God spoke directly to us at Sinai, we recoiled in fear (Exodus 20:15–16). We begged for God to speak to us through Moses. To hear the voice of God directly was too much for us to bear. Never again have we heard God's voice ring out so clearly throughout the world. Since that time God has used the voices of men, women, and children, Jew and non-Jew, to help instruct us on how to create a better world. God's voice did not go silent when the Bible became codified; it just required more work from us to be able to recognize it when we heard it.

God's call for justice and mercy, equality and compassion, is all around us. And just as it has always been, God's voice often comes to us in the form of flawed vessels and unexpected messengers. Just like the biblical prophets whose voices could be strident and intolerable or quietly pleading, today God's words can be heard in a singular voice straining to be heard above the din or in a chorus of voices raised in a song of inspiration that stirs us just when we need it, in the weeping of a child or even in the still small voice of our own conscience. These are some of the ways that God continues to speak to us and through us.

The words of the prophets have never been easy to hear, not only because of their sometimes overwrought style of speaking or their unceasing demands, but because we can feel the pain, anger, and righteous indignation that drives what they are saying. They make us look directly at, and feel, the suffering of the stranger, the widow, the orphan—the most vulnerable in our midst. They demand that we do not look away from that which frightens us or makes us uncomfortable.

Many go to synagogue for the safety and comfort of prayer and ritual. They want to find a refuge from the chaos and do not want the evils of the world to follow them inside the sacred walls. For them, the words of the prophets are upsetting to hear, a discordant voice ripping through the calm that they seek.

Just as our ancestors challenged the prophets, many today challenge their rabbis. "How dare you bring politics into the house of God!" they ask. But it is God who reminds us, through the voice of the prophets, that God is everywhere. God is to be found in the details of how we live, in the way we treat each other, and in the way we govern or allow ourselves to be governed, not just in the way we pray.

God is impatient with a society that is more concerned with empty ritual than with pursuing justice. Isaiah gives voice to this theme:

> Bringing oblations is futile, incense is offensive to Me. New moon and Sabbath, proclaiming of solemnities, assemblies with iniquity, I cannot abide. Your new moons and fixed seasons fill Me with loathing; they are become a burden to Me, I cannot endure them. And when you lift up your hands, I will turn My eyes away from you; though you pray at length, I will not listen. Your hands are stained with crime—wash yourselves clean; put your evil doings away from My sight. Cease to do evil. (Isaiah 1:13–16)

Amos also preaches that when our prayers and sacrifices are offered in a corrupt society, when our prayers are in opposition with our deeds, we will incur God's wrath:

> I loathe, I spurn your festivals, I am not appeased by your solemn assemblies. If you offer Me burnt offerings—or your meal offerings—I will not accept them; I will pay no heed to your gifts of fatlings. Spare Me the sound of your hymns, and let Me not hear the music of your lutes. But let justice well up like water, righteousness like an unfailing stream. (Amos 5:21–24)

The holy offerings that God wants most from us is a society where even the most vulnerable among us are protected. God is paying attention not only to what we say, but also to what we do. As my grandmother was fond of saying, "Don't tell me that you love me, show me that you love me." God does not want to hear empty prayers of praise; God wants to see us engage in acts of moral courage and righteousness that will bring healing to our world.

A disciple of the ancient prophets, Rabbi Abraham Joshua Heschel dedicated his life to bringing the prophetic message into the modern day. When he reflected on his experience of marching in Selma in 1965, his words were reminiscent of the biblical prophets: "For many of us the march from Selma to Montgomery was about protest and prayer. Legs are not lips and walking is not kneeling. And yet our legs uttered songs. Even without words, our march was worship. I felt my legs were praying."[3] What Rabbi Heschel described is the perfect response to Isaiah and Amos. What Heschel wrote about were the type of offerings, according to the prophets, that God is seeking from us; that the way we walk through the world and the actions we engage in should be a reflection of our sacred values.

When Rev. Dr. Martin Luther King Jr. used the words of the ancient prophets to call out to other members of the clergy, the ones who heeded his call were the ones who understood that people of faith cannot leave their morals at the door of their house of worship. They knew that how we act in the public square is an expression of our religious values, that our actions should be a manifestation of the prayers we offer and the sacred texts we read in our sanctuaries. These men and women of faith understood what our prophets knew: there is no distinction between the public and the private, no separation between religious values and political actions. The public and the private, our religious beliefs and our political actions, must be in harmony with each other.

Both in ancient times and today the "prophet" (religion) and the "king" (politics) play important roles, and both are accountable to the One who created us all. In America we have no kings, but we do have politicians who are tasked with implementing the will of the people, even as they try to influence and motivate us to act in the ways that suit their needs. While the prophet and the politician both need to motivate the community to act, their roles and the tools they use are very different.

Politicians sit at the center of society, inside the seat of power. They need to be popular with the people, to rouse them and to charm them so as to keep their job, a job that is all too often simply protecting the status quo.

However, a prophet does not work from the center of society, but from its edges. Prophets are not concerned with making a living or keeping their jobs or even their friends. The prophets have an eye on eternity, an understanding that they are part of an enduring covenant made at Sinai. The prophet seeks to shake us up, to agitate us into changing our ways, to move society closer to the vision of a world redeemed. Prophets are a social irritant. Theirs is that still small voice we hear at 3:00 a.m. that wakes us up with a gasp and a start, refusing to allow us to rest easy. Their language is meant to jolt us out of our comfort and our slumber so that we will not only look at the world around us, but really see it, try to understand it, and be moved by what we see. And then we are commanded to fix what we know to be broken.

So where does that leave the modern-day Jew? On one hand, we are neither the prophet nor the politician. But on the other hand, we have the opportunity to be both. Living in a democratic system means that "we the people" are the government, that each of us bears the responsibility of governance. Whether we are silent or we make our voices heard, we—the people—bear the ultimate responsibility of the government's actions and inactions. In a democracy, the "politician" is not *them*, it is *us*, and we have the ability to enact change and to be involved in the public discourse from within the democratic system, as well as be a moral voice giving criticism or praise.

The prophets remind us that we cannot shed our religious beliefs at the voting booth's curtain. We must heed the prophet's call and respond to the needs of the poor, the weak, and the stranger. We must do so both within the political system by voting, by building coalitions with other ethnic and religious groups, and by being educated citizens. And when our voices are in the minority, we can be like the prophet and agitate from the outside by making our concerns heard by our elected officials, educating others through social media, or taking to the streets to protest unjust laws.

But from whom do we hear the prophet's voice *today*? Of course it still calls out to us each Shabbat, but we need not wait to go to services to hear God calling out to us to do what is right. The rabbi is not the prophet, but is a teacher of the prophetic message. The rabbi, *like all of us*, has the responsibility to pay attention to our sacred teachings and to act on them. As Elijah learned so long ago, the voice of God is within each of us; it is the still small voice that is always there, if only we would stop and pay attention to it (I Kings 19:12).

Vision, Rage, and Rhetoric

Vision. Rage. Rhetoric. These are the blessings, and the curses, of the prophet. God grants the prophets vision—the gift of seeing what can be if only we do what we know to be right. Rage burns in a prophet's heart when we do not respond to the divine call to do justice and to love mercy. So the prophets plead, bargain, and rail against us with fiery rhetoric, trying to move us from our complacency and apathy.

The prophets enjoin us to bring holiness and wholeness into our world by actively looking for the sacred spark in everyone around us. They demand we understand that when we pay workers a living wage, when we create social service programs to care for the stranger, the widow, the orphan in our midst, when we feed the hungry, when we house the homeless, when we work together for the greater good, we *are* engaging in religious acts of faith and making sacred offerings to God.

The prophets each model for us different ways to teach, to lead, to prod, and to poke at our collective consciousness so that the divine vision can become an earthly reality. They offer us a vision of religion that is not limited to ritual, but a religion where our daily interactions can be elevated into sacred acts infused with *chesed* (grace and loving-kindness), *tzedek* (justice), and *rachamim* (compassion).

But what does the prophet need from us to be able to make God's vision a reality? Action. The prophet uses vision, rage, and rhetoric to move us, to inspire *us*, to goad *us* into getting out of our comfort zone and truly engaging in the world. God uses the voices of the prophets like a shofar blast, to wake us up, to rouse us out of our slumber and into action.

The vision, rage, and rhetoric of the prophets is not enough. It has never been enough. It is the sustained, collective *action* of the community that is needed to repair all that has been broken and to soothe God's anger at our communal apathy toward those who need us the most.

NOTES

1. Translations are adapted from *JPS Hebrew-English Tanakh* (Philadelphia: Jewish Publication Society, 1999).

2. The Days of Awe, the ten days from Rosh HaShanah through Yom Kippur.

3. Susannah Heschel, "Following in My Father's Footsteps: Selma 40 Years Later," *Vox of Dartmouth*, April 4, 2005.

ON TRUTH, TRUENESS, AND PROPHECY

The Discourse of Resistance

Rabbi Jonathan Cohen, PhD

It may be a passion for truth that lies at the heart of the determination to express one's truth in the face of opposition and power, let alone the courage to assume the risk entailed in dissidence and disruption. Expressions of resistance in the name of truth have long been admired and established as models of Jewish leadership and sacrifice. In our tradition, the prophetic voice has often been identified as exemplary in the struggle to confront dominant political forces as well as deeply ingrained cultural norms and religious practices with discomforting observations and insights. Yet, beyond the affirmation of divine revelation and general attachment to truth as an ideal, the definition of truth, the nature of our attachment to a truth, and our will and ability to perceive truth are not yet issues that attract sufficient rabbinic attention and study. Throughout the past century, a number of psychologists,[1] philosophers,[2] literary critics,[3] and scholars of history[4] have demonstrated that our perception of and attachment to truth are central to our construction of reality, as well as to our willingness to engage in public action and assume risk. Our conception of truth is also profoundly associated with notions of authenticity and reliability on the one hand, and with our experiences of verbal and nonverbal communication on the other. This essay explores Jewish reflections on the attachment to a cause that represents "truth," for this is a core component of activism and resistance.

The exploration, questioning, and definition of truth claims and the human capacities and limits with respect to the acquisition of knowledge and truth verification appear throughout halachah and in Rabbinic commentary, theology, and philosophy. These weighty matters and Rabbinic discussions of them merit serious consideration beyond what we can undertake here. This essay is an initial exploration of certain characteristics of the expression and reception of truth and truth claims, especially in the public sphere. The expression of truth in the public sphere is notable as a hallmark of the institution of prophecy. In the prophetic literature and in our reading of it, revealed truth (or Truth) emerges as the impetus for critique, for discourse that can be perceived to be seditious or treasonous, and resistance, even in the face of punishment or retaliation. Thus, it is to these aspects of prophecy that we turn our attention.

While resistance and countercultural discourse have over time emerged as standards of biblical prophecy in general, a small number of prophets have claimed their places as paradigms of courage and truth-telling. Among them we find the towering figure of Jeremiah. Presumed author of the scroll of Lamentations, which describes the desolation of Jerusalem, Jeremiah is the leading voice of warning to the city's ruler and people.

Jeremiah has attracted much attention in the context of Israel. In his magnum opus *The Law*, first published approximately a generation ago, in a section addressing human rights and focusing on the freedom of speech, my late grandfather H. Cohn commented that "the fate of great and courageous prophets was imprisonment (Jeremiah 26:8, 37:15), exile (Amos 7:11–13), or even death (Jeremiah 26:23) and however bitter their [perceived] fates—attempts to silence them all failed."[5] Before Cohn, Israel's "founding father" and first prime minister, David Ben-Gurion, also associated Amos and Jeremiah and identified them as true prophets (or prophets of truth—*n'vi-ei emet*, as opposed to the false ones—an interesting distinction in the writings of Ben-Gurion). For Ben-Gurion, these two leaders lived and acted during two grave, pivotal moments of Jewish history: the Assyrian expansion and conquest that led to the destruction of the Kingdom of Israel, and the Babylonian domination that resulted in the downfall of Judah. Highlighting their unique qualities, Ben-Gurion wrote that both prophets

> were also thinkers, and experts in the spheres of politics and state. Not only were they highly knowledgeable of the affairs of their nation, but also with respect to the affairs of neighboring peoples, and at times their national and international understandings were of greater value than those of kings, their ministers, and counselors.

Relating to the oppositional relationship between King Zedekiah and Jeremiah, Ben-Gurion identified the latter as "one of the greatest among the prophets of writing, if not the greatest among them."[6] Similar insights were expressed by Aryeh Simon, a leading Israeli educator, who pointed out that "among the unique attributes of the prophets is their lack of power and exposure . . . in the face of the wrath of office holders . . . Like Nathan before David, Jeremiah stood alone in opposition to an all-powerful king," uttering a stinging rebuke and accusing the king of corruption, abuse of power, and the shedding of innocent blood (Jeremiah 22:12, 22:17).[7]

More recently, in the introduction to his book on Jeremiah, Benjamin Lau opined:

> A small number of prophets were removed or harmed on account of their prophecy. First and foremost among them was Jeremiah. His life as a prophet was in danger more than once. The internal truth that resonated in him led him to extremity, to the point of treason against the Kingdom of Judah. . . . There is no doubt that the greatest prophet that has come upon us in the era of kingship before the destruction of Jerusalem, and also the most dejected, hated, and courageous among them was Jeremiah. He did not fear imprisonment, physical punishment, or death itself and chose to relate to his people the bitter truth to the end.[8]

These and other such expressions of admiration for Jeremiah reflect the strong connection various authors draw between the capacities for courage, for will and resistance on the one hand, and the attachment and commitment to the truth that the prophet must voice on the other.

Beyond the fascination and admiration that Jeremiah's literary legacy has generated, we still find occasional expressions of longing for those who would communicate to us the rude, unvarnished, dangerous, and painful truth. For example, Mike McCormack is a prominent Irish author and winner of the prestigious Goldsmiths Prize for 2016. In *Solar Bones*, he comments on the collapse of the Irish economy and its devastating aftermath for entire industries and for many of the republic's working people. He writes:

> Surely this was the kind of catastrophe prophets should have an eye for or some foreknowledge but didn't since it is now evident in hindsight that our seers' gifts were of a lesser order, their warnings lowered to a tremulous bleating, the voices of men hedging their bets . . . as they settled instead for . . . that cautionary note which in the end proved wholly inadequate to the coming disaster . . . without that shrill tone of indictment, theirs was never a song to hold our attention . . . when what was needed was our prophets deranged and coming towards us wild-eyed and smeared with shit, ringing a bell, seer and sinner all at once while speaking a language from the edge of reason.[9]

McCormack proceeds to provide examples of contemporary truth-telling, of the extraordinary determination, courage, and action that communicate an unyielding commitment to resist in the face of overwhelming power: that of an environmental campaigner who launched a hunger strike to protest against the laying of a pressurized gas pipeline in her region, and of the sole protester who stood in front of a column of tanks in Tiananmen Square in 1989.[10] These individuals—whose courage, strength, speech, and actions transcend accepted norms and etiquette in order to draw and capture attention—are arguably closer to the prophetic figure of Jeremiah than the "men hedging their bets" who McCormack critiques.

From this, we can direct our thoughts to yet another aspect of prophetic resistance: its unique and individual expression. Tractate *Sanhedrin's* tenth chapter includes a *sugya* concerned with Rabbinic distinctions between true and false prophets. There, using the unusual Hebrew word *signon*,[11] Rabbi Isaac teaches that one style or mode of expression may be transmitted (by God) to more than one prophet, but that no two (true) prophets use the same formula of words or the same precise expression to communicate their prophecies (Babylonian Talmud, *Sanhedrin* 89a). The Gemara adduces the examples of Jeremiah and Obadiah who both prophesy to Edom with the same message and whose prophecies are very similar (Jeremiah 49:14–17; Obadiah 1:1–5). Both employ the same rarely used phrases and evoke common images. However, as the Talmudic argument points out, the two prophecies remain distinct. The example of Jeremiah and Obadiah is presented in contrast to a biblical episode wherein a large number of (false) prophets use precisely the same formula in their collective prophecy (I Kings 22:6). This biblical citation and its context may be instructive and worthy of a brief digression: In the backdrop to this reference, Ahab, the king of Israel, lobbies Jehoshaphat, the king of Judah, to join him in launching a war against Aram in order to reconquer, or liberate, the heights of Gilead. In response to Jehoshaphat's demand that Ahab examine his battle plan's coherence with the will of God, Ahab calls upon the prophets, approximately four hundred of them, and asks whether he should launch a war in the Gilead. They all respond in unison, encouraging the Israelite king to wage war. Alarmed at the unified and one-sided endorsement of war by the "establishment prophets," Jehoshaphat famously asks whether there is not another prophet of God (*ha-ein poh navi l'Adonai od*) who may be consulted (22:7).[12] In response to the request for a second opinion, King Ahab concedes that there is one prophet whom he does not consult because he is a (fake news) critic and contrarian (22:8). Eventually Micaiah son of Imlah is summoned, and following an initial corroboration of the other prophets' statement and additional probing, this lone prophet predicts the defeat of the Israelite army and demise of the Israelite king. The prophet's message is dismissed, he is imprisoned, and the Israelite king enters the fray in disguise and is nevertheless killed by an arrow. That evening, the call goes out in the Israelite encampment for all fighters to retreat to their homes (22:9–18, 22:29–36). Further, the biblical text adds yet another important element: the revelation that it is God in God's divine counsel who is responsible for the deception of the Israelite prophets and that this deception is God's design to punish King Ahab (22:17–23). The Talmudic citation of King Jehoshaphat serves to show that the repetition of formulae, the complete coherence of the prophets' message, is one of the signs of false prophecy. At first blush, the implication is that true prophets internalize and personalize the received or inspired message in ways that render it unique.

All of this serves to reveal or emphasize that the prophet's inner sense of truth, the exceptional determination and strength of will, the personal and creative messaging, and even the ability to cross the boundaries of the acceptable and culturally appropriate, are not in themselves sufficient for the successful completion of the prophet's mission. As we learn from the biblical and Talmudic material, the prophet's truth must somehow be identified as "true prophecy" in order to be effectively communicated and to sway others. The success of the prophet's mission depends on it.

Here, Jeremiah's example is yet again instructive: Jeremiah's trial narrative relates the reaction of priests, prophets, and members of the public in the House of God to his act of resistance—meant as a harsh warning concerning the fate of Jerusalem and its Temple. Following an incendiary speech in the Temple compound, Jeremiah is seized and threatened with death (Jeremiah 26:8).[13] Only after the arrival of the ministers or elders, and the prophets and priests' call for Jeremiah to be executed, does Jeremiah speak in his own defense. Then, in reaction to Jeremiah's response, the ministers or elders exonerate him, while the crowds continue to demand his execution (26:9–16). In Cohn's view, the narrative reflects a constitutional crisis—a struggle for power between two branches of the judiciary: the priests and the judges—a conflict that reflects the assignment of potentially competing judicial powers to both groups (see Deuteronomy 17:9–12). In this view, the priests pronounce their judgment against Jeremiah, and it is later overturned by the elders-judges following Jeremiah's defense.[14] According to another view, this chapter's narrative describes a full-blown trial wherein the priests speak for the prosecution, and Jeremiah represents himself in these public proceedings.[15] While the substance of Jeremiah's message is the immediate cause of his prosecution (Jeremiah 26:11), the charge leveled against him is one of false prophecy: "Why did you prophecy in the name of the Eternal?" (*Madua niveita v'shem Adonai*; 26:9). Jeremiah's defense opens with the statement that God sent him to deliver these words in this Temple and city—*Adonai sh'lachani l'hinavei*—and concludes with a repetition of the same message (26:12; 26:15). However, in his closing iteration, Jeremiah adds the word "in truth" (*be-emet*) to his claim of divine mission. The reaction of the elders-ministers to the priests, prophets, and members of the assembled public leaves little doubt as to their view of Jeremiah: the phrase "he has spoken to us in the name of the Eternal our God" (26:16) reflects their acceptance of Jeremiah's truth claim, or his claim of prophetic authenticity. Indeed, the indication that Ahikam son of Shaphan seizes Jeremiah to protect him so that "the people" do not put him to death (26:24) suggests that while Jeremiah's truth claim is credible in the eyes of the political or judicial leaders assembled, it does not sway the judgment of the multitude. The trial does not end with a "slam dunk," a Nineveh-style change of heart, or with widespread recognition of the validity of Jeremiah's prophetic credentials, but rather with drama, tension, danger, and a general disbelief. Fortunately, for Jeremiah, his credentials and competence are accepted by those who sit in judgment, and his life is saved. In other words, Jeremiah's truth claim seems to resonate to some degree, but the people's inability to fully hear and understand him leads to defeat, destruction, death, and exile in the biblical narrative.

The tension that emerges from the material we are considering points to both the intrinsic value of (true) prophecy articulated with the force and personal passion it deserves, as well as to the significance of the reaction to it. Indeed, in certain cases, successful transmission and reception of the prophetic message constitute matters of life and death. The greater the opposition or enmity between the "truth-teller" and the potential recipient of her or his message, the greater the risk entailed with resistance. This dynamic is often reflected in our literature, but rarely more succinctly, elegantly, and effectively than in the writing of S. Y. Agnon. In a short story published posthumously, Agnon explores this dynamic, drawing upon common Jewish images and themes. His "Truth's Reward"[16] puts Rabbi Elazar Rokeach, who, following a Passover-related blood libel, advocates on behalf of his community, before a non-Jewish king. As if this situation were not sufficiently ominous to the twentieth-century Jewish reader, the story relates the arrival of a royal meal at the chamber of the king while the Jewish delegation waits for an audience. Reacting to the display of delicacies fit for royalty, the rabbi mutters, "If such is the lot of those who transgress against His will, all the more so for those who fulfill it." When the delegation is granted access to the king, he immediately asks the rabbi to repeat the comment he made when the food was arriving. Following silence and hesitation, the rabbi responds, explaining that he feels trapped: he would incriminate himself if he repeated his comment, on the one hand, and would endanger himself if he refused to do so, on the other; he would risk his life if the king heard his utterance, but he would compromise his integrity if he lied. Following the king's assurance to Rabbi Rokeach that he would not be harmed for revealing the truth, he relates and explains his words. In turn, the king's assurance of the rabbi's honesty contributes to his willingness to accept the rabbi's forceful truth claim with respect to the blood libel. Thus, at the start of this story, Agnon employs an oft-repeated trope of Jewish victimization and appeal to hostile non-Jewish authorities to set the stage for Jewish heroics against impossible odds, or perhaps for the expectation of miraculous deliverance through the feat of the inspired rabbi. Yet, the story ends with the undermining of ethno-religious roles and a redirection of the reader to the universal potential in the expression and reception of truth. Its conclusion suggests recognition and appreciation for an attentive, informed, and probing king whose good judgment of character offers an opportunity for the redemption of the rabbi and protection of his Jewish community. At the same time, while the rabbi's integrity is the *sine qua non* to the success of his mission, his utterance with regard to the royal meal does not testify to great discretion, let alone positive disposition toward the authorities. In other words, while the opposition between the rabbi and the king is exacerbated by the rabbi's comment about the catering, his comment is also authentic, or genuine, and contributes to the impression of his truthfulness. We may note that it is precisely the combination of the authenticity, truthfulness, and credibility of the undiplomatic rabbi along with the careful evaluation, consideration, and sense of fairness and justice of the non-Jewish king that leads to the desired outcome. The value of truth, shared between the rabbi and the non-Jewish judge-king, would save the Jews. Disregard or impatience for it, like that of a "jesting Pilate," would entail very different consequences.[17]

And so we return to the challenge of articulating a "truth" anchored in a deep and personal commitment, to mustering the capacity and courage to express this trueness in ways that fully communicate our message and its implications. While our discourse and action may transgress against customs and conventions in order to capture attention, our message also needs to be heard in such a way that it can be received and considered, rather than dismissed. We must recall the risk of retaliation and punishment and the willingness or resignation to sacrifice, as well as the realization that not all of our kings, judges, opponents, and other listeners always share the sense of justice and fairness we would wish to exhibit and to share ourselves. And as we consider these, it is incumbent upon us to recall role models of truth-telling and resistance.

One such figure of the twentieth and early twenty-first centuries is Vaclav Havel. Havel's *Living in Truth* is a testament to the clarity of vision and strength of character of one of Europe's leading dissidents. It is also an example of profound attachment to a personal truth and to the faith that it might be recognized by others. In this collection, he highlights some of the salient characteristics of opposition and resistance in the Soviet bloc and its association with truth.[18] Havel's essay "The Power of the Powerless" describes the functioning of the Soviet bloc, a system he labels post-totalitarian. He writes, "The principle involved here is that the center of power is identical with the center of truth." According to Havel, the system relies on a

> correct understanding of history anchored in an ideology that is incomparably more precise, logically structured, generally comprehensible, and . . . extremely flexible . . . that in its elaborateness and completeness is almost a secularized religion. . . . To wandering humankind it offers an immediately available home: all one has to do is accept it. . . . Of course one pays a dearly for this low-rent home: the price is abdication of one's own reason, conscience, and responsibility.[19]

The system maintains its power structure through ideological means, offering human beings the illusion of belonging to "something super-personal and objective . . . and greater than themselves," facilitating a self-deception that masks the degradation to which they are subjected. This web of prevarication relies on a systematic misuse of language, or "hypocrisy and lies," wherein

> government by bureaucracy is called popular government, the working class is enslaved in the name of the working class, the complete degradation of the individual is presented as his or her ultimate liberation . . . the use of power to control people is called public control of power, and the arbitrary abuse of the power is called observing the legal code.

Thus, the requirement to acquiesce, tolerate, and engage with the system requires the acceptance of a false reality, of "living a lie" in the form of an ongoing ritual. Further, collaboration with this intricate and overpowering web of deception—the willingness to follow the rules—strengthens and perpetuates the system, enabling it to survive.[20] For Havel, the power of dissidence and opposition is that it exposes the deception and sheds light on it. Deception maintains its hold until it is cracked and exposed. For Havel, "in the post-totalitarian system, living within the truth has more than a mere existential dimension . . . it also has an unambiguous political dimension."[21] Further, his notion of "living in truth" may be of value beyond the extreme conditions and circumstances of the post-totalitarian system that we associate with the Soviet bloc. He writes:

> A person who has been seduced by the consumer value system, whose identity is dissolved in an amalgam of accoutrements of mass civilization, and who has no roots in the order of being, no sense of responsibility for anything higher than his or her own personal survival, is a demoralized person. The system depends on this demoralization, deepens it, is in fact a projection of it into society.[22]

For Havel, demoralization is characterized by the undermining of the individual's moral compass and capacity for recognizing, articulating, and voicing truth in the face of overwhelming power; a demoralized person's attachment to truth and sense of authenticity and wholeness are compromised.

It should come as little revelation that the impetus to express one's truth is often anchored in the perception and utter rejection of a perceived lie. It is conceivable that Isaiah's expression of poetic outrage regarding those "who call evil good; and good evil; who present darkness as light; and light as darkness; who present bitter as sweet; and sweet as bitter . . . those who are so wise in their own opinions" (Isaiah 5:20–21) reflects a profound need to confront a pervasive misuse of language, an overwhelming deception, and the unchallenged justification of a false reality. It may be that Jeremiah's furious indictment of "foolish people, devoid of intelligence; they have eyes but cannot see; they have ears but cannot hear," and especially the judgment that "an appalling horrible thing has happened in this land: the prophets prophesy falsely, and the priests rule accordingly; and My people like it so" (Jeremiah 5:21, 5:30–31), all reflect an urgent, powerful, and aggressive need to expose a demoralized society overtaken by pretense and falsehood. And perhaps in this insight, in the acute sense of cognitive dissonance and doubt that generate discomfort and pain, we may find the beginnings of an understanding of the impulse for truth-telling and resistance. We are neither prophets nor children of prophets. Yet at certain moments in our history, some have seen and experienced the oppressive power of error, misconception, and duplicity. A number of the rabbis on whose shoulders we stand have raised their voices and acted to express their truth in the face of power and danger. May we be strengthened by their example. Inspired by prophets like Jeremiah, perhaps we should pray that we may find the courage to use our eyes to truly see, our ears to truly hear, and that when the darkness seems to spread, we may find the conviction and determination to speak out for the cause of light, learning, and justice, so that we may merit to live in truth.

NOTES

1. One of the pioneers in this area was Otto Rank, author of *Truth and Reality*, first published in German in 1927, and translated into English in 1936.

2. Starting with Hans-Georg Gadamer's *Truth and Method*, first published in 1960, and including the work of John Searle (especially in *The Construction of Social Reality*, especially chapter 9), as well as Bruno Latour and Pierre Bourdieu, to name a few.

3. For example, Geoffrey Hartman in *Scars of the Spirit*, especially in chapters 3, 4, and 9.

4. For example, Hayden White in *Metahistory*, first published in 1973, especially in chapters 1, 2, and 9.

5. Haim H. Cohn, *HaMishpat* [in Hebrew], 2nd ed. (Jerusalem: Bialik Institute, 1996), 532.

6. David Ben-Gurion, *Biblical Reflections* [in Hebrew] (Tel Aviv: Am Oved, 1969), 233.

7. Aryeh Simon, *Man in the Image* [in Hebrew] (Tel Aviv: Am Oved, 1991), 47.

8. Benjamin Lau, *Jeremiah* [in Hebrew] (Tel Aviv: Miskal–Yedioth Ahronoth & Chemed Books, 2010), 20, 21.

9. Mike McCormack, *Solar Bones* (Dublin: Tramp Press, 2016), 14.

10. Ibid., 14–15.

11. In the Jastrow and Ben Yehuda dictionaries the word is traced to Greek and to the Latin *Signum*, meaning "sign, watchword, or message."

12. Both Rashi and Ralbag in their commentaries explain King Jehoshaphat's distrust of the credentials of Ahab's prophets.

13. See Rabbi David ben Aryeh Leib's commentary, the *Metzudat David*.

14. "Priests and Judges," a lecture delivered in honor of Rabbi Zawi (Jerusalem, 1980), 21–22.

15. H. Angel, "Jeremiah's Trial as a False Prophet (Chapter 26): A Window into the Complex Religious State of the People," *Jewish Bible Quarterly* 45, no. 1 (2017): 15–16; Lau, *Jeremiah*, 120–26.

16. S. Y. Agnon, "Truth's Reward," in *A Shroud of Stories* [in Hebrew] (New York: Schocken, 1985), 127–28.

17. See Francis Bacon, "Of Truth," likely first published in 1625 in *Essayes or Counsels, Civill and Morall*.

18. Published in 1980, it is a collection of essays and correspondence, some of which was produced by Havel while imprisoned as a dissident. V. Havel, *Living in Truth* (London: Faber & Faber, 1980).

19. Ibid., 38–39.

20. Ibid., 42–46.

21. Ibid., 56–57.

22. Ibid., 62.

IMAGINING IMMIGRATION

The Stranger in Jewish Law and Lore

RABBI AARON D. PANKEN, PHD, *z"l*

A friend of mine whose parents were immigrants, Jews from Europe who came to America in search of safety, told me this story. His parents lived and worked in New York. They were not well off. His father died when he was young. His mother lived on, and in time my friend succeeded and became wealthy. He often used to offer his mother the chance to travel outside America. She never did. When eventually she died, they went back to recover the safety box where she kept her jewelry. They found there was another box. There was no key. So they had to drill it open. They wondered what precious jewel must be in it. They lifted the lid. There was wrapping and more wrapping and finally an envelope. Intrigued, they opened it. In the envelope were her U.S. citizenship papers. Nothing more. That was the jewel, more precious to her than any other possession. That was what she treasured most. So should America today.

—Tony Blair, former British prime minister,
My Journey: Tony Blair

The issues surrounding immigration are complex and multifaceted and go to the heart of what it means to hold the jewel of American citizenship Blair describes above. And yet, mixed into the standard questions of appropriate procedure for legally welcoming new immigrants are other thorny issues. Should amnesty or a path to citizenship be provided for the numerous undocumented immigrants already in this country? What rights and social benefits (health care, financial support, access to education, protection by local police) should they receive? What restrictions (quotas, voting, time frame, and process before citizenship) should be applicable to them? Should organizations like synagogues and churches offer them "sanctuary," a challenging term with a wide range of potential and legal interpretations? What is the just societal response to families in the United States illegally? And do we, as Jews, have specific knowledge or experience that compels us to act in certain ways?

The United States and other countries have struggled with this difficult tension for centuries. As Jews, we faced restrictions spurred by antisemitism enacted in the Johnson-Reed Act of 1924, which established strict quotas designed to prevent Jews from immigrating. At other times, Chinese, Italian, Irish, and German immigrants, as well as those professing Catholicism and other faiths, have faced severe limitations on entry to America. While being, in some respects, the quintessential immigrant nation, America does have a challenging record of restrictive immigration laws and, more recently, travel bans that seem unlikely to end anytime soon.

In this essay, I will selectively probe the Jewish tradition to explore the obligations, trends, and values it brings to such controversies in order to set a frame around what we might consider doing as Reform (or other sorts of) Jews in this challenging moment. The treatment here is not meant in any way to be exhaustive, but simply to refer readers to some of the most important texts and ideas that exist in the early Jewish canon. The hope is that then, informed by our tradition, we can continue the task of crafting a response to the immigration issues we now confront daily.

The Biblical Background: On Being a Stranger

The first hint of the trauma of being a stranger (Hebrew: *ger*) arises quite early in the Bible, in Genesis 15:13–16:

> [God] said to Abram, "Know now that your descendants shall be strangers in a land not theirs; they shall be enslaved and afflicted for four hundred years. But then I will bring judgment upon the nation they are serving; after that they shall go out with many possessions. . . . The fourth generation shall return here." (Genesis 15:13–16)

Being a stranger is constructed in starkly negative terms in this passage. While they are strangers residing outside their land, these future Israelites will be "enslaved and afflicted," with their only reward coming upon release in a monetary windfall. Further, God's judgment rests upon those who have enslaved them, indicating both the regular biblical privileging of Abraham's descendants over other peoples and, perhaps, a subtle condemnation of any oppressors who make miserable the lives of the Israelites. It is clear that sojourning temporarily in another land creates vulnerability that can only be resolved by the attainment of full resident status in one's own place.

Genesis 23:3–6 illustrates one particular challenge of being a resident alien in a foreign land and should sensitize readers to the vulnerability inherent in this situation:

> Then Abraham rose up from upon his dead [wife], and spoke to the Hittites, saying, "I am a resident alien [*ger toshav*] among you; sell me a gravesite among you, that I may bury my dead here." The Hittites answered Abraham, saying, "Hear us, my lord; you are the elect of God in our midst; bury your dead in any of our choicest graves. Not one of us will keep you from burying your dead by withholding a gravesite from you." (Genesis 23:3–6)

In the sadness of mourning his late wife Sarah as a *ger toshav*, a resident alien with limited rights to land ownership, Abraham experiences the pain of vulnerability when he has no access to the regular offerings for full citizens of the country. Burial plots, often organized in the ancient Near East by families or clans, required land, and this text suggests that *some* aliens, those with some sort of recognized stature within the community like Abraham, could receive access to a burial plot for beloved deceased relatives. Of course, the author or editor may be trying to raise the stature of Abraham in the reader's eyes in constructing the narrative in this manner. In any case, the aforementioned burial plot becomes the famous Machpelah, the cave in Hebron where most of the Patriarchs and Matriarchs are buried and that remains a holy site until this day.

While Genesis focuses on Abraham's trials as an individual moving from one country to another, Exodus 12:48–49 offers more quotidian information on entering a community or living in a foreign community:

> If a male stranger who dwells with you would offer the Passover [sacrifice] to the Eternal, all his males must be circumcised; then he shall be admitted to offer it; he shall then be as a citizen of the country. But no uncircumcised man may eat of it. There shall be one law for the citizen and for the stranger who dwells among you. (Exodus 12:48–49)

Two elements are of import here: first, that it is permissible to establish reasonable entry criteria and apply them to those who would wish to join a community or enter a country. In this case, circumcision provides the gateway through which an immigrant must pass to become part of the community. While this is not quite the complete conversion ceremony that develops later in Rabbinic literature, nor a full citizenship test, it does establish the fact that admission is accompanied by certain ritual or legal acts. Second, the text suggests a significant commitment to legal fairness—ensuring that the law applies to everyone equally. Based on these verses, it is clear that biblical law would not endorse the concept that aliens (legal or illegal) could be subject to different laws than citizens.

The Bible also commands citizens of a nation not to oppress the stranger who dwells with them in Leviticus 19. A related passage in Deuteronomy 10 goes even further, placing God in the role of enforcing against such behavior:

> When strangers reside with you in your land, you shall not oppress them. The strangers who reside with you shall be to you as your

citizens; you shall love each one as yourself, for you were strangers in the land of Egypt: I the Eternal am your God. (Leviticus
19:33–34)

For the Eternal your God is God supreme and Lord supreme,
the great, the mighty, and the awesome God, who shows no favor
and takes no bribe, but upholds the cause of the fatherless and the
widow, and befriends the stranger, providing food and clothing.—
You too must befriend the stranger, for you were strangers in the
land of Egypt. (Deuteronomy 10:17–19)

This text clearly forbids oppression of others because our people once
suffered it, and based on that experience, it is unthinkable and abhorrent to God to inflict it on others (see also Exodus 22:20, discussed
below). In fact, beyond simply avoiding oppression, one must actually
love strangers as God does, provide them with food and clothing, and
become their friends. Likened here to orphans and widows, the social
position of strangers was among the weakest in ancient society due to
their lack of protection within the reigning societal hierarchy. Recognizing this weakness and responding to it with kindness is a clear
biblical priority, in addition to an obvious moral imperative.

Once we move into the Prophets, the call for inclusion of strangers
grows even stronger. In Isaiah 56, the third and post-exilic section of
the Book of Isaiah, we read of a broad expansion of the contours of
welcoming strangers:

Let not the foreigner say, who has attached himself to *Adonai*,
"*Adonai* will keep me apart from God's people.". . . As for the foreigners who attach themselves to *Adonai*, to minister to God, and
to love *Adonai*'s name, to be God's servants—all who keep the Sabbath and do not profane it, and who hold fast to My covenant—I
will bring them to My sacred mount and let them rejoice in My
house of prayer. Their burnt offerings and sacrifices shall be welcome on My altar, for My house shall be called a house of prayer
for all peoples. Thus declares *Adonai*, who gathers the dispersed of
Israel: "I will gather still more to those already gathered." (Isaiah
56:3, 56:6–8)

Here, we see the possibility of a loyalty test, for it is only those who have attached themselves to serve and love God's name who may be full participants in the religious life of the Temple, even to the point of offering their sacrifices (through the priests, of course) on God's altar. The gathering of foreigners to worship God is seen as laudable; in fact it is part of the process of redeeming the world (see Isaiah 56:1). Thus, the inclusion of strangers, assuming their commitments are appropriate, is highly positive and desirable, leading to the ultimate redemption of the world.

Jeremiah 7:3–7 privileges ethical behavior over ritual acts, imploring those about to be exiled to Babylonia to change their actions to prevent the destruction of God's Temple in Jerusalem. Prominent among God's claims against them is the oppression of the stranger and other vulnerable parties:

> Thus said *Adonai Tz'vaot*, the God of Israel: Mend your ways and your actions, and I will let you dwell in this place. Don't put your trust in illusions and say, "The Temple of *Adonai*, the Temple of *Adonai*, the Temple of *Adonai* are these [buildings]." No, if you really mend your ways and your actions; if you execute justice between one person and another; if you do not oppress the stranger, the orphan, and the widow; if you do not shed the blood of the innocent in this place; if you do not follow other gods, to your own hurt—then only will I let you dwell in this place, in the land that I gave to your ancestors for all time. (Jeremiah 7:3–7)

It is downright remarkable to say that trust in the Temple is an illusion when weighed against ethical action on behalf of society's most vulnerable. Placing such words into Jeremiah's mouth, speaking with direct inspiration from God, raises the stakes even higher. It is hard to imagine a stronger statement of the import of supporting the foreigner, especially since the Israelites' continued dwelling in the land is now linked to their treatment of the stranger.

In sum, the biblical record offers clear preference for ethical behavior toward the stranger. Prohibitions against oppressing the stranger stand side by side with commandments to love and befriend the stranger. The text recognizes the intense vulnerability that accompanies dwelling in a foreign land and works hard to assuage it through concerted societal action. The inclusion of the stranger in ritual activities, plus the equalizing of widow, orphan, and stranger, serves to transform a natural human distrust of foreigners into a stance of welcoming, supporting, and loving them.

Rabbinic Literature: The Evolving Conception of the *Ger*

We now turn our attention to Rabbinic literature, comprising a series of postbiblical works written by the Rabbis in the Land of Israel and in Babylonia. These writings collect thousands of Rabbinic teachings, from roughly the first to the seventh centuries CE. The beginning phase, called the tannaitic period, stretches from 70 CE to 225 CE. The later period, from 225 CE through the seventh century CE, is known as the amoraic period. Both periods offer much in the way of information regarding the Rabbinic sense of compassion and the imperative to welcome strangers and immigrants.

The term *ger* (stranger) in Rabbinic literature is mostly understood to mean one who is either joining or has joined the Jewish people through some act of conversion. Many of the interpretations put forth of biblical passages are revised to focus on the act of becoming Jewish in this time. Despite this shift and the complexities it introduces, the conversion process is sufficiently akin to the dynamics of immigration, allowing appropriate Rabbinic texts about the *ger* to be useful in shaping our response to immigration issues today.

An early midrashic exposition on the Book of Exodus known as *M'chilta D'Rabbi Yishmael* (*Pisha* 15), completed during the tannaitic period, inquires as to why the biblical text includes the statement in Exodus 12:49, "There shall be one law for the citizen and for the stranger who dwells among you." In response:

> "There shall be one law for the citizen [and for the stranger who dwells among you]." Why is this said? Did not the text already

say (Exodus 12:48), "He shall then be as a citizen of the country"? Why should the text have to then say, "There shall be one law for the citizen"? Since it says, "If a stranger who dwells with you would make the *pesach* [passover] offering," this can only mean that with respect to *pesach*, the stranger obeys the same law. How do we know that this applies to all the other mitzvot in the Torah? The text says, "There shall be one Torah for the citizen and for the stranger." The text comes to make an equivalence between the stranger and the citizen regarding all the mitzvot of the Torah.

Moving far beyond simply ritual acts, this *M'chilta* passage now greatly expands the way strangers must be treated, demanding equality with respect to every commandment in the Torah! Criminal and civil laws, receiving charity and taking responsibility for others, and so much more devolve from this interpretation, suggesting that the stranger should both benefit from and be required to participate in every aspect of community life.

Another section of this same work (*N'zikin* 18) provides the most extensive tannaitic guidance on the way one ought respond to the stranger, starting with the sad yet natural human tendency to attack strangers by highlighting their differences:

> "You shall not annoy nor oppress a stranger, for you were strangers in the land of Egypt" (Exodus 22:20). You shall not annoy him, in words, and you shall not oppress him with money matters, that you may not say to him, "Yesterday you were worshiping Bel, Kores, Nebo, and behold swine was between your teeth, and now you speak against me!" And how do we know that if you annoy him he is permitted to annoy you? It is said: "For you were strangers"; from this Rabbi Natan would say, "Do not reproach your fellow with a fault that is also your own."

The Torah's use of two words, "annoy" and "oppress," opens up interpretive possibilities that reflect two of the standard tools embedded citizens employ to the detriment of foreigners: the use of language to harm them in words, and the crafting of negative narratives of immigrant history to harm them in monetary terms, whether in court, employment, or other venues. By reminding the newly arrived immigrant (in this case, one could also read this text as pointing to a convert as well) of his or her prior idolatry and lack of observance of kashrut, the citizen denigrates immigrants, pointing to their differences and making them less desirable as witnesses or as employees. In so doing, they lower the immigrants' ability to integrate and have access to fair and equal treatment in their society.

A further important point relating to the current immigrant situation emerges at the end of these lines, where there is a reminder that each citizen descends, at some point or another, from immigrants and that any accusation one can level against current immigrants could certainly have once been leveled at their ancestors at some point in history. Whether they came on the *Mayflower* or arrived last week, in the American context everyone (except, perhaps, for African Americans and others brought here against their will and, of course, Native Americans) fits neatly into only two categories: immigrant or descendant of immigrants. To fault others for their immigrant status is to reproach them for a fault you share and, therefore, the height of hypocrisy.

This is not universally accepted, though, as this passage then continues:

> Beloved are the strangers. For in so many passages, Scripture warns about them: "And a stranger you shall not annoy" (Exodus 22:20); "Therefore love the stranger" (Deuteronomy 10:19); "For you know the feelings of the stranger" (Exodus 23:9). Rabbi Eliezer says, "It is because there is an evil nature in the stranger that Scripture warns about him in so many passages." Rabbi Shimon bar Yochai says, "Behold, it says: 'But they who love God are as the sun, rising in might' (Judges 5:31). Now, who is greater, the one who loves the ruler, or the one loved by the ruler? We have to say it is the one whom the ruler loves, as it is said: '[God] loves the stranger' (Deuteronomy 10:18)."

Rabbi Eliezer's opinion suggests that immigrants are somehow deficient or wicked and that the reason the Torah must mention them so often is to overcome their suboptimal starting point as outsiders.

Surely there is an echo of this attitude in the language used against immigrants even today, despite the ample evidence to the contrary as to the hard work and incredible success so many immigrants have accomplished. Rabbi Shimon bar Yochai's refutation of Rabbi Eliezer's position is a reminder that God loves immigrants, based on Deuteronomy 10:18 and other evidence we have seen again and again in the Torah already. To behave appropriately, one must overcome one's base human instincts to isolate and distance immigrants and assume a stance of loving them as God does. Such a practice is a potent instance of *imitatio Dei*, modeling human behavior on the higher actions of the Divine.

This passage continues by highlighting the similarities rather than the differences between citizens and immigrants. It provides a long list showing how many verses of the Torah aim for equality and use the same language for both citizens and foreigners. Within the biblical text, both are called servants of God, ministers to God, friends, members of the covenant, and those who benefit from God's watchful guarding. This is meant, of course, to lower the walls between citizens and strangers and to ensure that citizens cannot in any way portray themselves as superior, thus taking advantage of the weaker societal position of the stranger.

The *M'chilta* then invokes a poignant reference to two of the greatest leaders of the Israelites:

> Abraham called himself a stranger, as it is said: "I am a stranger and a sojourner with you" (Genesis 23:4). David called himself a stranger, as it is said: "I am a stranger in the earth" (Psalm 119:19). And it also says: "For we are strangers before You, and sojourners, as all our ancestors were; our days on the earth are as a shadow, and there is no abiding" (I Chronicles 29:15). And it also says: "For I am a stranger with You, a sojourner, as all my ancestors were" (Psalm 39:13).

This is a very serious implicit critique of those who denigrate strangers. If Abraham, Judaism's essential founder, and King David, Judaism's greatest king, each saw themselves as strangers and sojourners, can later individuals really even begin to imagine themselves as superior to a stranger? Such chutzpah crosses all lines of acceptability.

Continuing on this theme, the text concludes:

> Beloved are the strangers. It was for their sake that our father Abraham was not circumcised until he was ninety-nine years old. Had he been circumcised at twenty or thirty years of age, only those under the age of thirty could have become proselytes to Judaism. Therefore, God bore with Abraham until he reached ninety-nine years of age, so as not to close the door to future proselytes. . . . And you find strangers also among the four groups who respond and speak before the One by whose word the world came into being (Isaiah 44:5): "One shall say: I am God's," that is, all of me is God's, and there is no mix of sin within me. "And another shall call himself by the name of Jacob," these are the righteous proselytes [*gerei tzedek*]. "And another shall write with his hand to God," these are the repentant sinners. "And [others] shall name themselves Israel," and these are the God fearers [among the gentiles].

Abraham's late circumcision (the moment he officially entered into the covenant with God) is to ensure that no door ever closes on a proselyte, a reminder that doors (borders, boundaries, etc.) are not to be slammed shut in the face of strangers; rather, they should be open to all, regardless of age. There is also, here, a delineation of the various levels of closeness to God and the people, whether as converts, righteous proselytes, repentant sinners, or God-fearing gentiles. This shows an awareness of the process of coming to be a part of a people and a respectful tolerance for people who are at different stages of moving from outside to inside. Fostering an ethos of openness, welcoming, and respect for immigrants wherever they are in the process is the ultimate aim of this discussion.

In a *baraita* (a tannaitic text), another vital set of guidelines emerges regarding converts to Judaism, which may be used to instruct our choices in how we regulate immigration:

Our Rabbis taught: A convert who comes to convert in this time, they say to him [sic] "What did you see that you came to convert? Don't you know that Israel at this time is afflicted, oppressed, swept away and troubled, and suffering comes to them?" If he says, "I know, and I am not worthy," we accept him immediately.

And we tell him some of the minor commandments [*mitzvot kalot*] and some of the major commandments [*mitzvot chamurot*], and we tell him of the sin of the gleanings, the forgotten sheaf, the corners of the field, and the tithe of the poor.

And we tell him the penalties associated with the mitzvot, saying to him, "Be it known to you that before you reached this level, you ate forbidden fat and you were not penalized with shortening of your life [*kareit*], you violated Shabbat and you were not penalized with stoning [*s'kilah*]; but now, if you eat forbidden fat, you are punished with shortening your life, and if you violate Shabbat, you will be stoned."

And just as we tell him about the penalties of the mitzvot, so too do we tell him about the rewards associated with them. We say to him, "Be it known that the world-to-come is made only for the righteous, and Israel in this time is unable to bear either too much good or too much suffering."

And we do not extend too much with him, nor do we enter into too many details with him.

If he accepted, we circumcise him immediately. . . .

When he heals, we immerse him immediately, and two wise students stand behind him and inform him of some of the minor and some of the major commandments. When he immersed and came up—behold he is like an Israelite in all matters.

And for a woman: two women stand her in the water up to her neck, and two wise students stand outside for her and inform her of some of the minor and some of the major commandments. (Babylonian Talmud, *Y'vamot* 47a–b)

Here we find the earliest outlines of the basic procedure for conversion to Judaism that continues to this day. Without going into too many of the fascinating details contained herein, consider the values that inform the actions of one bringing a new citizen into the Jewish people:

1. Inquiry: We are interested in the situation that brought this stranger to us. We ask: what did they see that caused them to consider joining?

2. Learning: We tell them about the requirements (mitzvot), pen-alties, and benefits of their new status, so they may be fully informed and oriented to their new life and aware of their role in the new society they join.
3. Acceptance/suitability: We have clear standards that they must adhere to before entry; otherwise we will not admit them.
4. Brevity: We do not extend too much into the details so as not to overwhelm them.
5. Immediacy: We do not delay their acceptance when they are ready, but welcome them quickly and efficiently without long waiting periods.
6. Ceremony: There is a clear moment in which their status changes, witnessed by members of the community on its behalf.

All of these values take into account the situation of the stranger or convert, rather than focusing on the position of the ones accepting the newcomer. While standards must remain high (one must actually know and commit to something to be admitted), the goal here is not to distance or reject strangers. Rather it is to provide them with the appropriate tools they need to survive in their new home as fully suc-cessful members of the new community. Imagine how different the world would be if analogous values were brought to bear on contem-porary questions of immigration.

It is clear that the arc of the classic Jewish sources bends toward welcoming and that we Jews, who understand from our long and tor-rid history what it means to be displaced and unwanted, have a clear obligation to understand the plight of strangers and welcome them. That is, predominantly, what Jewish sources, both early and late, com-mand us to do.

There are at least two additional factors that must also be taken into account from our tradition. First, we are obligated under Talmudic law to follow the law of the land, a principle known as *dina d'malchuta dina* (the law of the land is the law; see Babylonian Talmud, *N'darim* 28a; *Gittin* 10b; *Bava Kama* 113a–b; *Bava Batra* 54b–55a). Law made by a legitimate government body is to be obeyed. This coexists, of course, with the prophetic instinct to oppose and respond to laws considered unethical or improper, whether through civil disobedience or other necessary means, though decisions as to when a law's toxicity rises to this level are complex and multifaceted. Neither knee-jerk protestation nor simple obedience is an obvious choice, especially when human beings face serious harm or seek asylum from those bent on depriving them of life or liberty.

A second principle that demands recognition in this debate is the inalienable right a community has to protect itself. If an individual approaches you who may be intent on doing harm to your family or you in your home, Exodus 22:1 says, "If a thief is seized while tunneling and beaten to death, there is no bloodguilt in that case." Expanding the purview of this biblical passage to an entire society, I find it plausible to read Jewish tradition as offering us the unassailable right to protect our family and community. That is to say, I believe it to be reasonable within Jewish tradition to prohibit the absorption of strangers who bear indications that they are intent to harm those of their new host country. Examples would include, among others, proven terrorists, spies from nations hostile to the host nation, those involved in violent crime, or those with serious communicable diseases. The thornier questions come when individuals are suspected of bearing these or other dangers, without clear proof. Responding to rumors or suspicions or giving in to blanket accusations of entire countries or religious groups is clearly not the way to make immigration decisions. Balancing the obligation to welcome and assist the stranger with the necessity of protecting those already living in the country is unlikely to make for easy cases. Our obligation is to ensure each stranger a fair hearing, free of the influence of unsubstantiated rumor, prejudice, or suspicion, yet analyzing the real and present threats for the sake of the safety and security of the nation.

What then of the illegal immigrant who crossed the border surreptitiously and may live with a mixed family of legal and illegal status? One can read Jewish tradition to say that there should be some pathway established to welcome these immigrants to citizenship as well.

Simple and widespread expulsion would go against the grain of our history. To see them as criminals and call for police forces to remove them with no due process is to deny them their humanity and to erode our democracy. Rather, we should establish thoughtful laws and procedures that evaluate illegal immigrants and, where appropriate from a security and safety perspective, offer them an entryway into citizenship. We need only glance back at our own history to know the serious pain that comes with such denial and expulsion. We cannot allow it to happen to others without appropriate legal protection, no matter how they happened to arrive in this country.

Sanctuary movements, where municipal, state, religious, and other organizations provide safe places for immigrants to prevent the federal government from expelling them or, in some cases, even interviewing them, offer both a highly effective form of protest and a very complicated set of legal challenges. The concept of sanctuary arose first in the Bible, in Exodus 21:13, when God commands the Israelites to allow someone who kills another unintentionally to flee to designated cities of refuge to avoid retribution from the family of the deceased. Later texts, paralleled by Christian ideas, envision religious places such as synagogues and churches as such places of sanctuary from improper prosecution. In the present moment, it appears that the entire concept of sanctuary goes strongly against the law of the land; and yet, a valid argument can certainly be made that sanctuary is something we ought to be offering to individuals who are caught up in this system without options.

No short essay can expect to cover completely the challenging issues immigrants and host countries face today. For each of the questions treated here, there are numerous others and endless permutations. Suffice it to say that Jewish tradition demands that we prioritize the needs of immigrants, welcoming and helping them when we can, balanced with the needs for security and safety in our own nation. Yes, we should remain obedient to the law of the land, but we must be unafraid to confront it and, potentially, to violate it if necessary, when real lives are at risk. Obligations arise from history, and we who have been slaves and strangers, wanderers and outsiders, simply cannot be silent in the face of persecution and hatred rendered to others.

We must surely be judicious with the jewel of citizenship, but we must also be committed to protect the world's most vulnerable and offer them life, liberty, and safety. The very word "Hebrew" (*Ivri*) comes from a root for "those who cross over" from one place to another, quintessential immigrants from the start. If this is our essence, how can we not stand up for those who walk these paths in contemporary life?

IN EVERY GENERATION

The Obligations of Our Exodus

RABBI JONAH DOV PESNER

We Will Build a World of Love

I write these words only hours after being arrested in the grand rotunda of the Russell Building of the United States Senate. Nearly one hundred Jewish clergy and leaders joined in song and prayer, demanding that the United States Congress pass the DREAM Act, which would grant citizenship to the nearly eight hundred thousand Dreamers who came to the United States as children and are every bit American as my own daughters. As we sang "Olam Chesed Yibaneh" ("We will build this world with love") over and over again, hundreds of Dreamers stood cheering us on from the balcony, ringing us like a human halo. In an intentionally ironic twist on the famous cry from Moses to Pharaoh, we chanted, "Let our people stay!"

When we were handcuffed, removed by the Capitol Police, and placed under arrest, we understood that we were following directly in the footsteps of our ancient Israelite ancestors. Ironically, our being put into fetters was inspired by the Hebrew slaves, who rose up from their slavery in Egypt and cast off the chains of Pharaoh's bondage in their journey to redemption. As our hands were locked in cuffs and we were led away, we chanted the verse taken from the Song at the Sea "*Ozi v'zimrat Yah, va-y'hi li lishuah*," "God is my strength and might, and will be my salvation" (Exodus 15:2). There seemed no words more fitting than those our ancient Israelite ancestors sang as they passed through the parted seas of their redemption.

In Every Generation

Even as we were led into police custody, our group understood that we were walking in the footsteps of countless generations of Jews before us, generations who internalized the Rabbinic mandate in the Passover Haggadah that "it is incumbent on every generation to see itself as if they themselves—every person—had personally escaped from Egypt" (Babylonian Talmud, *P'sachim* 116b). Our deeds of civil disobedience were an act of *moral resistance* to the injustices being perpetrated on the Dreamers, along with tens of millions of other immigrants and refugees. We acted on the *spiritual authority* inherited from recent leaders like Rabbis Richard Hirsch, Abraham Joshua Heschel, and Maurice Eisendrath, who marched with Dr. Martin Luther King because they internalized the most often repeated commandment in all of Torah: "You shall love the stranger, because you were strangers in the land of Egypt" (Leviticus 19:34). Jews have marched throughout history because the core narrative of our people, the defining master story of our tradition, is the archetypal tale of redemption. Our Exodus from Egypt is the story of the transformation of the world-as-it-is, in which "strangers" are continually crushed by oppression, into the world-as-it-should-be, one where all people know justice. The power of the Jewish master narrative lies in its inherent call to every generation to live empathy; because our ancestors were strangers, we—in this era, and in every era—are to love the stranger.

In their brilliance, the Rabbis created ongoing rituals to ensure that the Exodus would remain the core Jewish narrative, to make certain that every generation would experience the empathic call of the

Exodus and internalize its teaching to love the stranger. Grounded in the Torah's requirement that "you shall teach your child on that day, 'It is because of what God did for me when I went free from Egypt'" (Exodus 13:8), the Passover seder and the telling of the story through the Haggadah are in essence an annual replay of the Exodus drama in which all participants play the roles and experience redemption. It is significant that in contemporary Jewish life, perhaps the most observed Jewish ritual by most modern Jews—regardless of affiliation, background, or level of observance—is the Passover seder. Bookstores stock seemingly endless versions and publications of the Haggadah that retell its master narrative; there are continuously created videos, puppets, toys, and myriad other tools to help tell this sacred story. Countless Jewish organizations create supplementary readings related to modern themes of injustice to be included in the Haggadah, in the retelling. New rituals are added every year. One of the first was the now classic orange on the seder plate as a symbol warning against the exclusion of women and oppression of LGBT folks. One more recent was the acorn, as a symbol of solitary confinement and the plague of mass incarceration. Across the country, organizations and individuals invite people of other faiths to learn the story of our Passover seder. I still smile remembering when I hosted then Massachusetts governor Deval Patrick (an African American and Christian) for seder. As I began to explain the various rituals and symbols to the governor and his family, he looked at me and scolded, "Jonah—do you think this is my first seder?"

Beyond Passover, the Rabbis also ensured that our master narrative would be retold weekly on Shabbat with the chanting of the *Kiddush* at the family dinner table. Weekly we chant, "In love and favor, You made the holy Shabbat our heritage as a reminder of the work of Creation. As first among our sacred days, it recalls the Exodus from Egypt." The blessing serves a weekly reminder that even as we in freedom celebrate the joy of Creation, we must remember our roots as slaves. In essence the Rabbis were reminding us that slaves can neither taste the sweet joys of the Sabbath nor appreciate the miracle of Creation, as these are a privilege reserved for those who are free. The Rabbis were well aware that though the Torah allowed for slavery even after the Exodus, the system mandated that slaves participated in the Sabbath rest on the seventh day (Deuteronomy 5:14). The Rabbis also ensured that we would be reminded of the lessons of our Exodus no fewer than three times daily: we praise God for our redemption from Egypt in the celebratory Song at the Sea during the *Mi Chamochah*, and at the conclusion of this *G'ulah* liturgy, we pray for the redemption of all those still oppressed—"*Adonai* redeemed Jacob from a hand stronger than his own. Praised are You, *Adonai*, redeemer of Israel." Our prayer links redemptions past to those we await in the future.

The Exodus links past to future in more ways than just liturgically. Before our protest on Capitol Hill, we gathered at a nearby church to prepare to stand up for DACA, for Dreamers. I addressed the assembly of leaders and told the story of my grandma Fannie. She came to the United States in 1916, fleeing the pogroms of Russia when she was only sixteen years old. She used to tell me stories of her childhood, how her father had to dig a hole under the floorboards of their house so she would have a place to hide when the Cossacks would come to rape the girls and kidnap the boys for the czar's army. Voice trembling, I relayed the story my grandma Fannie used to tell as she witnessed the rabbi of her town tied by his beard behind a horse and dragged to his death. My grandma Fannie courageously came to America on her own as a sixteen-year-old, because she too was a dreamer; she dreamt of her redemption from the crushing antisemitic hatred of the old country, in search of a modern "Promised Land." As I retold the story, I was reminded that Jews not only retell the master story of redemption throughout our ritual and cultural life; we have relived it throughout history. Our history has served to reinforce the most central exhortation of our Exodus narrative: we are obligated to love the stranger *as ourself*.

Among the many gleanings of the Exodus narrative that ground Jewish life and values, three stand out as the sources of the *spiritual authority* demanding that Jews resist injustice and champion morality in every age (and regardless of the challenges we face). First, we learn not only that resistance is required by our faith and experience, but also that it is always possible. Second, we are reminded that our empathy extends beyond the "stranger" to all those who are vulnerable in our midst. Finally, we instill in our souls that the Exodus is not simply about freedom from bondage; our master story culminates with the agency to enter into a covenantal community in which all people are bound to one another.

Resisting Injustice

The Exodus story begins in earnest with a new king in Egypt who does not know Joseph. This Pharaoh, perceiving a military threat, convinces the Egyptians to enslave the growing Hebrew population. His oppression becomes genocide when the new Pharaoh orders the Hebrew midwives to kill all the newborn boys. The response of these midwives, Shiphrah and Puah, is remarkable and echoes across eternity: *they resist.* Shiphrah and Puah refuse Pharaoh's evil decree. Their resistance is especially noteworthy because the Hebrew midwives were likely the least powerful members of the Egyptian hierarchy, and refusing an order from Pharaoh should have resulted in mortal consequences. However, the Torah explains that Shiphrah and Puah averted punishment through their seemingly ridiculous claim that "the Hebrew women are not like the Egyptian women: they are vigorous. Before the midwife can come to them, they have given birth" (Exodus 1:19). Not only do the midwives escape Pharaoh's punishment, but instead their households thrive. The success of Shiphrah and Puah is mitigated by Pharaoh's single-mindedness: failing to force the midwives to commit genocide, Pharaoh turns instead to the Egyptian people. The Egyptians obey.

It would seem that the Torah includes the brief story of Shiphrah and Puah into the longer narrative of the Exodus in order to juxtapose their response to Pharaoh's cruel act of injustice with Egyptian complicity. The presence and power of Puah and Shiphrah make the point clear: resistance to injustice is *always* possible. In the case of our Exodus, even the least powerful are able to thwart a seemingly omnipotent tyrant.

The moral resistance to Pharaoh continues in the very next passage of our master story, as two more women, a mother and a sister of a Hebrew baby, evade the genocidal decree and place a male child into a basket in the Nile River. A fifth woman—the daughter of the very Pharaoh himself—rescues the baby, names him Moses, and raises him in the Pharaoh's palace. Miriam, Yocheved, and Pharaoh's daughter join Shiphrah and Puah as proof that moral resistance is possible. As the Exodus story continues, Moses, Aaron, the elders, and finally all the Israelites rise up and—despite the many crushing setbacks and moments of terrified doubt—succeed in refusing to accept their oppression. The continual lesson of our Exodus story, and the continuing legacy of these five remarkable women, is that resisting injustice is always possible.

Protecting the Vulnerable

Just as the Rabbis codified rituals and responsibilities for every generation to identify with the experience of slavery and redemption, so too did they highlight and reinforce our obligation to empathy. The Sages teach that the most commonly repeated commandment in the entire Torah is to love the stranger, since we were strangers in the land of Egypt. The very foundation of this obligation, written in the Torah itself, is to have empathy with the vulnerable, whose experience we share. In the Book of Exodus, in a moment not long after the parting of the sea and the encounter at Sinai, God commands, "You shall not wrong nor oppress a stranger, for you were strangers in the land of Egypt." The text continues in the subsequent verse, saying, "You shall not ill-treat any widow or orphan" (Exodus 22:20–21). The Torah connects our experience of slavery with a command to have empathy for all those who are least protected by society. Widows, orphans, and strangers lacked ancient patriarchal protections, were almost completely without power, and often suffered terribly. It is worthy to note that the Torah doesn't stop with an obligation to "tolerate" or even to "protect" the stranger. Instead, our obligation, as we are commanded, is to *love* the stranger. Over and over again, the biblical text connects our experience of slavery with a radical empathy for all those who suffer.

Creating a Covenantal Community

The master story of our redemption from slavery in Egypt begins with a cry *and* an awakening. Not only are we suffering the oppression of bondage, but Hebrew babies are being cast in the Nile river to die! Pharaoh's own daughter hears one of those babies cry, rescues him, and then raises him as a privileged Egyptian. His life is uneventful until his eyes open and he awakes. As it is written:

> When Moses had grown up, he went out to his kinsfolk and witnessed their burdens. He saw an Egyptian beating a Hebrew, one of his kinsmen. He turned this way and that and, seeing no one about, he struck down the Egyptian and hid him in the sand. (Exodus 2:11–12)

Moses becomes aware of who he is. Moses knows he belongs to the community of Israel, to the wider family of all those oppressed. He becomes enraged at the injustice. And, despite his privilege, he acts.

In that same chapter of our master story, there is another cry and another awakening: "The Israelites were groaning under the bondage and cried out. . . . And God heard their moaning, and God remembered the covenant with Abraham and Isaac and Jacob" (Exodus 2:23–24). Suddenly, God awakes. Just as Pharaoh's daughter heard the crying baby about to die, God hears God's own crying children. Just as Moses had seen the injustice they suffered, now God too can see. Remembering the covenant, God becomes enraged at the injustice and is spurred to action.

How could God have forgotten? What took so long? Avivah Zornberg teaches, "The basic requirement of freedom ('redemption') is the awareness of 'exile,' the groan of conscious alienation."[1] The Israelites' cry wakes God, but theirs is the cry is of a people who themselves have woken up to their own plight. Redemption begins with a cry; redemption begins when God, Moses, and the people of Israel wake up to resist the reality of oppression. They become aware of injustice. They are enraged. They are ready to act. But this is only the beginning.

God cannot act alone. Moses encounters God, appearing in a bush that burns but is not consumed. God calls Moses to confront Pharaoh and free the Israelites. But Moses refuses. He claims he cannot speak for God, since he stutters. He realizes that neither Pharaoh nor the Israelites will listen if he cannot articulate the story of their redemption. God expands the leadership, deputizing Aaron and later Miriam. As Israel moves from suffering to redemption, more shared leadership emerges. The circle of relationships widens.

The circle of relationship, the centrality of covenant, is seen in Rashi's interpretation of a midrash from the collection *Sh'mot Rabbah*, in which Moses asks God why the Israelites deserve redemption. God's response is almost as startling as Moses's question: "Why do the people deserve to be freed from Egypt? They are destined to receive the Torah at this mountain three months after their liberation from Egypt" (Rashi's commentary on Exodus 3:12, citing *Sh'mot Rabbah* 3:4).

God tells Moses that we merited redemption not because *of what was*, but because of *what was to be*. The purpose of liberation from bondage was not an end in and of itself; it was a means for us to receive Torah at Mount Sinai. The purpose of liberation is Torah: Torah is the articulation of the story of redemption, from Creation through liberation. Our central text is a collection of ethical and ritual laws; our Torah reflects the opposite of slavery. Our Bible is the articulation of a blueprint for an empowered people creating a society of justice and godliness.

Redemption culminates at Sinai. In hearing the words of the Torah, Israel as a community is able to not only rethink the past, but also to imagine a better future. It is what Zornberg calls "an encounter with the Face of the Other."[2] Each individual soul, each "I," met the Ultimate Thou, the Infinite: God. The content of that encounter, as recorded in Torah, is an ethical framework. It is both a retelling of the story of the past and a series of laws providing a standard of justice for future human interaction. The encounter with God, the Ultimate Other, serves as a model for encountering any other.

Assembled at the mountain, the Israelites respond to God with one voice: "*Naaseh v'nishma!*" "All this we shall do, and we shall hear!" (Exodus 24:7). Now their redemption is complete, for the wordless cry of suffering at the beginning of Exodus is replaced by the empowered call of individuals ready to follow the commandments whose goal is to make us holy, make us godlike in treating our fellow. The wordless cry is replaced by dialogue. God articulates the vision and the people reply—"All this we shall *do*, and we shall *hear!*"—the people stand ready not only to act, but to listen, to remain in the dialogue, as the story of redemption continues to be told. The God-human dialogue becomes the paradigm for humanity, bound by listening to the common story and a willingness to act.

Now Israel is worthy of redemption, for in receiving Torah, by entering the dialogue, the Israelites can imagine a better future, they can articulate the story of their liberation, and they can see in the face of the other, the face of God. They have gained the power of relationship, relationship whose content is divine.

Our Shared Story

The Exodus from Egypt, the master story of our tradition told and retold from generation to generation, is a template for all redemption. First and foremost, it teaches that redemption is possible. It begins with a cry, as those who suffer become aware of their suffering. It continues with rage at the injustice and a willingness to act. It requires leadership and relationships. As the circle of leadership and participation widens, the community gains power. The people must begin to articulate their story—both the story of their outrage and the story of the just society that they can imagine for themselves and each other. Redemption culminates, as the people stand in relationship together, bound by a new, shared story.

In his seminal book *Exodus and Revolution*, Michael Walzer understood the timeless, repeating quality of the story, concluding that the Exodus taught us three things: "First, that wherever you live, it is probably Egypt. Second, that there is a better place, a world more attractive, a promised land. And third, that the way to the land is through the wilderness."[3]

The Reform Movement prayer book *Mishkan T'filah* has adapted Walzer's teaching with a prayer for redemption, read in connection with *Mi Chamochah*, which celebrates the redemptive act of the parting of the sea:

> Standing on the parted shores of history
> we still believe what we were taught
> before ever we stood at Sinai's foot;
>
> that wherever we are, it is eternally Egypt
> that there is a better place, a promised land;
> that the winding way to that promise
> passes through the wilderness.
>
> That there is no way to get from here to there
> except by joining hands, marching
> together.[4]

The historic arc of redemption that brought our Israelite ancestors from slavery into the freedom of covenantal community has inspired countless generations of Jews to resist injustice, have empathy with all those who suffer, and join together for a better world. Our master story has been retold and relived in the Russel Office Building, on the

Edmund Pettis Bridge in Alabama, and in countless generations of our people's history when we have stood up and countered injustice in the name of our story, our history.

There is an oft-repeated joke in Jewish life that explains how every holiday has the same basic story: They tried to kill us, we won, let's eat! While there is truth underlying this saying, I would posit that it misses the *ikar* (the deeper point) of the central Exodus narrative and the Jewish historical experience that ensued. I would argue a better saying might be:

> They tried to oppress us.
> We successfully rose up in resistance.
> Now, let all people eat.

NOTES

1. Avivah Gottlieb Zornberg, *The Particulars of Rapture: Reflections on Exodus* (New York City: Knopf Doubleday, 2011), 33.
2. Ibid., 304
3. Michael Walzer, *Exodus and Revolution* (New York: Basic Books, 1986), 149.
4. Michael Walzer, from *Mishkan T'filah*, ed. Elyse D. Frishman (New York: CCAR Press, 2007), 157.

· Part Two ·

Moral Resistance

Section A
Moral Commitments

ECONOMIC JUSTICE AND THE SOCIAL SAFETY NET

Rabbi Marla J. Feldman

"Entitlements." This loaded word, meaning "a legal right to benefits," has come to be code for those who oppose government spending for social welfare programs. The term has become a metaphor for the struggle between capitalism and socialism, pitting those who have against those who have not. It conjures up images of hardworking citizens who have "earned" their wealth being put upon by those who would "leech" off society and unfairly drain communal resources.

There was a time when Americans took pride in the Great Society programs that helped to level an unjust playing field and we celebrated our nation for embedding the best of human nature into the fabric of government policies and programs. In today's political climate, however, these principles are often maligned. We find ourselves forced to justify the core ideas inherent in the social safety net programs that reflect our Jewish community's historic commitment to caring for the poor, the elderly, the vulnerable, and the stranger.

There is no single economic theory that characterizes the Jewish community—our pews are filled with capitalists and socialists, fiscal conservatives and "spend-and-tax" liberals alike. We will not find specific guidance within Jewish texts as to which health-care plan is divinely inspired or a requirement that governments provide food stamps, energy assistance, or tax credits to the poor. The Bible does not mandate Medicaid, Medicare, or Social Security. Nonetheless, Jewish teachings most certainly provide ethical guidelines by which to judge such matters and contain a blueprint for how a society should care for those who are vulnerable or needy.

The question of whether Jewish tradition supports the idea of entitlements has a rather simple answer: yes. Jewish text, tradition, and history embrace the concept of economic justice and the mandate to establish a social safety net. Nonetheless, reasonable questions arise regarding to what one is entitled, who may be eligible, and who is obligated to pay for that safety net.

What Must Be Provided?

Among the earliest biblical injunctions pertaining to our obligations in this arena are the guidelines found in a section known as the Holiness Code in the Book of Leviticus. Leviticus 19 begins a collection of ethical mandates regulating human society—a blueprint for communal relations. The verses begin with the words *K'doshim tih'yu*, "You shall be holy, for I, the Eternal your God, am holy" (Leviticus 19:2). And what does it mean to be holy? The subsequent verses include many of the basic principles that define human relations, including leaving the corners of our fields for the poor and needy, a basic duty of care for those who are disabled and elderly, treating the non-citizen among us as one of our own, maintaining courts of justice, and fairness in the workplace. The commandment to "love your neighbor as yourself" is first found within this code. The rules and principles contained in the Holiness Code are necessary to establish a just society, one that fulfills our covenant with God to be a holy people.

It is important to note that these commandments are not optional; we are told that the corners of the field *shall* be left for the poor and the stranger. The provisions do not outline the expectations of charitable giving, nor do they articulate an aspirational guideline for what one might choose to do to live an exemplary life. The bounty at the edges of the fields and the gleanings left behind after the harvest are not gifts of the owner of the field. Rather, this share of the field *belongs* to the poor and needy, who are, indeed, entitled to a share of the communal resources.

Admittedly, there is an element of charity involved in the giving of their portion. The actual size of the corners is not predetermined and remained a matter for discussion, with some sages arguing that as little as one-sixtieth of the field was sufficient and others asserting that the amount should be fixed based on the need in the community.[1]

It is noteworthy that the commandments of the Holiness Code are directed at "you" written in the plural, collective form; *all* of you shall be holy. These laws are not imposed upon us as individuals, but rather are commandments directed to the community at large, as a collective entity. We have a *communal* obligation to maintain a safety net that provides for the basic human needs of all our citizens. The community must establish fair laws that preserve the rights of the individual while protecting the community as a whole. It is a collective responsibility to provide for those who need assistance and to maintain a just foundation for society.

The underlying principle of the community's obligation toward those who are needy is embedded throughout Jewish text and tradition. There is a clear recognition that there will always be vulnerable members of society who rely on others for their well-being and that the community must step up to provide the necessary care. Perhaps we find such reminders repeated throughout the biblical texts precisely because this was not always a popular message. For example:

> If, however, there is a needy person among you, one of your kin in any of your settlements in the land that the Eternal your God is giving you, do not harden your heart and shut your hand against your needy kin. Rather, you must open your hand and lend whatever is sufficient to meet the need. Beware lest you harbor the base thought, "The seventh year, the year of remission, is approaching,"

so that you are mean and give nothing to your needy kin—who will cry out to the Eternal against you, and you will incur guilt. Give readily and have no regrets when you do so, for in return the Eternal your God will bless you in all your efforts and in all your undertakings. For there will never cease to be needy ones in your land, which is why I command you: open your hand to the poor and needy kin in your land. (Deuteronomy 15:7–11)

These principles were not merely aspirational admonishments intended to encourage good behavior. By the Rabbinic period we see that Jewish law had institutionalized these principles by requiring the establishment of soup kitchens, charitable funds, clothing funds, and other ancient safety net programs within every community. By way of example:

> The Gemara asks: **And do we require** that one live in a city for **twelve months for all matters? But isn't it taught** in a *baraita*: If one lives in a city for **thirty days**, he must contribute to the **charity platter** from which food is distributed to the poor. If he lives there for **three months**, he must contribute to the charity **box**. If he lives there for **six** months, he must contribute to the **clothing** fund. If he lives there for **nine** months, he must contribute to the **burial** fund. (BT *Bava Batra* 8a)[2]

The Sages wrestled with the meaning of the biblical mandate to provide "sufficient to meet the need" found in the Deuteronomy passage above, and they expanded upon the basics of food and clothing to include other life essentials to which those in need were entitled. Not only did they regulate what should be given, but also the manner in which it was given. Many of these regulations are encapsulated in Maimonides's treatise *Hilchot Mat'not Aniyim*, (Laws of Gifts to the Poor) within his *Mishneh Torah*, for example:

> One is commanded to give to a poor person according to what he lacks. If he has no clothes, they clothe him. If he has no utensils for a house, they buy [them] for him. If he does not have a wife, they arrange a marriage for him. If [the poor person] is a woman, they arrange a husband for marriage for her. Even if it was the custom

of [a person who was rich but is now] a poor person to ride on a horse with a servant running in front of him, and this is a person who fell from his station, they buy him a horse to ride upon and a servant to run in front of him, as it is said, *Sufficient for whatever he needs* (Deuteronomy 15:8). You are commanded to fill whatever he lacks, but you are not commanded to make him wealthy.[3]

The Sages were also well aware of the risk that some might take advantage of the community's generosity, and they developed guidelines for proper investigation of needs. Nonetheless, knowing the scourge of hunger, the initial presumption was to take those in want at their word and feed them first, ask questions later:

If a poor person who is unknown [in the area] has said, "I am hungry; please feed me," they do not check into his background lest he be an impostor, but rather they feed him immediately. If he was naked and said, "Clothe me," they do check on his background lest he be an impostor, but if they know him, they clothe him according to his honor immediately and they do not check on him.[4]

In addition to the provision of basic human needs such as food, housing, and clothing, the social safety net as understood in Jewish tradition extends to other aspects of daily life including, for example, access to medical care and education.[5] Although a detailed examination of every such entitlement is beyond the scope of this essay, suffice it to say that Jewish law and tradition recognize the obligation of a community to provide for the basic needs of its residents.

Who Is Eligible?

In most of these passages, it is clear that the discussions revolved around obligations within the homogeneous Jewish communities in which our community dwelled for much of Jewish history. The *ger toshav* (resident alien) who lived within the community was granted the same social welfare rights and obligations as other residents. Other than that, there was not much interaction between Jews and non-Jews.

Through the medieval period, local rulers would impose taxes for security and to fill their coffers, while the communal charitable institutions were left primarily to local governance. One might argue, therefore, that the duty to provide for the needy extended only to one's own faith community, and not the general public. While that was, indeed, largely the case through Jewish history, even as early as the Mishnaic period the Rabbis articulated the requirement to provide a basic level of support for non-Jews as well. This duty of care was justified as *mipnei darchei shalom*, "for the sake of the ways of peace." It is unclear if the nuance of this dictum is to suggest the least one must do in order to maintain civil relations or a universalistic message about basic human rights. Nonetheless the idea that every person, regardless of insider or outsider status, was entitled to a basic level of care was embedded within our tradition at an early stage:

> The mishnah teaches: **One does not protest against poor gentiles** who come to **take gleanings, forgotten sheaves, and the produce in the corner of the field, which is given to the poor** [*pe'a*], although they are meant exclusively for the Jewish poor, **on account of the ways of peace.** Similarly, **the Sages taught…: One sustains poor gentiles** along **with poor Jews, and one visits sick gentiles along with sick Jews, and one buries dead gentiles** along **with dead Jews.** All this is done **on account of the ways of peace,** to foster peaceful relations between Jews and gentiles. (BT *Gittin* 61a)[6]

Other expectations of things we must do "for the sake of the ways of peace" included comforting mourners, helping non-Jews hide their property from robbers, providing a bride's dowry, and offering a eulogy when one has died (JT *Gittin* 33a).

Although Jewish law is imposed only on members of the Jewish community, it is noteworthy that our tradition also holds expectations that non-Jews will follow certain basic principles of social behavior. The section of the Talmud noted above (JT *Gittin* 33a) specifically notes that non-Jews should maintain their own tax collections to serve the basic needs within their own communities.

Who Should Pay?

The overarching principle that runs through these texts is the basic tenet that the vulnerable in society are entitled—yes, *entitled*—to receive the basic necessities of life. If they are unable to provide for themselves, the community is obligated to provide for them. Access to a share of communal resources is a right accruing to everyone in society ordained by God, and not subject to the goodwill one might, or might not, have toward the needy. And so, as Jews we are obligated to create communities in which all members of society have their basic needs met.

All of this being said, a candid review of Jewish tradition leaves open the question of who must pay for establishing and maintaining the social safety net. The basic principles are clear: every member of the Jewish community is obligated to contribute a portion of his or her resources to those who are in need, and every Jewish community is obligated to maintain the societal structures necessary to implement these principles in a just and fair manner. Jewish law, however, does not speak to requirements imposed upon secular governments, with the exception of the seven basic Noachide Laws. These laws included prohibitions on idolatry, blasphemy, murder, incest, theft, and eating live flesh and required the establishment of a legal system to ensure these laws are followed (BT *Sanhedrin* 56a–b).

It was generally understood since ancient days that the governing authority was responsible for safety and security and would levy taxes for those purposes. While secular governments are not obligated under Jewish law to provide a social safety net, in a democracy it is the citizens who determine the proper role of government. As full citizens of American society, the Jewish community's traditional obligation to provide for the welfare of each member of the community provides a moral model that may be extended to our expectations of our government. The Great Society safety net was established in the United States by those citizens who share the perspective of Jewish tradition that the community has an obligation to sustain the most vulnerable members of society.

Why Should We Provide a Social Safety Net?

Jewish tradition not only describes the basic safety net that must be established for all members of society, but also provides insights as to why we should do this. On the most basic level, the reason is because God commands it, and generosity is required of us whether or not we feel it in our hearts. Yet we are nonetheless promised benefits in the world-to-come for fulfilling this requirement, articulated in such proverbs as "Wealth is of no avail on the day of wrath, but righteousness saves from death" (Proverbs 11:4) and "One who is generous to the poor makes a loan to God; God will repay one one's due" (Proverbs 19:17). This notion is beautifully described in a midrash on Psalm 118:19, "Open the gates of righteousness for me":

> At the time of judgment in the future world everyone will be asked, "What was your occupation?" If the person answers, "I used to feed the hungry"—they will say to him, "This is God's gate; you who fed the hungry many enter." "I used to give water to those who were thirsty"—they will say to him, "This is God's gate; you who gave water to those who were thirsty may enter." "I used to clothe the naked"—they will say to him, "This is God's gate; you who clothed the naked may enter" . . . and similarly with those who raised orphans, and who performed the mitzvah of *tzedakah*, and who performed acts of caring, loving-kindness. (*Midrash T'hillim* 118:17)

The reverse is also forewarned in Jewish tradition. If we fail to provide for the poor and vulnerable within our midst we will face God's wrath:

> Thus speaks the God of hosts, saying: Render true judgment, and show loving-kindness and compassion every man to his brother. And do not oppress the widow, nor the orphan, the stranger, nor the poor; and let none of you plot evil against his brother in your heart. But they refused to listen, and turned a stubborn shoulder,

and stopped their ears that they should not hear. And they made their hearts like adamant stone, lest they should hear the Torah, and the words which the God of hosts has sent in God's spirit by the former prophets; therefore a great wrath came from the God of hosts. And so, as God cried, and they would not hear, the God of hosts said: So they cried, and I did not hear; but I scattered them with a stormy wind among all the nations whom they did not know. Thus the land was desolate after them, so that no man passed by nor returned; for they laid the pleasant land desolate. (Zechariah 7:9–14)

There is a pragmatic rationale offered for these societal standards as well. A Rabbinic version of the dictum "What goes around comes around," commenting on Deuteronomy 15, cited above, notes that we ourselves will benefit from or suffer by the nature of the society we create. Whether in our lifetime or in the lives of our descendants, if we create a community that cares for the poor and needy, that safety net will be there for all those in need, which may one day include our own families. But if we fail to create that ideal society, then we will suffer the consequences of a harsh and hard-hearted world when the wheels inevitably turn:

> **It was taught** in a *baraita* that **Rabbi Elazar HaKappar says: A person should always request** divine **mercy with regard to this condition** of poverty, **for if he does not come** to a state of poverty, **his son will, and if his son does not come** to such a state **his grandson will,** as it is stated: "You shall surely give him and your heart shall not be grieved when you give to him, **for due to this thing [*biglal hadavar hazeh*]** the Eternal your God will bless you in all your work and in all that you put your hand toward" (Deuteronomy 15:10). With regard to this verse, the *Tanna* **from the school of Rabbi Yishmael taught:** Due to [*biglal*] this thing means that **it is a wheel [*galgal*] that turns in the world,** upon which people continuously rise and fall. . . . In a similar vein, the Gemara relates that **Rabbi Chiya said to his wife: When a poor person comes** to the house, **be quick to give him bread so that they will be quick** to give bread **to your children.** (BT *Shabbat* 151b)[7]

Whether we bring these principles and values into the public institutions of civic life is a political matter. Jewish law does not require us to do so. Jewish text and tradition, however, obligate us to establish communities in which every member of society enjoys the basic life essentials, whether that comes from the government, through our taxes, or from our own charitable institutions. Jewish tradition does not celebrate unlimited acquisition and consumption of wealth, nor does it promote tough love for the poor. "Let them pull themselves up by their bootstraps" is simply not a Jewish value. Instead, we are admonished to remember that there will always be some who are needy among us, whether because of financial hardship, disability, or disadvantage, and God commands us to care for them. The challenge of economic justice is great. Our meeting this challenge will determine nothing less than the very nature of the society we will bequeath to our children and to future generations.

NOTES

1. See, e.g., Maimonides, *Mishneh Torah, Hilchot Mat'not Aniyim* 1:15.

2. English translation from The William Davidson digital edition of the Koren Noé Talmud, with interpolated explanatory commentary by Rabbi Adin Steinsaltz. Literal translation of the text appears in bold; commentary appears in plain type. Even-Israel. https://www.sefaria.org/Bava_Batra.8a.

3. Maimonides, *Mishneh Torah, Hilchot Mat'not Aniyim* 7:3, based on BT *K'tubot* 67b; from *Gifts for the Poor: Moses Maimonides Treatise on Tzedakah.* trans. Joseph B. Meszler, ed. Marc Lee Raphael (Williamsburg, VA: College of William and Mary, 2003).

4. Maimonides, *Mishneh Torah, Hilchot Mat'not Aniyim* 7:6, based on BT *Bava Batra* 9a, from *Gifts for the Poor.*

5. On health-care matters, see, e.g., *Shulchan Aruch, Yoreh Dei-ah* 335–36. On education, see, e.g., BT *Shabbat* 119b, for discussion of the importance of education; and Maimonides, *Mishneh Torah, Hilchot Talmud Torah* 2, for detailed instructions on educational requirements.

6. The William Davidson Talmud, with interpolated explanatory commentary by Rabbi Adin Steinsaltz Even-Israel, https://www.sefaria.org/Gittin.61a.

7. The William Davidson Talmud, with interpolated explanatory commentary by Rabbi Adin Steinsaltz Even-Israel, https://www.sefaria.org/Shabbat.151b.

HEALTH CARE AS A JUSTICE ISSUE

A Healthy System Starts with Healthy Jewish Values

RABBI ADAM F. MILLER

Today's debate around health care, and specifically access to health care, can also be found within the pages of classic Jewish texts. While Torah, *Tanach*, Mishnah, and Talmud may not employ the modern terminology of single-payer systems, insurance coverage, concierge medicine,[1] or rising pharmaceutical costs, they do explore the question of health-care access for all patients. Examining the textual sources, one learns that an obligation exists for physicians to care for the sick and provide access to medical care. At the same time, the entire community is required to provide the funds necessary so that all individuals may receive emergency care and lifesaving medicine. Along with the communal obligations, each individual is required to perform some level of preventative care for themselves.

Abba Umna represents the most well-known Talmudic example of a doctor analogous to the medical practices that exist today. The Sages begin this conversation by noting that Abba the Bloodletter[2] receives more respect than the great rabbis of his era. Curious why Abba receives such adulation, the text leads into the discussion of Abba's deeds that merited him this level of honor. Later, the Sages will send students to test Abba and determine if he is truly as altruistic as he appears to be. We read in the Babylonian Talmud, *Taanit* 21b:

> The Gemara asks: **And what were these** righteous **deeds of Abba the Bloodletter?** The Gemara explains **that when he would perform a matter** of bloodletting, **he would bring in men separately from women,** for reasons of modesty. **And he had** a special **garment that had a slit in the place of the incision [kusilta]** where the bloodletting instrument was inserted. **When a woman came to him, he would have her dress in that garment, so that he would not see her** exposed. And furthermore, **he had a hidden place** where he worked, **where** customers **would place the coins [p'shitei] that he would take** as his fee. In this manner, **one who had** money **would throw it there,** while **one who did not have money was not embarrassed.**[3]

From the description of Abba's practice, one realizes that his workspace consisted of two distinct areas: the room in which he ministered to his patients and the waiting/exit room. This point is key, as Abba Umna's payment box, described in this translation as a "hidden place . . . where customers would place the coins that he would take as his fee," is located such that Abba cannot see the transaction. As a result, what a patient pays remains a mystery. Additionally, there is no one present to request or demand a fee on behalf of the doctor. It suggests that payment for medical services is performed on the honor system, left up to the individual to determine the value of Abba's treatment and provide compensation relative to the patient's ability to pay. The assumption was that those with more resources would deposit larger quantities, while those with less means would deposit smaller amounts into the box.

One should also note that payment is procured only *after* Abba Umna has performed his actions on the patient. As the doctor, Abba accepts all patients, regardless of each one's financial situation.[4] It is only as a patient departs that he or she places coins into the hidden box. This hidden "honor system" contrasts greatly with the model often employed today, in which doctors check off services performed and charge according to a preset price scale. Although the medical practitioners may not take payment directly, their staff is tasked with collecting appropriate payment or insurance documentation prior to a patient's leaving. In some offices, especially in urgent care centers, payment is required *prior* to even seeing the doctor, making financial insecurity a significant hurdle to receiving medical treatment.

Jewish texts support the work of Abba Umna and other physicians to treat the sick. The Sages explore whether a human being has the right to have their illness treated. In the ancient world, illness was often seen as a form of punishment—that the sins of the soul appeared as disease in the body. This belief is most famously demonstrated by the story in which Miriam contracts leprosy as punishment for having spoken against Moses. It is only when Moses begs God to heal her that she is cured of the disease (Numbers 12:1–15). Within this construct, one could argue that only God could remove illness or cure disease. Those divine actions would come in response to sacrificial offerings made by those who had transgressed and were now suffering. As such, human attempts at healing would be understood as interference with divine justice.

In contrast to that viewpoint, the Talmud says: "Whoever is in pain, lead him to the physician" (BT *Bava Kama* 46b), and the Rabbis adopt the approach that human beings can, in fact, minister to the sick:

> **As it is taught, the school of Rabbi Yishmael says:** "When the verse states **And shall cause him to be thoroughly healed [*v'rapo y'rapei*]**" (Exodus 21:19), it is derived **from here that permission is granted to a doctor to heal**, and it is not considered to be an intervention counter to the will of God. (BT *Bava Kama* 85a)

Later Jewish legal codes take this message even further, not only enabling a physician to treat illness, but making treatment of the sick an obligation that the doctor must perform. Maimonides (a physician himself) based his ruling on the phrase in Deuteronomy 22:2 "and you shall restore it to him." In its original context, the "it" in question is property, but the Rabbis understood this to refer to restoring one's body to health as well:

> … because it is a religious duty, that is to say, a physician is obligated by law to heal the sick of Israel. This is included in what [the

Sages] said in explanation of the verse, "And you shall restore it to him" (Deut. 22:2)—to include his body, that if he saw him lost and he can save him, he must save him with his body or with his money or with his knowledge... (Commentary on *Mishnah N'darim* 4:4)

Nachmanides went a step further, justifying not only the physician's obligation to prevent loss of life but also to provide medical care for general wellness using the Leviticus mandates, "do not stand idly by the blood of your neighbor" (19:16) and "you shall love your neighbor as yourself" (19:18). As the contemporary Talmudic scholar J. David Bleich wrote:

Nachmanides also finds that the obligation to of the physician to heal is inherent in the commandment "And you shall love your neighbor as yourself" (Leviticus 19:18). As a specific instance of the general obligation to manifest love and concern for one's neighbor, the obligation to heal encompasses not only situations posing a threat to life or limb or demanding restoration of impaired health, but also situations of lesser gravity warranting medical attention for relief of pain and promotion of well being.[5]

The overriding mandate of *pikuach nefesh* ("saving a soul/a life") is frequently used as a basis for the doctor's requirement to heal. According to the following legal text from the *Shulchan Aruch*, the doctor is required to address the medical needs of all those who come seeking assistance:

The Torah gave permission to the physician to heal; moreover, this is a religious precept and is included in the category of saving life [*pikuach nefesh*]. And if the physician withholds his services, it is considered as shedding blood. (*Shulchan Aruch, Yoreh Dei-ah* 336:1)

"Shedding blood" is a euphemism for taking a life, meaning that if a doctor refuses to see a patient, that doctor is held liable for having contributed to the death of that individual. This liability exists outside the ability of the sick person to provide financial remuneration for any services rendered. Of course, the texts recognize that a doctor does not have unlimited availability and there would need to be sufficient doctors available for this standard to be upheld. But this model of ensuring coverage and mandating that doctors treat patients whether they can afford payment or not appears to contrast strongly with our present-day experience of concierge medicine, limited appointment availability, and payment prior to treatment.

Part of the reason for the strict obligation placed on doctors is the Rabbis' realization that a doctor sits in the critical position between life and death. The Sages understood that proper diagnosis and treatment of a patient's illness were essential to preventing the possible loss of life. As such, a doctor lives with the constant reminder that they always must act to save a life, even if such acts require them to violate other commandments. The legal concept of *pikuach nefesh* is often derived from two texts in *Tanach*: "You shall keep My laws and My rules, by the pursuit of which human beings shall live: I am the Eternal" (Leviticus 18:5); and "I gave them My laws and taught them My rules, by the pursuit of which human beings shall live" (Ezekiel 20:11). Each text emphasizes the value of life, to the extent that if a direct conflict arises between observing God's laws and preserving life, *pikuach nefesh* takes precedence in most cases.[6]

The importance of protecting life is further emphasized in the Mishnah and Talmud. One text in Mishnah illustrates the value of a single life: "Whoever destroys a single life, it is as if one has destroyed an entire world. Whoever saves one life, it is as if one has saved the entire world" (*Mishnah Sanhedrin* 4:5).[7] A text in the Babylonian Talmud (*Yoma* 84b) explores the conditions under which one may violate commandments in order to preserve life. The exceptions include moving a fallen wall on Shabbat to save a child, extinguishing a fire on Shabbat, feeding a pregnant or sick person on Yom Kippur, and even providing unclean food (read: not kosher) to prevent someone from dying of starvation. Therefore, a doctor may provide medical care on Shabbat or Yom Kippur to those who are sick. In today's modern world, this would include the use of electronic medical equipment on

Shabbat and even driving or riding in an ambulance en route to life-saving medical treatment.

The use of *pikuach nefesh* as the source of the doctor's obligation to heal does, however, raise some complications. Situations that are not life-threatening would not meet the legal justification inherent in the concept of *pikuach nefesh*. One cannot violate Jewish law to relieve minor discomfort or pain if those ailments do not endanger the person's life. For present-day situations, this means that a patient seeking elective surgery or treatment for ailments that are deemed minor may not be included within the same obligation for a medical professional. In such cases, a doctor's requirement to provide access to these treatments may be more limited and thus the doctor could make them more dependent on an individual's ability to provide funding.

Up to this point, the texts appear to be placing all responsibility for care on the medical professionals who are meeting with patients. While the doctors might have a particular professional obligation to save lives, it would be unreasonable to assume that they were also obligated to shoulder the entire financial burden for patients who could not afford their care. Abba Umna provides one model for collecting payment, but his identification as an exemplary individual leads one to believe that he was unusual in his approach. Recognizing that the care of the sick should be an obligation shared by all in the community, Jewish legal texts emphasize the importance of providing *tzedakah* for those who are ill. We read in the *Shulchan Aruch*:

> There are those who say that the commandment to [build and support] a synagogue takes precedence over the commandment to give *tzedakah* [to the poor]. However, the commandment to give money for the youth to study Torah, and to the sick among the poor, takes precedence over the commandment to build and support a synagogue." (*Yoreh Dei-ah* 249:16)

Here we find that before a community builds a brick-and-mortar synagogue, it is more important for there to be a community fund that allows all those who are sick to have the resources they need to pay

for care. This suggests a solution to the problem of obligating doctors to care for all patients and still being able to provide for their own
well-being. The doctor may charge all patients for services rendered.
Community funds for medical care will make it possible for all patients,
even those of lesser means, to fairly compensate medical professionals.

Indeed, this system of communal support for health care actually
occurred in Jewish communities throughout the ages. Rabbi Eliezer
Waldenberg, a towering authority in twentieth century halachah on
medical issues, writes:

> It has been enacted that in every place in which Jews live, the com-
> munity sets aside a fund for care of the sick. When poor people
> are ill and cannot afford medical expenses, the community sends
> them a doctor to visit them, and the medicine is paid for by the
> communal fund. (*Tzitz Eliezer* 5:4)[8]

And while some texts suggest that these obligations apply only to
providing for Jews who are ill, others suggest that the poor who are
to be cared for are not just the Jewish poor. Rabbi Nissim of Gerona
(Barcelona, 1320-1380) notes that health care funds are specifically
designated for the "poor of the world" and not only for the "poor of
the city."[9]

Other scholars develop these ideas even further. Rabbi J. David
Bleich, a leading halachic scholar at Yeshiva University who has written
extensively on medical issues, justifies the obligation to use tax funds
when needed to support medical care:

> The community clearly has an obligation to provide for the medi-
> cal needs of the indigent. This establishment of a fund to defray
> medical expenses represents both a needed social amenity as well
> as a charitable obligation, and the community is fully empowered
> to levy a tax for either purpose.[10]

In response to a question about the obligation to provide care for
indigent patients, the Central Conference of American Rabbis (CCAR),
the Reform rabbinic leadership association in North America, issued a
responsum[11] that included the following excerpt:

Still, the duty to save life does not necessarily fall upon the physician as an individual. The commandment of *pikuach nefesh* is addressed to all of us, not just to a particular class of persons; the physician has no greater obligation than does anyone else to save life. This is a key element in the Jewish legal theory which permits physicians to be paid for their work: when a positive commandment is incumbent upon all members of the community, no one person can be required to perform it for free. Physicians are entitled to reasonable compensation because, though they render a service that only trained professionals are allowed to administer, they are the agents of the community. The mitzvah they perform is our mitzvah, not just theirs. Like others who provide vital public services, they are the means by which each of us fulfills the individual responsibility to save life. *Thus, if it costs money to perform the mitzvah, that expense ought to be borne by the community, by all of us together, and not by doctors alone. It is arguably unfair to require that physicians treat indigent patients without adequate compensation* [emphasis added].[12]

There are several noteworthy elements in this responsum text. Doctors are given respect here, as was Abba Umna in the Talmud, for their level of expertise, training, and willingness to embrace the mitzvah of caring for the sick. Referring again to the idea of *pikuah nefesh*, saving a life, it is emphasized that this positive commandment is incumbent upon every person: "The mitzvah they perform is our mitzvah, not just theirs." Therefore, the authors indicate that physicians are entitled to reasonable compensation because they are acting as agents of the community as a whole. It would not be reasonable or acceptable to assume that doctors alone should bear the financial responsibility today with respect to caring for indigent patients. While the doctor must treat those patients, it is the community's responsibility to ensure that the doctors are fairly and justly compensated for their sacred work.

Although medical professionals and the community are given the lion's share of responsibility with respect to health care, there is also an individual component that bears exploration. There is an obligation put on the individual to have ownership over the quality of one's own health. Maimonides writes, "One has a positive obligation to avoid anything that is injurious to the body, and to conduct oneself in ways that promote health." (*Mishneh Torah, Hilchot Dei-ot* 4:1). This teaching requires each individual to perform what today we would call preventative medicine and self-care. One should not engage in behaviors that are detrimental to one's health, such as smoking, excessive drinking, or the use of drugs. This could be further extended to include things that permanently harm or damage the body, as well as engaging in risky behaviors that open one to potential illnesses (such as unprotected sexual encounters) or include significant potential for injury (e.g., base jumping, skydiving). We are also called to maintain our health through positive behaviors. This would include eating a nutritionally balanced diet, exercising on a regular basis, and visiting regularly with medical professionals to monitor and maintain one's health.

There are two contemporary applications of this teaching from Maimonides to the current issues involved in health-care access. First, it is possible to conclude that preventative care should be made available for individuals. Each person should be able to engage with medical professionals to maintain and manage their health in a positive and proactive manner. In contemporary language, this calls for annual exams and testing as necessary for an individual to fulfill his or her obligation. Second, although Maimonides does not explore the issue, this focus on preventive steps the patient should take leaves one to wonder how this individual obligation relates to the community obligation to provide medical access. The text does not address whether failing to uphold one's responsibility for self-care would negate or lessen the community's responsibility to provide health-care access. This question is relevant today with respect to whether those who engage in risky behavior (such as smoking, not exercising, or avoiding annual doctor visits) should be penalized financially with higher fees for medical access.

As we return to the broader issues of health-care access, Jewish texts offer valuable insights into our modern discussion. One gleans from these sources that access to health care, for curative and preventative medicine, is a human right. Doctors act as agents of our society to provide support for the sick and bear the responsibility of saving lives. A doctor may not turn away a patient whose life may be in danger. While working in this capacity, doctors must be fairly and justly compensated for their efforts on behalf of the broader community. Individuals should pay for their medical expenses when they can, and the community (via its government) is obligated to provide funds for those in financial distress. This funding is to provide the resources necessary so that all individuals may receive critical health-care access for emergency, lifesaving medicine as well as preventative care.

Additionally, each woman and man operates with the positive obligation to maintain personal well-being through good nutrition, exercise, preventative care, and refraining from behaviors that risk one's health. In order to fulfill this obligation, individuals must rely on health-care professionals to provide accurate health education, as well as have access to the services and resources necessary to maintain their own well-being.

In the Talmudic ideal for medicine, exemplified by Abba Umna, doctors would see all patients seeking care. Compensation would be based on what the patient was able to pay, rather than on a strict fees chart.

At the same time, Jewish legal texts did not require or guarantee that all individuals receive the same level of health-care access. While all would receive minimum care, those with more resources could certainly purchase increased access for elective surgeries and treatments for non-life-threatening ailments.

The Sages and leaders of the Jewish people over the last two millennia could not have imagined the complex health-care system that has evolved in modern society. Yet, the sacred texts examined above demonstrate that the Jewish values on health care remain relevant, offering vital guidance for us today. Rather than get caught up in logistical and political quagmires, we should return to our values when determining how to address health care. Jewish texts teach us that doctors, patients, and society all bear the responsibility for maintaining our health and caring for all those who have been created in the image of God. The ideal system would start with these values, providing necessary health-care access for all individuals in a society. There would be recognition that financial supplementation from the community will be necessary, as not every individual has the same level of means. At the same time, individuals would accept responsibility for their role as partners in maintaining personal health, aided by education from medical professionals and available resources. A healthy system for health care starts with maintaining good values.

NOTES

1. Concierge medicine is the health-care model in which a patient and doctor establish a relationship with an annual retainer fee. The doctor provides on-call care, with limited patient load, in return for the retainer.

2. Bloodletting was a common practice of the time. Blood in ancient Jewish belief was seen as a source of both purity and impurity. This approach to medicine existed through the world and was not unique to the people Israel.

3. English translations of the Talmud in this essay are taken from The William Davidson digital edition of the Koren Noé Talmud (plain text), with interpolated explanatory commentary by Rabbi Adin Steinsaltz Even-Israel (bold text). https://www.sefaria.org/texts/Talmud.

4. Later in the same Talmudic text, the Sages note that Abba Umna would go out of his way to provide financial support to students of Torah (who were known to be poor), often giving them coins after treating their ailments.

5. J. David Bleich, *Judaism and Healing: Halakhic Perspectives* (Jersey City, NJ: KTAV Publishing, 2002), 4, citing Nachmanides, *Torat Haadam, Kisvei Ramban* 2:48.

6. Exceptions include: committing idolatry, sexual immorality, and murder. *Sefer HaChinuch* 296:1.

7. This teaching appears in the context of a debate on the use of capital punishment. It is intended to discourage witnesses from providing false or misleading testimony.

8. Jill Jacobs, *There Shall Be No Needy: Pursuing Social Justice through Jewish Law and Tradition* (Woodstock, VT: Jewish Lights, 2010), 171–72, quoting the 17th c. scholar Rabbi Rafael Mordechai Malchi.

9. Ibid., 172. Ran, *She'elot U'tshuvot* 1, *Dibbur hamatchil*, "V'haben hayoresh."

10. J. David Bleich, "Survey of Recent Halakhic Periodical Literature: Medical and Life Insurance: A Halakhic Mandate," *Tradition* (Rabbinical Council of America) 31, no. 3 (1997): 64

11. A responsum is a legal text that consists of a question and an answer. This model allows individuals to bring particular concerns or questions on how a Jewish law or teaching should be observed to a rabbi or rabbinic authority. In this case, the

question was posed by one rabbi, on behalf of a congregant, to the larger rabbinic authority of the CCAR.

12. CCAR Responsum 5754.18, "Physicians and Indigent Patients," W. Gunther Plaut and Mark Washofsky, *Teshuvot for the Nineties* (New York: CCAR Press, 1997), 373–80. https://www.ccarnet.org/ccar-responsa/tfn-no-5754-18-373-380/.

DO NOT SEPARATE YOURSELF
FROM THE COMMUNITY

RABBI LYNNE F. LANDSBERG, *z"l*

It is a bittersweet honor to introduce the work and words of Rabbi Lynne F. Landsberg, brilliant, implacable, loving and fierce advocate for the rights of people with disabilities both in the Jewish community and beyond. The sweetness is in having had the opportunity to learn from and be led by this luminous, courageous champion of justice whose accomplishments and vision were held in the highest esteem by so many. The bitterness is in having to write these words after Rabbi Landsberg's death in February of 2018. We had planned to write this chapter together and had begun to draw upon her past speeches and publications when a diagnosis, treatment, and then a virulent return of cancer cut our work short. It is ironic and perhaps also *beshert* that Rabbi Lynne Landsberg's teaching included in this volume begins with the sentence, "This text begins with the word *zachor*, remember." It is we who now must and will remember her as we strive to continue the work of leaving no one behind, of bringing people with disabilities into positions of leadership and of changing attitudes that prevent us from appreciating the full humanity and irreplaceability of every human life.

The first time I heard Rabbi Landsberg speak before a large gathering I remember being mesmerized at her elegance, her humor, her passion, and the depth of her Judaic learning as she told the story of her work to help the ADA to become law well before her own near-fatal car accident that left her in a coma and with traumatic brain injury. She had created a path to participation and dignity for others that proved to be one she would also travel. Rabbi Landsberg was pivotal in moving forward the Union for Reform Judaism's efforts to bring the issue of disabilities rights and inclusion to the forefront of our movement's attention when Rabbi Richard Address, who was then Director of the Department of Jewish Family Concerns, and I, then associate director, drew together a group of disabilities advocates, including other true luminaries in doing transformative work, to develop programs, symposia, and educational materials for congregations, camps, and other organizations. Rabbi Landsberg's political acumen, her wisdom, her tough resolve, always balanced by zany humor and an incredible ability to connect and offer solace and joy to others, guided us and impelled us forward. Even when some of us felt discouraged at the enormity of the task before us and the difficulty of getting others to see this as a civil rights and social justice issue, she spurred us on. Through the years I turned to Rabbi Landsberg for information, encouragement, strategy, and wisdom as I became director of the URJ Presidential Initiative on Disabilities Inclusion, a position created partly as a result of her continued and successful effort to keep us all effectively focused upon our shared goals. I benefited from and contributed to Hineinu, a collaborative work group bringing together representatives from the major Jewish movements to share in disabilities inclusion efforts that Rabbi Landsberg co-founded. Her words that are included in this volume, her laughter, her moral authority, and her depth of Jewish knowledge all continue to guide me and so many others. And, perhaps most importantly, because of her efforts, there is noticeable progress being made since she wrote these words in 2012. I am certain that those who read her words now will also "remember" and carry her influence with them.

Rabbi Edythe Held Mencher

> Remember what Amalek did to you on your journey after you left Egypt—how, undeterred by fear of God, he surprised you on the march, when you were famished and weary, and cut down all the stragglers in your rear.
> —*Deuteronomy 25:17–18*

This text begins with the word *zachor*, "remember." Why must we remember Amalek? This passage from Deuteronomy is read on the

Shabbat preceding Purim. The Book of Esther, which we read on Purim, introduces us to Haman as an Agagite (Esther 3:1). And the prophetic reading on Shabbat Zachor (I Samuel 15:1–34) tells us that Agag was the king of the Amalekites (v. 20). So, we infer that Haman was a descendant of Amalek.

The Hebrew word that is translated as "stragglers" in more modern translations (or "enfeebled" in the 1917 Jewish Publication Society translation), *necheshalim*, appears only once in the *Tanach*. In fact, the root, *chet-shin-lamed*, never appears again. Contemporary biblical scholars like Gunther Plaut, *z"l*, postulate that *necheshalim* was most likely originally meant to be *nechelashim* (root: *chet-lamed-shin*), "weak." So, the difficult to translate *necheshalim* is probably the result of a transposition of the letters *shin* and *lamed*.

Ibn Ezra would never consider the possibility of a mistake in the *Tanach*. So he takes the word *necheshalim* to mean "those who did not have the power to walk," suggesting that the root of this word, *chet-shin-lamed*, might have the same meaning as the root *chet-lamed-shin*. Similarly, Rashi understands the word to mean "those who lack strength" but adds "on account of their sin."

It is very fitting that our study of this passage of Shabbat Zachor often falls during the month of February, which is Jewish Disability Awareness Month, affectionately called JDAM. And we need not look far to find the connection between this special month and the reading of Zachor.

Who were the "stragglers in your rear"? They were the slow, the weak, the enfeebled—the invalids. In ancient times, these people were in fact considered invalids, *in*valid human beings.

We know this because the Israelites abandoned them, leaving them on their own to struggle at the rear of the Exodus.

Let me put it another way. People who couldn't keep up with the rest of the Israelites could also have been their children. But their children were *not* among the stragglers. The Israelites made sure their children were within their reach or were being carried—always with them in the midst of the group.

Yet, were the Israelites hand in hand with those with disabilities? Were those with disabilities tended to in any way? No, in fact, they were left behind because they were considered *in*valid human beings.

We moderns can explain this away by saying that this was the mindset of the ancient Israelites. Today we do not connect disability with sin. However, the invalidation of people with disabilities remains a modern bias. Where are the "stragglers" today? Unfortunately, our American society—including many Jewish communities—continues to leave them behind.

In January 1999, I was involved in a devastating automobile accident. I barely survived and I sustained a traumatic brain injury. After brain surgery, six weeks in a coma, and four months in the hospital, I came home with twenty-four-hour nursing. Years and years of intensive rehabilitation followed.

People who survive traumatic brain injury have to reestablish pathways from the brain to the body. In order to do this, many have to learn *everything* all over again. I had to *re*learn how to walk, *re*learn how to talk, actually *re*learn my ABCs and how to read, *re*learn how to concentrate and focus, *re*learn how to perform basic daily activities, and *learn* how to compensate for a failing memory.

For the past thirteen years I have been attempting to *re*learn Hebrew. In order to prepare my simple introductory thoughts about Shabbat Zachor, I had to literally *re*learn how to study text. Two years ago, with a great deal of help from a close colleague, sitting with me in my home office, I seriously studied text for the first time in over a decade. As simple as it seems, this little bit of study was exhilarating! I still cannot do it alone.

Over the years, I've slowly *re*learned how to live. But the traumatic brain injury has left me with persistent physical and cognitive challenges. Now, I walk with a cane and require assistance with minor tasks, and my speech therapist says I must speak slowly to be understood. For a New Yorker, that is the hardest part.

When I reentered the world, I was shocked at what I learned.

Before my injury, I belonged to one minority that was cohesive, strong, articulate, and definitely heard—the American Jewish community. What I learned was that I now belong to a second minority that is daily the victim of discrimination, and though about ten times larger than the American Jewish community, *this* minority remains almost invisible and barely heard—Americans with disabilities.

In my former life, I was the associate director of the Religious Action Center (RAC). In 1990, I, along with other Washington advocates from the interreligious community, worked on a huge new bill that I never, in my wildest dreams, thought would directly affect *my* life. In 1990, the religious community helped Congress pass the Americans with Disabilities Act, now called the ADA. The ADA is known as *the* civil rights bill for Americans with disabilities.

The Americans with Disabilities Act mandates access to public buildings, but it cannot mandate access to the human heart. We people with disabilities remain "undesirables" or, at best, outsiders in every basic sphere of life: education, recreation, social life, religious life, and especially employment.

Even now, almost twenty-two years after Congress passed the Americans with Disabilities Act, discrimination still permeates the lives of people with disabilities.

The ADA successfully tackled only two of the three issues that had stopped Americans with disabilities from living full lives: (1) it abolished public physical barriers, making the outside world accessible; and (2) the ADA allowed children and adults to learn through mandatory accommodations in public schools and universities across the nation.

However, the ADA attempted *un*successfully to tackle its third goal to abolish discrimination. Years and years after the ADA was passed, there is much that needs to be dealt with. These things are not as tangible as physical or programmatic improvements and they are harder to define. They are subtle and not so subtle acts of discrimination, like negative attitudes, a lack of awareness of the basic needs of people with disabilities, social exclusion, and outright employment discrimination.

The reality is that adults with disabilities in the United States, who number over fifty million, disproportionately experience poverty. Compared to people without disabilities, a greater percentage of people with disabilities are more impoverished, unemployed, and less educated. We Americans are all alarmed at the national unemployment rate we hear about every day through the media. However, nowhere in any newspaper article, editorial, op-ed, talk show, or TV news outlet is it ever mentioned what national disability rights groups have repeatedly voiced—that the national unemployment rate for people with disabilities is almost double the rate of those without disabilities. And, that doesn't even count people with disabilities who have never been able to get a job.

In fact, for the last fifty years, two-thirds of Americans with disabilities of working age who *can* work and *want* to work are unemployed or underemployed, recession or no recession. There is a joke in the disability community that Americans with disabilities are the only Americans who *want* to pay taxes.

The ADA of 1990 and the later ADA Amendments Act made outright employment discrimination illegal. Even though it is illegal, it still exists.

We Jews must understand and admit that we, too, discriminate by not demanding that Jews with disabilities have equal access not only to our synagogue front doors, but to all things Jewish, including jobs. Synagogues rightly worry about access to the bimah but what about jobs on the bimah, or jobs in Jewish organizations, or jobs in Jewish social service agencies, or jobs in Jewish schools, or jobs in Jewish camps? The list goes on and on.

It would be very hard for the Jewish community to discriminate against Jews with disabilities seeking jobs if the job seekers presented outstanding Jewish resumes. But the only way that Jews with disabilities can build such resumes is by being offered a great Jewish education beginning at an early age and continuing through Jewish schools of higher learning. But most synagogue religious schools and many Jewish day schools do not accommodate and, therefore, do not educate kids with special needs.

Maimonides taught, "Every member of the people of Israel is obligated to study Torah—regardless of whether one is rich or poor, physically able or with a physical disability!" (*Mishneh Torah, Hilchot Talmud Torah* 1:8). He added: "The great sages of Israel included wood choppers, water drawers and the blind" (ibid 1:9). He taught that over nine hundred years ago!

Today Jews with disabilities are a distinct segment of our community whom the Jewish world is choosing not to serve. Jewish communities all over the country shut Jews out by not altering all physical barriers. We shut Jews out by continuing non-inclusive programming. We shut Jews out by simply not inviting them to volunteer or to join groups like sisterhood or youth group or to use their talents in leadership positions or actual Jewish jobs. We shut Jews out by maintaining attitudes of discomfort and disdain.

We Jews would never *consciously* do it, but are we *un*consciously putting a stumbling block before the blind?

Congregational leaders often say they do not need accommodations more than a ramp because no one in their congregation has other disabilities. However, it is a fact that there are fifty-four million Americans (that's nearly 20 percent!) who have disabilities. And the percentage of Jews with disabilities is undoubtedly commensurate with this.

If so, then where are the Jews who need more than a ramp? Where are the Jews who are deaf? Where are the Jews who are visually impaired? Where are the Jews with intellectual disabilities? Where are the Jews with cognitive or psychological disabilities?

They are not in our synagogues because they perceive they are not wanted there. They feel this way, perhaps, because our synagogues have no sign language interpreters. Our synagogues have no Braille prayer books or Braille signs anywhere. Our synagogues do not offer any material in large print—not prayer books, not service programs, not bulletins. Only a few synagogues have religious school classes for kids with special needs. Even fewer have the same for adult education. Fewer still offer any programs, trips, or religious services that are designed to include people with all types of disabilities.

"Equal access to all things Jewish" means more than a ramp. It means physical and *programmatic* access. Programmatic access includes, but is not limited to, all kinds of Jewish education: religious school, day school, youth group programs, adult education, retreats, conferences, and informal education like camps.

And equal access means rethinking what the Jewish community provides and how we provide it.

Even if every synagogue or Jewish community event is physically and programmatically accessible, we still shut Jews out if we don't publicize the fact that "all are welcome" by using accessibility symbols on *all* of our announcements.

You may publicize an excellent event that gets someone's attention, but they do not want to call the synagogue or the JCC to ask if their disability will be accommodated or to ask if they will be able enter the building or to ask if they can use the facilities.

We must use the appropriate symbols on all of our announcements: on our fliers, on our websites, in our advertisements and our bulletins. And on all registration material and invitations, we must include information about how to request accommodations and by what date we need to know what accommodations are needed.

One of the Jews whom we have shut out is Martin Kroessel, who was born with cerebral palsy. His account is a painful one. He says:

> The hardest obstacles I have been forced to cope with over the years were not my own physical limitations, but the attitude of other people. For instance, when I was six my parents tried to enroll me in an afternoon *talmud Torah*. The administrators of the school refused to accept me because they felt that I did not have the intellectual capacity to successfully take part in the program. Since then I have earned degrees at both the undergraduate and graduate levels and I [have been] accepted as a student in the Graduate School of Journalism at Columbia. (Personal communication)

He then tells us something that we should all find disturbing. He says:

Most of the people with disabilities I know can be described, at best, as being indifferent to their Judaism. And who can blame them? Throughout the life of a person with a disability, barriers are encountered to active participation in Jewish life. . . . Most synagogues and other communal institutions are ill prepared to deal with people with disabilities. It is a tragic irony that while lay and religious leaders profess to be concerned about assimilation, the Jewish community remains content with a situation that makes it impossible for a large number of Jews who happen to have disabilities to be affiliated with communal institutions.

All of us preach and teach *Al tifrosh min hatzibur*, "Do not separate yourself from the community" (*Pirkei Avot* 2:5). We know it is an *aveirah* (sin) to separate yourself from the community. If we do not make the community accessible for Jews with disabilities, we are forcing our stragglers to assimilate, and we are held responsible.

As Michael Chernick, professor of Talmud at Hebrew Union College–Jewish Religion Institute in New York, told me, we are responsible for much more than enabling Jews with disabilities to separate themselves from the community. If we make the Jewish community inaccessible for them, we are the reason why they are not fulfilling many mitzvot. Most halachic authorities say the obligation to pray is a Rabbinic requirement. Since *t'filah b'tzibur* (praying with a minyan) is the preferred way to fulfill one's obligation to pray, it would be incumbent upon the community to make it possible for someone who is disabled to be able to fulfill the obligation of prayer (like saying *Kaddish*) in the best possible way, that is, with a minyan.

A Jew who is deaf is required to recite the *Sh'ma* and its attendant *b'rachot* (blessings) not because he or she can hear the *Sh'ma*, but because others can hear him or her saying the prayer, "Hear, O Israel." But how could people who are deaf follow a service without someone signing the service for them or a projected image of the siddur on a screen with a pointer indicating exactly where people are currently praying? And because the *Bar'chu* requires a minyan, providing full access including transportation to the synagogue would be the congregation's obligation.

Though people with disabilities were widely exempted from the performance of mitzvot in the time of the Mishnah and Talmud, modern developments and technology have enhanced the capabilities of people with disabilities and have given them the status of obliged persons in many, if not most, areas of Jewish observance.

Regarding the principle of corporate responsibility, *areivut*, each Jew is responsible to help his or her fellow Jew to observe mitzvot. Therefore, we are required to aid people with disabilities to fulfill all the mitzvot that are incumbent upon them.

One who *prevents* a person from performing a mitzvah (*hamonei-a et chavero milaasot mitzvah*) has sinned grievously. According to Dr. Chernick (personal communication), under Jewish law that was practiced in autonomous Jewish communities, such a person would be either fined or excommunicated. This indicates the extreme seriousness of restraining a fellow Jew from performing the acts that bring him or her closer to God and/or Jewish communal life.

Therefore, a community that does little or nothing to aid people with disabilities to fulfill the mitzvot that others without disabilities can easily perform has committed a serious violation of halachah and of Jewish moral values. Such a community at best does not understand what its Jewish obligations are or at worst is morally culpable for the ill treatment of the most vulnerable.

If we want to make changes in our community in order to include Jews with disabilities, we must begin by opening the eyes of Jews without disabilities and help them understand that they have to change their attitudes. There is a saying in the disability community that goes, "Before ramping buildings, you've got to ramp attitudes." We have got to encourage our communities to change their attitudes from "pity" to "possibilities."

In fact, it says exactly that in our texts! *Midrash T'hillim* (commenting on Psalm 82:3, "Defend the poor and the orphan, do justice to the afflicted and needy") says, "It does not say, 'Have pity on them,' but 'Do justice to them.'"

A year and a half after my accident, David Saperstein made me gasp when he told me that he wanted me back at the RAC as soon as I was ready. The possibility of my returning to the RAC with a traumatic brain injury seemed inconceivable—and yet the thought of my contributing again to the Jewish community, as well as the opportunity to think and learn and actually become productive, was as irresistible as it was frightening.

I returned to the RAC and soon realized that there were no longer religious voices in the coalitions working for the civil rights of people with disabilities. After the ADA passed in 1990, religious groups thought that it was a done deal. But through my experience as a new member of this minority, I knew differently. So we at the RAC helped form the Jewish Disability Network, an advocacy coalition made up of the Washington representatives of all the national Jewish organizations and religious movements.

A nationally recognized organization, the American Association of People with Disabilities (the AAPD) used the Jewish Disability Network as a model in establishing its Interfaith Disability Advocacy Coalition (IDAC).

People often ask us: What more legislation do you need? Wasn't the Americans with Disabilities Act enough?

We tell them even now, more than two decades after the ADA, Senator Tom Harkin (D-Iowa), an original sponsor of the ADA, says, "With the ADA, we have climbed the mountain and reached the top, but we still have not fully arrived at the Promised Land."

So try to understand my mixed feelings as I travel around the country. I am happy to find some synagogues beginning to become aware of and include people with disabilities. However, I am concerned that we Jews can ultimately model positive behavior, but that does not make it law. I see the role of the Jewish community as going beyond inclusion to real political advocacy.

My greatest wish is to take what I've learned from my experience and sound a wake-up call to the whole Jewish community that (a) Jewish people with disabilities are out there alone, and they need to be embraced by our communities, and (b) all people with disabilities need our political advocacy.

We must come together as a religious community and help all Americans recognize that people with disabilities are people first, people who are not to be defined by their disabilities. People with unlimited potential.

So let us move beyond building ramps to building effective political advocacy. Let us join hands, hearts, and voices to ensure the civil rights—in fact, the human rights—of all the stragglers.

NOTE

This essay is adapted from a talk originally delivered at the Brickner Rabbinic Seminar, February 15, 2012.

WHAT REPRODUCTIVE JUSTICE
MIGHT LOOK LIKE

Rabbi Emily Langowitz

The American public, in many ways, understands the religious voice on sexuality and reproductive health to be the sole property of the Christian Right. This comes as no surprise; when the media discusses contraception, it turns to the voices of Catholic leaders six times as often as to those of women's health professionals.[1] In the 2016 election season's vice presidential debate, candidates Tim Kaine and Mike Pence, both white Christian men, shared their religious positions on abortion and how they influence an approach to policy. Writer and pro-choice activist Katha Pollitt wrote an op-ed in the *New York Times* critiquing the application of faith-based principles to women's reproductive rights:

> I wish we didn't so often discuss abortion rights in the context of religion. We're not a Christian nation, much less a Catholic or evangelical one. Why should women's rights have to pass through the eye of a theological needle? . . . It's discouraging that we are still talking about abortion as a matter for biblical exegesis.[2]

Yes, and no.

What Pollitt accurately identifies is the androcentric nature of public discourse on reproductive health, particularly when it comes to religious justifications for or against women's reproductive choice. That much of Judaism's sacred canon can be attributed to solely male authorship is problematic when discussing *any* topic, but doubly so when considering an issue that so directly affects women and individuals with uteruses. But Pollitt conflates the specific way that Pence and Kaine rely on their faith with the broader way that religion guides both our moral decision-making and our pursuit of justice. And in assuming that the religious voice on abortion is a Christian one, she points to the same problem highlighted above: conservative Christian voices currently dominate our society's moral discourse on reproductive choice.

Some would argue that the solution for such an imbalance would be to fully excise religion from public political discourse. It is my belief, however, that the antidote to a conservative religiously driven political agenda on reproductive rights is not a call for the removal of faith from public life, but the presentation of a platform of reproductive choice firmly rooted in a different understanding of religious values. As progressive religious leaders, then, we have both the opportunity and the moral responsibility to offer nuanced religious language in discussing abortion and all facets and stages of the reproductive life cycle.

This chapter will focus on the issue of abortion and how it has been presented across centuries of Jewish text and history. This focus is due to the unique place abortion has taken as the touchstone moral issue at the heart of most debates on reproductive rights. But though the theological and ethical implications of a woman's choice to maintain or end a pregnancy are particularly laden in public and political opinion, this chapter also seeks to expand the dialogue by embracing the framework of reproductive justice. Such a framework was initiated by a group of black women in Chicago who, in 1994, sought to center the voices and concerns of marginalized groups in the dialogue around "the human right to maintain personal bodily autonomy, have children, not have children, and parent the children we have in safe and sustainable communities."[3] The framework of reproductive justice requires that we consider abortion, yes, but also that we expand our understandings of the societal structures necessary for all people to make caring decisions about their own bodies, their lives, and the lives of their families. Reproductive justice's expansive awareness of the reproductive life cycle will also help us think with expansiveness about what interpretive choices have been made in selecting and reading the religious texts that guide the Jewish discussion of abortion.

Before I undertake such an expansion, however, first a brief overview of the development of the Jewish discussion on abortion from biblical text through the modern era. It should be noted that though I seek to move this discussion beyond the justification of reproductive choice based on text alone, in many ways Jewish textual and halachic tradition lends itself to being pro-choice. This is reflected in the widespread support for the legalization of abortion within the Jewish community.[4] Our tradition is, at its core, cognizant of the humanity and agency of a pregnant person, and such a focus can only be enriched by the sharing of our own stories and the inclusion of previously marginalized voices as sacred additions.

The central biblical text that has informed the Jewish response to abortion appears in the Book of Exodus, one verse among many in a chapter that details various laws around damages. Sandwiched between the appropriate punishment for beating a slave and rules for the proper way to handle a dangerous ox are two verses that set the stage for centuries of Jewish thought on abortion. Exodus 21:22–23 reads:

> When individuals fight, and one of them pushes a pregnant woman and a miscarriage results, but no other damage ensues, the one responsible shall be fined according as the woman's husband may exact, the payment to be based on reckoning. But if other damage ensues, the penalty shall be life for life.

From this short passage, later interpreters come to significant conclusions about the difference in status between a woman and her fetus. The Torah demands retributive justice in two different forms depending on which "being" is accidentally destroyed in the fight. For the miscarriage of the fetus, the husband exacts a monetary fine, while for the death of the mother, the text demands a measure-for-measure punishment of *nefesh tachat nafesh* (life for life).[5] From this, later authorities derive the principle that a woman has the full status of a *nefesh*, while the fetus has a lesser status. This focus on status differential greatly influences the development of Jewish positions on abortion.

Though the passage from Exodus is an essential starting point for Jewish conversations on abortion, later halachic discourse draws extensively from passages of the Oral Law (tannaitic and amoraic materials). These sources expand on the question of maternal and fetal status, and some consider what is at stake for the mother in the potential termination of a pregnancy. Again, it should be noted that none of the authors of Rabbinic literature conceived of abortion in the modern sense; the materials from the Mishnah and Talmud consider a specific mode of terminating pregnancy that excludes any present-day understandings of nonmedically indicated abortions. Dr. David Kraemer, an ethicist and Talmud professor at the Jewish Theological Seminary, writes powerfully on this issue: "The halakhic authorities of old were not asking our questions about abortion. Can we justify deriving instruction when the analogies are so inexact and the circumstances so different?"[6] My answer to Kraemer is as follows: This material is of its own time and place. It has been interpreted to fill a certain need based on a certain paradigm for how moral (and legal) decision-making gets made. And yet, it is still deeply relevant for post-halachic considerations in that it guides our understanding of both the hurdles there are to overcome (feminist and otherwise) and the incredible potential there is in using sacred text (ancient, new, sacred as broadly defined as possible) to ask modern questions of how Judaism will help fashion our lives.

There are several key texts from the Mishnah and Talmud that directly relate to the termination of a pregnancy. They can loosely be categorized around three different considerations: the status of the fetus, potential concerns for the mother's welfare, and broader concerns for how Jews should approach abortion given the stances of other groups in society. *Mishnah Ohalot* 7:6 concretizes the implicit language of Exodus 21:22–23. It states that the life of the woman takes precedence in difficult childbirth and that the fetus may be dismembered to save her as long as its majority remains in the womb. Only when the majority of the fetus has emerged, alive and intact, can it be considered a *nefesh*:

> If a woman is having difficulty in childbirth, one cuts up the fetus inside her and takes it out limb by limb, for her life comes before its life. If most of it had come out, one does not touch it, for one does not push off one life for another. (*Mishnah Ohalot* 7:6)

This text implies that there is precedent for performing an abortion up until the moment of childbirth, even if, as Kraemer notes, this is not exactly what the source intended in its time. As Rabbi Mark Washofsky, a leading Reform legal scholar, argues, "The Jewish legal sources, by drawing the distinction between mother and fetus, *allow us to make the moral judgment necessary to permit any abortion.*"[7]

The Babylonian Talmud, in *Sanhedrin* 72b, complicates this mishnah and the way its strong definition of the status differential between mother and fetus could constitute a blanket approval of abortion. The passage in the gemara introduced by a statement from Rav Huna presents the idea that a fetus might be considered a *rodeif*, a "pursuer," when childbirth endangers the mother. Rav Huna believes that a pursuer can be killed to save the life of the pursued, even without warning. The gemara continues with a challenge from Rav Chisda to Rav Huna that directly references the mishnah from *Ohalot* 7:6:

> Rav Chisda challenged Rav Huna, saying, "If its head came out, one does not touch it, for one does not push off one life for another." Why [should this be the case]? Isn't it [the fetus] a pursuer? (BT *Sanhedrin* 72b)

Rav Chisda wants to understand the seeming contradiction between Rav Huna's categorization of the fetus as a *rodeif* and the injunction in *Mishnah Ohalot* 7:6 against harming the fetus upon emergence. If the fetus is truly a pursuer, argues Rav Chisda, then it should be permissible to kill the child after it has been born if it mortally threatens the mother. Rav Huna counters by claiming that in the case of difficult childbirth, the fetus is not a direct pursuer; rather, the fetus's endangerment of the mother represents the fact that the heavens themselves are her direct *rodeif* ("There it is different, for the heavens pursue her"). The gemara is inconclusive on how the fetus should be labeled, but this debate between Rav Chisda and Rav Huna serves to complicate the way future rabbis will consider abortion. When can the fetus be considered a *rodeif*, and is it *necessary* for the fetus to intentionally place the mother in mortal danger for action to be taken to terminate the pregnancy? These two Rabbinic sources introduce a complex dialectic, which guides the future development of Jewish thought on abortion.

The Talmud does not confine its consideration of maternal need when terminating a pregnancy to mortal danger alone. The mishnah and gemara from BT *Arachin* 7a–b consider the proper procedure for dealing with a pregnant woman who has committed a crime worthy of the death penalty. Through this process, the text once again asserts the diminished status of the fetus while in the womb and grants permission for ending a pregnancy on those grounds.

Thus far we have seen that Judaism's sacred canon offers a limited number of texts that directly deal with the termination of a pregnancy. These texts present certain specific cases that depict the potential abortion scenarios relevant to that historical time period: accidental miscarriage, maternal mortality in childbirth, and pregnancy that would impede the administration of just, court-ordained punishment against the pregnant woman. In all of these cases, the texts agree that abortion is acceptable, though they differ on their modes of presentation and the principles invoked. The questions focused on in these texts center around the determination of fetal status and how it impacts the mother's status and physical health. We will see now how early medieval commentators expanded these cases and the impact their positions have in forming lenient and stringent tendencies in the development of Jewish thought on abortion.

The great split between lenient and strict opinions on abortion originates in the difference between Rashi and Rambam (Maimonides)'s commentaries on the fetus-as-*rodeif* concept. The Talmud, in BT *San-hedrin* 72b, presents Rav Huna's assertion that a fetus can be considered a *rodeif* and thus can be destroyed to save the life of the mother. Rashi's comment on the passage invokes *Mishnah Ohalot* 7:6, which permits the dismemberment of the fetus in cases of difficult and dangerous childbirth. He continues:

> Any time that [the fetus] has not gone out into the air of the world it is not a *nefesh*, and it is possible to kill it and save its mother.

Rashi states explicitly his opinion: the fetus may be destroyed not because it qualifies as a *rodeif* (who is a living, breathing person whom one may still kill to preserve another's life), but because it is not a full *nefesh* while in the womb. This sets the precedent for more lenient opinions because it cites the fetus's diminished status as legitimate justification for abortion, not the fatal harm it causes the mother.

Maimonides makes a slight variation in the *Mishneh Torah*, which will have lasting consequences for the Jewish interpretive tradition on abortion. In *Hilchot Rotzei-ach uShmirat Nefesh* (Laws of the Murderer and Preservation of Life) 1:9, Maimonides writes on the same case of a woman in mortal danger while in childbirth. Unlike Rashi, he makes a particular distinction about the fetus's status as *k'rodeif*, "like a *rodeif*." His full statement makes no mention of the fetus as a non-*nefesh* while in the womb—only that like Rashi and *Mishnah Ohalot* 7:6, he feels the fetus gains protection as soon as its head emerges, for one *nefesh* does not take precedence over another. Thus, there is an implicit acknowledgment that the fetus has not been a *nefesh* prior to its emergence from the womb, but Rambam's explicit use of *k'rodeif* is the strongest influence on his later readers. More stringent rabbinic opinions on abortion will flow from Maimonides's focus on this specific rendering of fetal status; they argue that abortion can only be permitted in situations where the fetus literally acts as a *rodeif*, causing immediate threat to the woman's physical life.

Beyond the medieval period and through the modern era, the Jewish discussion on abortion is carried out predominantly through the halachic literature of *sh'eilot* and *t'shuvot*. Rabbis are asked about specific abortion cases and apply a combination of legal reasoning, personal preference, and societal pressure to the Jewish textual tradition. The offerings of this responsa literature are varied, and there is a great deal of textual and interpretive material that upholds a partial pro-choice agenda. According to even the strictest of rulings, an abortion must be performed if the life of the mother is at stake. Beyond that, there is a vast range of acceptable scenarios in which a woman could seek a halachically permissible abortion. Despite this relatively positive summary, the halachic process remains born of and carried out in a patriarchal power structure, and there is still a stigmatization of abortions for nonmedical reasons. What, then, should a contemporary, feminist, post-halachic Jewish discussion on abortion look like? How can we, as a movement, ground ourselves in a Judaism that represents the values of Reform and honors the humanity of those making reproductive decisions for themselves?

The desire to expand beyond the extant Jewish discussion on abortion does not, it should be noted, solely exist outside of the halachic framework. Before presenting my vision for how we, as progressive Jews, can engage in the task of reproductive justice from a Jewish perspective, it is worth seeing how a leading Orthodox feminist thinker has dealt with the issue from within a halachic worldview. Blu Greenberg's 1976 essay "On Abortion" is still one of the most progressive Jewish pieces I have read on the topic of reproductive choice. Greenberg's writing reflects many of the principles of reproductive justice; she is aware of the complex social and economic dynamics that surround women's reproductive choices. Greenberg demands that Jewish thinking and activism move beyond the relatively narrow scope of reproductive scenarios presented in halachic discourse. She sees grounds for embracing abortion as an appropriate decision even in nonmedically indicated scenarios. Greenberg writes:

> [When] conditions do exist, such as the need to support self and/
> or husband through school, the need for time for a marriage to
> stabilize, overwhelming responsibilities to other children and so
> forth then abortion should be seen as a necessity rather than an
> evil. Many mitzvot (commandments) are interdependent functions
> of timing and of the conditions which they regulate.[8]

This statement is trailblazing beyond its respectful expression of the
many factors that influence women's reproductive choices. The conclusion of Greenberg's position radically destabilizes the halachic categories typically applied to women. First, women are not obligated,
according to the rabbis, in the biblical command to procreate. Second, women are considered exempt from all commandments that are
positive and *time-bound*. Thus, Greenberg's framing for the validity of
nontherapeutic abortions is a model for how we might explore anew
the principles that have guided us in our work for reproductive justice.
And the reproductive justice framework itself, which asks us to center
marginalized voices in our work, demands that we center voices that
have been marginalized from tradition as well.

I believe that though the sources discussed above provide backing
for a pro-choice position, the Jewish canon on reproductive justice can
and should be expanded. We do this by using the lived experiences of
fellow Jews and fellow human beings to reread our sacred sources in a
new way. As part of a project I undertook in writing my rabbinic thesis
at Hebrew Union College–Jewish Institute of Religion, I interviewed
nearly twenty individuals who had a strong connection to reproductive
choice: those who had had abortions, who had seriously contemplated
abortion as part of their reproductive decision-making, or who had
worked or volunteered in a medical, legal, or pastoral capacity around
this topic. In the same way that the lives of the rabbis of halachic tradition influenced their interpretations of Jewish texts, the stories of these
individuals (and many others) can and should be legitimate bases for
continuing to evolve our religious language of reproductive choice and
reproductive justice. In speaking with them, I found five central themes
that served as through-lines across their interviews.

The themes I found aligned with the arc of sacred Jewish storytelling. They began with creation, moved through the familial narratives of Torah, touched on the methodologies of the Rabbinic interpretive tradition, and closed with redemption. They emerged from the commonalities in contemporary stories but clearly have resonance with the broader Jewish narrative far beyond the present day. These themes set the groundwork for new language to define ethical principles around a robust Jewish ethic of reproductive choice. They are as follows:

- **Creation:** The power of centering the experience of a pregnant body in the tradition. This principle demands that we acknowledge the childbearing body as a source of divine creative power; the sacredness of the reproductive process mirroring divine creation requires that a pregnant person be granted the same agency and autonomy as God maintains while creating the world. I will discuss this theme in more depth below.

- **Bodily integrity:** The ethical mandate for the inviolability of the pregnant body and women's sacred right to control the parameters of their own lives through control of their physical health and well-being. As Dr. Lisa Guenther, professor of philosophy at Vanderbilt University, writes in her work on Emmanuel Levinas's concept of the Other and its application to reproduction, "What if we grounded women's reproductive freedom not on the assumption of an autonomous subject who owns her body and therefore has a right to choose, but rather on the ethical sensibility of an always-already embodied self whose very exposure to the Other calls for justice and equality, and *therefore* for women's right to choose?"[9] Guenther understands pregnancy to be an act of hospitality—a principle central to Judaism—and for that hospitality to be ethically sound, it cannot be coerced.

- **Transmission:** Reproductive history as a covenantal heritage. Many of those interviewed for my thesis, and indeed most women I've interacted with anecdotally, have been told stories about the reproductive history of the women in their families.

The Torah focuses on the transmission of Judaism as a biological inheritance, passed from Abraham's seed down through the generations. But the heritage of female reproductive decision-making can be understood as an equally sacred covenantal inheritance. The passing down of a lineage amounts to more than genetic replication; it includes elements of spiritual, religious, and ethical transmission as well.

• **Choice:** Decision-making is a religious value. Our tradition emphasizes the need to place the power for personal and spiritual development in the hands of human beings. Nowhere is this more apparent than in the very famous Talmudic story known as the Oven of Achnai (BT *Bava M'tzia* 59a–b). In the story, a halachic argument ends with the majority declaring that "we pay no attention to a heavenly voice," meaning that decision-making is no longer in the heavens. God sanctions such a conclusion by smiling and stating, "My children have defeated Me; My children have defeated Me." The central role of human decision-making in the religious tradition need not be relegated solely to the halachic realm. Choice, in all aspects of human existence, but particularly in such a life-changing realm as reproduction, deserves to be seen not just as a legal necessity but as a moral and religious requirement.

• **Justice:** The question of who controls the power in the world of reproduction is not just a personal one—it is a broader justice issue. This returns us to the framework with which I opened this chapter. Women's ability to make choices about their lives, their families' lives, and their futures is imperative for a just society. Our tradition demands that we seek justice in our world—we ought to expand such a call to read: "Reproductive justice, reproductive justice you shall pursue."

This is just a brief overview of how this research could influence our religious language around reproductive rights. Such an ethical framework might be expanded to show that it is possible to find a space that can hold the complicated nexus of our tradition's voices, our marginalized stories, and the ethics of our contemporary society in harmony. Take, for example, creation, the first theme outlined above. Typically, the verse in Genesis 1:27, which tells us that God creates humanity in God's own image, is read as a caution against the destruction of the human form. And it certainly reminds us to be aware of the inherent sacredness of human lives. But we might also read it in its context as a verse that supports the sacredness of the human power for creating life *in the image of how God creates life*. And how does God create life in the first chapter of Genesis? By using God's voice—speaking truth into being. By discerning what of that which has been created can be called "good." And by choosing to *stop*—God determines when the creative process will not continue. In reading our ancient texts guided by the questions of contemporary experience, we see that we affirm God's image when we ensure that reproductive justice is present in our society: when women and all individuals have the capacity to make choices for how they create life, when they will not create life, and what must be in place for their lives to be truly good.

This textual rereading is just one of many ways to integrate the tools of reproductive justice into our lives as progressive Jews. As people of faith, we have a responsibility to counteract the dominant societal narrative that assumes that religion is *against* abortion, reproductive and sexual health access, and reproductive justice. This means that the work we do is twofold: to speak out and reclaim the public narrative around religion and reproductive justice, and to continue to take action that ensures that all people have the access to the information, health care, and services that will reflect their dignity as creative agents made in the image of God.

NOTES

1. Rev. Debra W. Haffner, *A Time to Embrace: Why the Sexual and Reproductive Justice Movement Needs Religion* (Westport, CT: Religious Institute, 2015), 47.

2. Katha Pollitt, "Can Women Be Trusted on Abortion? Two Men Weigh In," *New York Times*, October 5, 2016, A27.

3. SisterSong: Women of Color Reproductive Justice Collective, "Reproductive Justice," sistersong.net/reproductive-justice/.

4. Eighty-nine percent of Jews support the statement that abortion should be legal in all or most cases, the highest number among all American religious groups and even those who are "unaffiliated" (75 percent). See Haffner, *A Time to Embrace*, 17.

5. There is some dispute about whether this indicates killing the man who accidentally kills the pregnant woman or simply exacting a fine equivalent to her life's value, but either way, it means that the woman is a *nefesh* and the fetus is not.

6. David Kraemer, "Jewish Ethics and Abortion," in *Exploring Judaism: The Collected Essays of David Kraemer* (Atlanta: Scholars Press, 1999), 271.

7. Mark Washofsky, "Response: 'Abortion, Halacha, and Reform Judaism,'" *Journal of Reform Judaism* 28, no. 4 (1981): 18. Emphasis mine.

8. Blu Greenberg, "Abortion: A Challenge to Halakhah," *Judaism: A Quarterly Journal of Jewish Life and Thought*, 25 (Spring 1976), 204.

9. Lisa Guenther, *The Gift of the Other: Levinas and the Politics of Reproduction* (New York: State University of New York Press, 2006), 143.

TOWARD LGBT LIBERATION

Rabbi Rachel Timoner

When, over the coming generations, human beings seek hope that social transformation is possible and that campaigns for justice can prevail, they will find evidence in our time through the changing status of lesbian, gay, bisexual, and transgender people. In less than a century, tens of millions, possibly hundreds of millions, of American hearts and minds have changed, and with them the norms, standards, language, cultural images, and laws of our society and of countries around the world. If we survey the fifty years between 1967 and 2017, we would see a revolution in perspectives about LGBT equality. We would also see that social progress produces backlash and that the forces of fear and retrenchment rise up precisely when human consciousness is in the midst of a dramatic leap forward. We would see that homophobia and transphobia are inextricably linked to sexism and misogyny, and that true *tikkun* (repair, healing) on these social problems will be intertwined. Finally, we would see that Judaism and the Jewish people have a particular role to play in that *tikkun*.

Judaism has played both a regressive and a progressive role in relation to lesbian, gay, bisexual, and transgender equality. The Hebrew Bible is the primary text used to justify bias, discrimination, and hatred against LGBT people. On the other hand, progressive Jewish movements, like the Reform and Reconstructionist Movements, have been at the forefront in advocating for change. This combination means that Jews have a particularly powerful role to play in achieving equality for LGBT people.

In 1967, *CBS Reports* aired an episode entitled "The Homosexuals." In it, Mike Wallace presented the results of a *CBS News* poll that found that two-thirds of Americans described their reaction to homosexuality as "disgust, discomfort, or fear" and that a majority believed homosexuality should be criminally sanctioned. Concluding the hour, Wallace said:

> The dilemma of the homosexual: told by the medical profession he is sick; by the law that he's a criminal; shunned by employers; rejected by heterosexual society. Incapable of a fulfilling relationship with a woman, or for that matter a man. At the center of his life he remains anonymous. A displaced person. An outsider.

The CBS special was clearly biased about gays, but it was also portraying an accurate picture of America. In 1967, sex between two consenting adult men was a felony in forty-nine of fifty states, punishable by a lengthy prison term. The American Psychiatric Association classified homosexuality as a mental disorder until 1973 and then in 1980 added Gender Identity Disorder as a new diagnosis. When I was growing up in the 1970s and '80s in Miami, Florida, "gay" and "lesbian" were words filled with shame. For a parent, the idea that one's child could end up gay, lesbian, bisexual, or transgender was feared as one of the worst fates imaginable. Not many years earlier, lobotomies were performed on LGBT people. Shock therapy and drugs like thorazine were still in use to make gay and trans youth conform.

When I ran a peer talk line for lesbian, gay, bisexual, and transgender youth in the early 1990s, I saw firsthand the impact of this stigma on LGBT youth. They faced rejection and threats from their families and peers—many beaten, kicked out of their homes, and, in rates much higher than the general population, suicidal. In the 1970s, it was legal to discriminate against LGBT people in employment and housing in all fifty states. Nowhere was it legal for same-sex couples to marry. In fact, when attorney Evan Wolfson, founder of Freedom to Marry, proposed a national campaign for gay marriage in the mid-1990s, we laughed him out of the room. Couples like my wife Felicia and me, who have been together twenty-five years, truly never imagined that we would legally marry in our lifetimes.

And then, through strategic, long-term advocacy, legal action, and activism by LGBT people, things began to change. From the time that the first domestic partnership laws were passed in Berkeley, West Hollywood, and San Francisco in the 1980s, to the decriminalization of homosexual sex in all fifty states in 2003,[1] to 2015 when all fifty states began to recognize and license marriage between same-sex couples,[2] and 2016 when transgender people were allowed to openly serve in the military, many strides have been made toward full equality for LGBT people in the United States.

Societal attitudes have changed concomitantly, largely because LGBT people have had the courage to come out to those around them. In 1977, only 56 percent of Americans thought gay men and lesbians should have equal rights in employment; by 2008, 89 percent thought so. In a 2012 poll, 36 percent of respondents said that their perspectives on same-sex marriage changed significantly in their lifetimes. In the last decade, awareness of transgender identity and gender fluidity has become widespread. However, the work for trans equality continues. Only 11 percent of respondents in a 2015 poll by the Williams Institute report knowing someone transgender; and 78 percent of transgender people report mistreatment or discrimination in the workplace. Increased visibility is beginning to lead to increased understanding of the spectrum and fluidity of gender identity, but laws and institutions are still far behind.

The Role of Judaism and the Jewish People

In a 2012 Gallup poll, by far the greatest percentage of those Americans who opposed same-sex marriage said they were against it because "the Bible says it is wrong."[3] The Hebrew Bible, Judaism's foundational text, known as the Old Testament by Christians, is the source—or the excuse—for much of the anti-gay bias in this country and around the world. The legal concept of sodomy, used among other things to criminalize gay male sex, comes from the story of Sodom in the Book of Genesis. But as Rabbi Steven Greenberg writes, despite the common perception that the sin of Sodom was rampant sexual vice, Jewish literature has largely rejected this reading. The prophet Ezekiel locates the sin of Sodom in its inhospitality, its cruelty, and its perversion of justice, not in homosexuality. Ezekiel describes Sodom as arrogant and insensitive to human need.[4]

The most quoted biblical texts prohibiting gay sex are Leviticus 18:22, "Do not lie with a male as one lies with a female; it is an abhorrence [to-eivah]," and Leviticus 20:13, "If a man lies with a male as one lies with a woman, the two of them have done an abhorrent thing [to-eivah]; they shall be put to death—they retain the bloodguilt."

The Jewish people can make an important contribution to LGBT equality by offering strong ethical and halachic reinterpretations of these Levitical texts. Many rabbis argue that rather than intending to condemn homosexuality, the Hebrew Bible intended to condemn sexual actors who did not honor their sexual partner. Rabbi Bradley Artson writes:

> In antiquity, there was no categorical distinction of humanity into heterosexual and homosexual as secular orientations. . . . The great revolution of the Torah in the realm of sexuality is to insist that sexual expression is legitimate only within the confines of a commitment to the sexual partner as a complete person.[5]

Rabbi Nancy Wiener writes:

> As Reform Jews, we affirm that sexual intimacy should be mutually expressive for those involved. To consider the needs of a sexual partner, to engage in sexual behavior solely to satisfy one's own needs or to enhance one's position—personally, economically, or as a means to assert one's power over another—would be to fail to

recognize the partner as created *b'tzelem Elohim*, in the image of God. . . . Sexual behaviors that fail to respect the inherent holiness and dignity of a sexual partner, that are built on lies and falsehoods with the express intent of leading someone to act in a way she or he would otherwise avoid, that exploit power differentials, that mistreat or abuse others, and that violate another person's sense of trust, faith, or boundaries may be considered *to-eivah*.[6]

In "The Halakhah of Same-Sex Relations in a New Context," Rabbis Myron Geller, Robert Fine, and David Fine provide a halachic reinterpretation. They observe that all of the forbidden sexual relationships in the Torah are excluded from marriage because of the societal standards of the time. You were not allowed to have sex with someone you could not marry. Marriage was centered on the importance of procreation. Since two men could not procreate, two men could not marry. Since two men could not marry, two men could not have sex. In other words, sexual relations between two men was considered a *to-eivah* because marriage between two men was not possible, and marriage between two men was not possible because two men could not have children. The authors point out that gay men now have options for procreation and that societal standards about sexuality have changed significantly from the time of the Torah. Further, *to-eivah* is an attributed, not inherent, characteristic, meaning that it therefore has the potential of being temporary. Given that it was based on societal standards and procreative options of the time, and that those standards and options have now changed, same-gender sex is no longer a forbidden category. They say:

What is clear to us is that the use of the תועבה [*to-eivah*—abomination] term in the Bible may apply only to a specific society and within that society to a specific and limited period of time in its history. . . . Just as the ancient Israelites could not envision a world without slavery, so could they not imagine a society where two men or two women could live together in a recognizable consecrated relationship and raise children. Just as the Rabbis understood that monetary interest could no longer be considered usury in a currency-based economy, so do we understand that same-sex relationships can no longer be considered תועבה [abomination]. And just as the Rabbis limited the application of biblical laws (such as the proscription of the Canaanites . . .) because of changed societal circumstances, so are the rabbis of today able to limit the prohibition of משכב זכר [a man lying with a man] and related laws in a society such as ours where same-sex couples are able to fulfill the intentions of the Torah, that is, to strive to achieve holiness in their relationships and to build families.[7]

A similar position was taken by the Responsa Committee of the Central Conference of American Rabbis many years earlier in 1996:

But while "abhorrence" may be a proper reaction toward many of the forbidden sexual unions (*arayot*), it does not apply to the case of homosexuality, for the issue cited in the sources as rationales for the prohibition fail to strike us as convincing on moral grounds. This is especially true in that we, unlike our ancestors, are aware of the possibility of committed, stable, monogamous and loving relationships between members of the same gender.[8]

In addition to the dreaded Levitical texts, Deuteronomy 22:5 is misused to justify discrimination against trans and gender nonconforming people. It reads, "A woman must not put on man's apparel, nor shall a man wear woman's clothing; for whoever does these things is abhorrent to the Eternal your God." Rabbis Elliot Kukla and Reuben Zellman explain that according to the great medieval commentator Rashi, such dress is prohibited only when it will lead to adultery. According to Maimonides, a twelfth-century codifier of Jewish law, this verse is actually intended to prohibit cross-dressing for the purposes of idol worship.[9] Kukla and Zellman write:

Classical Jewish scholars do not accept such a justification for narrow-mindedness. Neither should we. Rather, we can flip mainstream understandings of our verse on their head and understand it as a positive mitzvah, a sacred obligation to present the fullness of our gender as authentically as possible.[10]

Long before ethical and halachic reinterpretation of these Torah texts was under way, the Reform Movement was advocating for the rights of LGBT people in the public sphere. The movement has taken stands repeatedly for LGBTQ equality since 1965, when the Women of Reform Judaism (WRJ) passed a resolution calling for the decriminalization of homosexuality. In 1977, the Union for Reform Judaism and the Central Conference of American Rabbis passed their first resolutions calling for human rights for homosexuals. Since then, the Reform Movement has supported inclusion of gays and lesbians in the rabbinate and cantorate, marriage equality, elimination of discrimination within the armed forces and the Boy Scouts, and support for comprehensive nondiscrimination and civil rights legislation. In March 2000, the Central Conference of American Rabbis made history by becoming the first major group of North American clergy, as an organization, to give its support to rabbis choosing to perform same-gender ceremonies. In 2008, the first trans rabbi was ordained by Hebrew Union College–Jewish Institute of Religion. In 2015, the Union for Reform Judaism adopted a resolution calling for equal rights of transgender and gender nonconforming individuals, and the Religious Action Center recently released a guide to better inclusion of transgender and gender nonconforming members and their families.

Where We Go from Here

As of this writing, a sizable backlash against LGBT equality is under way. Since the Supreme Court legalized gay marriage nationwide, more than one hundred pieces of virulently anti-gay legislation have been introduced at the local, state, and federal levels. Soon after taking office, the Trump administration reversed an Obama administration policy of interpreting Title IX, the law that prohibits sex discrimination in education, to include transgender students in schools. Meanwhile, lesbian, gay, bisexual, and particularly transgender youth continue to face unsafe environments in schools, including a lack of accommodations for gender identity. The Employment Non-Discrimination Act (ENDA), which would ban discrimination in the workplace based on sexual orientation and gender identity nationwide, has been introduced in almost every Congress since 1994 but has not yet even come to a vote. Over 1.6 million youth are homeless in the United States, and as many as 40 percent identify as lesbian, gay, bisexual, or transgender. In the first five months of 2017 alone, fifteen trans women of color were murdered, but few of these deaths were covered by the media. Though astounding progress has been made, LGBT liberation is far from reality.

In the 1970s, the movement for LGBT equality was called Lesbian and Gay Liberation. The movement's leaders imagined not just a time in which LGBT people could live safely and equally in a heterosexual, cis-gendered world but, as the word "liberation" suggests, they imagined a world freed from constricted sexual and gender categories. Working for many years in the battered women's movement, Suzanne Pharr came to see the ways in which women were controlled by men through economics, violence, and homophobia. In her 1997 book titled *Homophobia: A Weapon of Sexism*, Pharr argues that sexism is maintained through the societal promise that women will not suffer violence or economic hardship if we attach ourselves to a man to protect us. "When the male abuser calls a woman a lesbian, he is not so much labeling her a woman who loves women as he is warning her that by resisting him, she is choosing to be outside society's protection of male institutions and therefore from wide-ranging, unspecified, ever-present violence."[11]

Pharr points out that there are only two circumstances in which men are allowed to be openly physically affectionate with other men in our society: sports and war. For many men, these are highlights of their lives, and they think of them with great nostalgia. Pharr suggests that gay men (and I'd add, some trans people) are the objects of extreme hatred and fear because they have broken ranks and are seen as traitors to male dominance. "When we see the fierce homophobia expressed toward gay men," Pharr says, "we can begin to understand the ways sexism also affects males through imposing rigid, dehumanizing gender roles on them."[12]

What Pharr shows us is that it's not just LGBT people who suffer from homophobia and transphobia, and it's not just women who suffer from sexism, but that cis-gendered, heterosexual people, and cis-gendered heterosexual men in particular, also have a great deal to gain from a freeing of these rigid categories and an acceptance of the full range of human sexuality and gender expression.

Tikkun

As I write these words, both the United States and Israel are in full-scale battles for their futures. The fight over an egalitarian prayer space at the Kotel is a fight over nothing less than the identity of the Jewish people. Do the ultra-Orthodox, who insist on the subjugation of women, speak for and represent Judaism and the entire Jewish people? Or will liberal Jewish movements assert our Judaism and our status as representatives of the majority of the Jewish people, with a shared commitment to the full equality of women and LGBT people? In the United States, will women lose our right to control our own bodies, or will our people rise up to demand full equality and reproductive rights for people of all genders? Sexism is at the root of these divisions among the Jewish people and the American people. And homophobia is a weapon of sexism.

Jews have a vital role to play in the *tikkun* that is needed both for the Jewish people and for the American people. First, we must assert our pluralistic, egalitarian vision for Judaism and the Jewish people. Second, we must teach an interpretation of the Hebrew Bible that allows for the full humanity, dignity, and expression of people of all sexual orientations and genders. Third, we must advocate in the public sphere for the liberation of LGBT people and all people from heterosexism, homophobia, transphobia, and sexism.

The extraordinary sea change in LGBT rights of the last fifty years sets us up to imagine a next fifty years in which the words gay, lesbian, bisexual, and transgender carry no stigma or shame; in which schools are safe and accommodations are available for every student, regardless of gender or sexual orientation; in which no one is homeless and LGBT youth are no more likely than anyone else to run away or be kicked out of their homes. Let's start to imagine a world in which men can love other men and be affectionate as brothers, friends, or lovers and still be "real men." Let's envision a world where women can stand up for their rights and their bodies—and can be independent and assertive without stigma—regardless of sexual orientation. And let's create a world in which all forms of gender expression are open to everyone. The Jewish people have a unique and vital role to play in bringing that world into being.

NOTES

1. Supreme Court decision in Lawrence v. Texas.
2. Supreme Court decision in Obergefell v. Hodges.
3. Gallup, November 26–29, 2012, "What are some of the reasons why you oppose legal same sex marriage?" Religion/Bible says it is wrong 47%; Marriage should be between a man and a woman 20%; Morally wrong, have traditional beliefs 16%; Civil unions are sufficient 6%; Unnatural/Against laws of nature 5%; Undermines traditional family structure/mother and father 5%. Frank Newport, "Religion Big Factor for Americans against Same-Sex Marriage," Gallup, December 5, 2012, http://news.gallup.com/poll/159089/religion-major-factor-americans-opposed-sex-marriage.aspx.
4. Steven Greenberg, "The Real Sin of Sodom," in *Sacred Encounters: Jewish Perspectives on Sexuality*, ed. Lisa J. Grushcow (New York: CCAR Press, 2014), 20.
5. Bradley Shavit Artson, "Enfranchising the Monogamous Homosexual," in *Kulanu: All of Us, A Program and Resource Guide for Gay, Lesbian, Bisexual, and Transgender Inclusion*, rev. ed., ed. Richard F. Address, Joel L. Kushner, and Geoffrey Mitelman (New York: URJ Press, 2007), 196, 201.
6. Nancy H. Wiener, "A Reform Understanding of *To-eivah*," in Grushcow, *Sacred Encounters*, 37–38.
7. Myron S. Geller, Robert E. Fine, and David J. Fine, "The Halakhah of Same-Sex Relations in a New Context," Rabbinical Assembly, 13, 18, https://www.

rabbinicalassembly.org/sites/default/files/assets/public/halakhah/teshuvot/20052010/geller_fine_fine_dissent.pdf.

8. "On Homosexual Marriage," responsum 5756.8, in *Reform Responsa for the Twenty-First Century: Sh'eilot Ut'shuvot*, vol. 1, *1996–1999/5756–5769*, ed. Mark Washofsky (New York: CCAR Press, 2010), 223.

9. Maimonides, *Sefer HaMitzvot, Lo Taaseh* 39–40.

10. Elliot Kukla and Reuben Zellman, "To Wear Is Human: Parashat Ki Teitze," TransTorah, 2006, http://www.transtorah.org/PDFs/To_Wear_Is_Human.pdf.

11. Suzanne Pharr, "Homophobia as a Weapon of Sexism," in *Race, Class, and Gender in the United States: An Integrated Study*, ed. Paula S. Rothenberg (London: Macmillan, 2004), 181.

12. Ibid.,172.

"NOTHING WILL BE OUT OF THEIR REACH"

Sexual Harassment, Sexual Assault, and Gender Power Imbalance

RABBI JILL L. MADERER

In the year 2018 many high-profile women have accused high-profile men of sexual harassment or sexual assault. It has been important for our nation to see prominent men held accountable for the abuse of power manifested in their sexual misconduct. Yet, with so much reckoning in celebrity circles, we need to be cautious against responding as if it were *their* problem. Sexual harassment and assault, and the imbalance of gender power that is at the root of it all, are all of our problem. It's in our neighborhood, our school, our workplace, our desk chair. The imbalance of gender power devalues women and robs men as well as women of choices in their work and in their lives. We all need to learn and grow in order to take steps to dismantle gender power imbalance.

Judaism's ancient and patriarchal tradition does not always provide a road map for gender justice. We confront inequality and inconsistency. Yet, we also encounter teachings about responsibility and power, which can inform Jewish values that relate to sexual harassment and assault. Sexual harassment and assault are about power and can be targeted at men and gender nonconforming individuals as well as at women; the texts in this essay are applied mostly to harassment and assault directed at women.

Responsibility

In our tradition, when a woman is raped, who is responsible? Deuteronomy 22:23–27 offer a problematic, yet also instructive teaching that differentiates between a possible rape that occurs in a setting with potential witnesses versus a setting without likely witnesses:

> In the case of a virgin who is engaged to a man—if a man comes upon her in town and lies with her, you shall take the two of them out to the gate of that town and stone them to death: the girl because she did not cry for help in the town, and the man because he violated another man's wife. . . . But if the man comes upon the engaged girl in the open country, and the man lies with her by force, only the man who lay with her shall die, but you shall do nothing to the girl. The girl did not incur the death penalty, for this case is like that of one party attacking and murdering another. He came upon her in the open; though the engaged girl cried for help, there was no one to save her.

In a town, a betrothed woman is considered complicit in an illicit sex act because she should have screamed out to stop the advance.[1] In a field, she is considered innocent because even if she screamed out, it would have been to no avail.

The implication that the silent woman in the town should be blamed is tragically problematic. The lack of a scream is not equivalent to consent. The Torah cannot know how every woman communicates consent.

Medieval commentator Nachmanides seems to understand this problem in his interpretation:

> If we see that a girl who has been grabbed by a man fights him with all her strength, crying and pulling at his clothes and his hair to try to escape his clutches but does not call out to others for help, I do not see why she should be stoned. The text is simply referring to what commonly happens.[2]

I hear Nachmanides expressing something of humility; although he still seeks signs of resistance, he admits he cannot know how she would communicate protest. Therefore, Nachmanides does not take the requirement literally. Perhaps in his humility, Nachmanides offers a small opening for future generations to admit they do not understand. Taken even further, perhaps he lays the ground for future generations to learn to "believe her."

Today, we understand that consent is not the absence of protest; it is an affirmative communication. Ours is not the first generation to shamefully ask victims and survivors of sexual assault, "What were you wearing?" As troubling as it is to see, our tradition, too, sometimes blames the victim. Adding a painful commentary to an already problematic text, medieval commentator Rashi explains the scene as he understands it: "One comes upon her in town. That is why he slept with her—because she was out and about. An open door invites a thief. Had she stayed home, this would not have happened to her."[3] Stay home. Rashi's victim blaming is an assault not only on consent, but on a woman's agency in her world.

Still, the cruel text is not without a worthwhile message. Consider the power of the townspeople. In our own time, it is not a woman's obligation following a sexual assault to publicly accuse the man.

With deep respect to the brave women who have spoken out, I do not believe women should carry the burden to repair the damage from sexual misconduct and abuses of power. We all carry that burden. Here's where the Deuteronomy text can be not only problematic, but also profoundly instructive. Consider what the text implies about the *townspeople*.

In her article "The Inner Scream: Rabbinic Voices on Sexual Assault," Rabbi Aviva Richman teaches, "The rabbis interpret the scream as an indication of the critical role of a third party—the person who is supposed to hear the scream and intervene to prevent this act of violence."[4] The burden is on the third party. Who is the third party? Who is the bystander? The town! *All of us. We are all responsible.*

Power

In our tradition, where can we find women's power present or absent? In the Babylonian Talmud, in *Sanhedrin* 75a, the Rabbis tell this story:

> A man once saw a certain woman, and his heart was so consumed by burning desire for her that his life was in danger. When the doctors were consulted and said, "His only cure is that she shall submit," the Sages said, "She should not yield. Let him die."
>
> Then when the doctors said, "Let her stand naked before him," the Sages answered, "She should not yield. Let him die."
>
> When doctors said, "Let her converse with him from behind the fence," the Sages said, "She should not yield. Let him die."

While we may be relieved to see the text reject the exploitation of women's bodies to benefit men's sexual desires, the text still reveals the tragic problem we have yet to overcome in our own time: the problem of the imbalance of power. When it comes to situations involving sexual harassment and assault, power is of the essence. The man and the doctors assumed they had the right to even propose exploitation—they held the power. No one asked the woman for her point of view—she held no power.

Nineteenth-century Talmudic commentator Rabbi Yaakov Ettlinger, in his work *Aruch LaNer*, points out, "The Gemara makes no mention of the woman's own disgrace, because she might have forgiven the man. . . . She had no authority to forgive him, however, on behalf of relatives in distant lands."[5] Concerned not for the woman's own dignity, but about the disgrace of her family, Rabbi Ettlinger unintentionally highlights the absence of the woman's voice in the text. He makes clear: a woman holds so little power that even her dignity is not her own.

Much of power comes with voice, and women's voices on sexual harassment and assault are missing from classic Jewish texts. The experience of rape and its aftermath is absent. So for the victim or survivor's voice we turn to modern texts, such as Marge Piercy's "Rape Poem":

There is no difference between being raped
and being pushed down a flight of cement steps
except that the wounds also bleed inside.

There is no difference between being raped
and being run over by a truck
except that afterward men ask if you enjoyed it.

There is no difference between being raped
and being bit on the ankle by a rattlesnake
except that people ask if your skirt was short
and why you were out alone anyhow.

There is no difference between being raped
and going head first through a windshield
except that afterward you are afraid not of cars
but half the human race.

The rapist is your boyfriend's brother.
He sits beside you in the movies eating popcorn.
Rape fattens on the fantasies of the "normal" male
like a maggot in garbage.

Fear of rape is a cold wind blowing
all of the time on a woman's hunched back.
Never to stroll alone on a sand road through pine woods,
never to climb a trail across a bald
without that aluminum in the mouth
when I see a man climbing toward me.

Never to open the door to a knock
without that razor just grazing the throat.
The fear of the dark side of the hedges,

the back seat of the car, the empty house
rattling keys like a snake's warning.

The fear of the smiling man
in whose pocket is a knife.
The fear of the serious man
in whose fist is locked hatred.

All it takes to cast a rapist is seeing your body
as jackhammer, as blowtorch, as adding-machine-gun.
All it takes is hating that body
your own, your self, your muscle that softens to flab.

All it takes is to push what you hate,
what you fear onto the soft alien flesh.
To bucket out invincible as a tank
armoured with treads without senses
to possess and punish in one act,
to rip up pleasure, to murder those who dare
live in the leafy flesh open to love.[6]

Because the oldest texts in our tradition so often strip women of power, they can be unhelpful and even offensive in our search for guidance about how to repair the gender power imbalance that is at the root of sexual harassment and assault. I do not apologize for those texts. Instead, I turn elsewhere. The Torah does offer a message about how to address abuses of power, and we can apply this message to the gender power imbalance.

In the Torah's story of Babel (Genesis 11:1–9), the people of the city endeavor to build a tower with its top in the sky, in order to make a name for themselves. God sees and responds, "If . . . this is how they have begun to act, then nothing they may propose to do will be out of their reach" (Genesis 11:6). Nothing out of their reach. Unchecked power. When God sees unchecked power, *God dismantles it*. This is a lesson we can take from the Torah: when we see unchecked power, *we must dismantle it*. When we see the unchecked power that enables devaluing women with microaggressions, insults, or inequality such as comments about women's looks, greeting women in the workplace with a hug rather than a handshake, calling women in the workplace "girls," using women's first names rather than earned titles, the telling or tolerance of sexist jokes, unequal hiring practices and mentorship pipelines, all-male panels, or a lack of parental leave for men, we must dismantle it. The power imbalance, misuse, and abuse that enable inequality are the same that enable sexual harassment and assault.

Studies show that most people do not speak up when they experience or witness sexual harassment. Why such silence? I believe women are trying to protect their *dignity and are afraid* their character will be put on trial. Where is this fear rooted? In *reality*. In our formative years, my generation witnessed the Anita Hill hearings,[7] and every generation of women has witnessed character attacks, unprepared human resources offices, and untrained ethics committees. For accountability and deterrence, all of our institutions will need to heed the call of the story of Babel. All of our societal—including Jewish communal—institutions will need to dig deep and dismantle gender power imbalance.

Yet it is not only the institutions; it is every one of us who can heed the message of Babel. Every one of us can influence the culture where we have power. Where do you have power? Where do you have status? Where do you have the most to lose? When you see a woman harassed or any vulnerable person harmed by someone in power, someone who can strip you of your power, your money, your friends, your dignity . . . will you accommodate the predator, or will you allow yourself to notice? Will you keep silent, or will you speak up? Are you ready to make a sacrifice in order to dismantle the gender power imbalance?

It's All of Our Problem: Repentance

When a woman is harmed by someone in power, are you sure you see it? So pervasive is inequality that we have grown accustomed to it. So normalized, often it does not even catch our attention.

The first step to taking responsibility for sexual harassment and assault in our society is to shine a light on our bias—so often implicit bias, therefore almost impossible to see. Yet, Psalm 90 prods us to try, as the Psalmist calls to God, "You can see our concealed darkness; You can see our concealed shortcomings, in the light of Your face." Why does our Hebrew Bible make this point that God can see our concealed shortcomings? Perhaps the psalm is reminding us about what *we* do *not* easily see, challenging us to dig deep to find our shortcomings, so they are no longer concealed from our own understanding. That's how we grow. The Psalmist's cry would urge us to see our own concealed darkness, our own concealed shortcomings.

May we reveal concealed shortcomings in our society, our institutions, and ourselves, that we may dismantle the gender power imbalance at the root of sexual harassment and assault.

NOTES

1. A discussion of the problem with a law that defines this as an illicit sex act, preventing women from owning their own sexuality and from choosing a sexual partner, is not included in this article, but is related in its connection to gender power.

2. Michael Carasik, *The Commentators Bible: Deuteronomy* (Philadelphia: Jewish Publication Society, 2015), 152.

3. Ibid.

4. Aviva Richman, "The Inner Scream: Rabbinic Voices on Sexual Assault," *Times of Israel*, August 30, 2017.

5. *Talmud Bavli: The Schottenstein Edition*, vol. 48 (New York: ArtScroll, 2002), 75a-1.

6. Marge Piercy, *Circles on the Water: Selected Poems by Margie Piercy* (New York: Knopf, 2009), 164–65.

7. Attorney and professor Anita Hill accused now-justice Clarence Thomas of sexual harassment when he was being considered for the United States Supreme

Court. In October 1991 an all-male, all-white Senate committee grilled Anita Hill. Senator Arlen Spector (*z"l*) accused her of being "unfair" to bring such an accusation, and committee chairperson Senator Joe Biden neglected to bring a sexual harassment expert witness, leaving Anita Hill to *explain* what sexual harassment *is*. So many women watched, praying that we would never find ourselves sitting in the seat she occupied—not in a Senate hearing, not in a courtroom, not in an HR office. Senator Spector, a friend to women's reproductive rights in many other seasons, *misused* his power then. And Senator Biden, now an advocate for women, *abdicated* his power then.

GENDER PAY EQUITY

Rabbi Mary L. Zamore

Nearing the end of their graduate studies, two friends interviewed with the employers who had come to their school during job search season. After they accepted offers for their first positions, the friends, a man and a woman, compared notes about the interview process, discovering that they were both offered the same job. Strangely, the man was offered markedly more salary than the woman, although neither could figure out why. Both newly minted graduates had the same degree from the same school, the same training, similar work experiences, and comparable skills. Between the two candidates, there was only one difference that could explain the disparate salary offers—gender.

It would be tempting to think that this vignette was from the 1970s or '80s, when a substantial wave of professional women entered the American workforce, breaking barriers in many sectors, but it is not. This true story of gender pay inequality happened recently. It is easy to see the injustice in a specific narrative, but this story happens every day, without acknowledgment, across the world. Throughout their careers, frequently without even knowing it, many women earn less than their male colleagues. In the United States alone, according to the U.S. Census Bureau data for 2015, women working full-time were typically paid 80 percent of what men were paid.[1] This earnings ratio varies across the nation, with New York having the smallest gap at 89 percent and Wyoming the largest at 64 percent. It is important to note that women of color suffer a much larger wage gap, with Hispanic and Latina women, for example, being paid only 54 percent of what white, male workers were paid in 2015.[2] The American workplace is evolving and the wage gap is narrowing, but at the current rate of change, women will not reach full pay equity with men until 2152.[3]

Pay equity is not a women's issue alone, although women suffer financially when they are paid less than what they deserve. Pay equity is not a family issue alone, although families suffer when the sole bread earner is underpaid, especially since the percentage of women-headed households has increased from 1 in 10 in 1960 to 4 in 10 today.[4] Of course, families with multiple incomes also suffer when women are underpaid. Pay equity is not just an employment issue. Less income coming into any household means less money for food, housing, health care, and education. Yet, the pay equity issue is not just about the resources available to women and their families. When workplaces throughout the world underpay women, it reflects an imbalance in the overall worth placed on women. Surprisingly, as will be discussed later, the Reform Movement itself has a persistent and troubling pay gap among its professionals. Pay equity is ultimately an issue of justice. Judaism envisions society as built on justice. This is reflected in the expectation of fair compensation.

According to the biblical narrative, from the moment that God punishes Adam in the Garden of Eden, proclaiming, "By the sweat of your brow shall you eat bread, till you return to the earth" (Genesis 3:19), God dooms humanity to work but also ensures a solid relationship between toil and reward. Human beings work, expecting to reap the benefits proportionally. Considering Genesis 29, the narrative of Jacob working for his future father-in-law, the reader fills with moral outrage as they learn of Laban's trickery, depriving Jacob of his proper payment of Rachel as wife after his laboring for seven years. (Yes, of course, the modern reader is equally filled with outrage over the idea of paying for a wife, but the ancient narrative itself points the reader toward abhorring Laban's exploitation of Jacob.) The reader cringes as Jacob patiently works for another seven years to reap his intended reward. Then, just as the reader believes there is no justice, Jacob prepares to leave his father-in-law's domain to return to his own homeland and rejects Laban's payment for his twenty years of labor. Instead, Jacob proposes, "Do not pay me a thing. . . . Let me pass by all your flock today, removing from it every spotted and speckled kid . . . that will be my payment" (Genesis 30:31–32). When Jacob's wise breeding practices yield him an abundant flock, it appears the divine plan is that Jacob should be paid more than fairly.

Ancient Jewish sacred texts, of course, do not approach employment laws with the understanding of modern feminism and therefore do not address gender pay equity directly. However, the moral insights implied both by Jewish law and by the tradition's ethical standards do provide a path to equal pay for women. The Torah is clear that employers must treat employees ethically. Part of the section of the Torah referred to as the Holiness Code enjoins, "You shall not defraud your fellow [Israelite]. You shall not commit robbery. The wages of a laborer shall not remain with you until morning" (Leviticus 19:13). Meanwhile Deuteronomy 24:14–15 commands, "You shall not abuse a needy and destitute laborer, whether a fellow Israelite or a stranger in one of the communities of your land. You must pay out the wages due on the same day, before the sun sets, for the worker is needy and urgently depends on it; else a cry to the Eternal will be issued against you and you will incur guilt." These two sections of Torah clearly command that we not oppress workers by withholding wages. They also recognize the power dynamic of the employer/employee relationship. Employees will frequently work under conditions that include unfair wages because they need employment and have little or no choice. They depend on the money due them for their work in order to sustain their lives. Even thousands of years later, many people today work paycheck to paycheck.[5] Their wages sustain them and their family with an urgent immediacy. At all socioeconomic levels, the employer has more control than the employee. As highlighted in the verses above from Leviticus and Deuteronomy, the Torah protects employees with laws forbidding *oshek*, the oppression of workers, which includes withholding salary. Ultimately, not paying a female worker fairly is a type of withholding. The worker has produced the quantity and quality of work demanded of her position, and yet because of her gender, she is being paid less.

When an employer places a specific monetary value, a salary, on an individual's contribution to the workplace, there are several factors informing that decision.[6] Salaries are shaped by demand, prevailing rates in the same or similar communities, training, experience, education, and skills of the employee, as well as potential productivity and contribution of the employee. The process by which salaries are set can be likened to weighing and measuring commodities, as the goal in setting a salary should be to eliminate any arbitrary factors like prejudice or bias to reflect the employee's true contribution to the workplace. In addition to being the source of ethical treatment of workers as discussed above, the Holiness Code also instructs on the use of fair weights and measures. Leviticus 19:35–36 states, "You shall not falsify measures of length, weight, or capacity. You shall have an honest balance, honest weights, and honest *eifah*,[7] and an honest *hin*.[8] I am the Eternal your God who freed you from the land of Egypt." These verses echo the language used earlier in Leviticus 19:15, which enjoins the Israelites to judge fairly: "You shall not render an unfair decision: do not favor the poor or show deference to the rich; judge your kin fairly." As Rashi points out in his commentary on verse 35, both Leviticus 19:15 and Leviticus 19:35 begin with the same words, *Lo taasu avel bamishpat*, which can be translated, "Do not render an unfair judgment." This repetition draws a connection between legal judgment and judgment in commerce through the measuring tools used daily.[9] Rashi emphasizes, "If he deals falsely in measuring, he is as one who corrupts justice and is called unrighteous, hated and abomination, accursed and detestation."[10] These verses can guide us to understand that employers must "weigh" and assign salary in an ethical manner, avoiding the gender bias that still pervades our society and workplace.

Fair weights and measures are a great concern throughout Jewish texts. The Levitical laws are expanded in Deuteronomy 25:13–16 with the following commandment:

> You shall not have in your pouch alternate weights, larger and smaller. You shall not have in your house alternate measures, a larger and a smaller. You must have completely honest weights and completely honest measures, if you are to endure long on the soil that the Eternal your God is giving you. For everyone who does those things, everyone who deals dishonestly, is abhorrent to the Eternal your God.

The strong language here damns those who corrupt commerce through unethical practices by using one set of weights or measures for buying and another for selling. This disreputable practice allows the merchant to have an unfair advantage in all exchanges. The Babylonian Talmud, in *Bava Batra* 88b–90a, discusses the steps the merchant, as well as the ordinary homeowner, must take to ensure that their measures are just. The Talmud points out that the Deuteronomy text commands owning weights and measures that are *sh'leimah vatzedek*, "perfect and just" (Deuteronomy 25:15). The doubling of the adjectives is interpreted as signifying two practices concerning the weights and measures. The first is that they should be accurate; the second that the seller should always over-measure, meaning measuring accurately and then adding a bit more (BT *Bava Batra* 89a). These two practices ensure that the seller does not cheat the buyer, deliberately or inadvertently.

If the moral underpinnings of these rules are applied today to gender pay equity, it should become the responsibility of employers to guarantee that they are paying female employees fairly. Just as the Talmud's instruction that fair measurements include two parts, measuring accurately, plus adding a bit more, to ensure ethical business practices, employers need to be scrupulous in assigning salaries to female workers, perhaps even overpaying by a bit to safeguard they are not underpaying and therefore perpetuating the gender pay gap. The question every modern employer must answer is not "Am I paying my female employees fairly?" but instead "How do I know that that I am paying them fairly?" The former question too often becomes impressionistic: "Do I think or feel that I am paying the equal and fair wage?" This question is too easily answered in the affirmative. The latter question requires thought and research to ensure that salaries offered to female employees are truly equal with the market range offered to white men. As in the matter of weights and measures, the responsibility to ensure "perfect and just" wages should be on the employer, who must use multiple methods to ensure ethical employment. Employers should not ask what employees were paid in their prior positions or how much they wish to earn in the new position.[11] Instead, employers should utilize salary studies to set wages. Many employers use implicit bias inventories, self-administered tests which help individuals reflect on the biases they unwittingly harbor,[12] before engaging in the hiring or review process to reduce the impact of bias on hiring, promotion, and salary. Being able to identify those subconscious biases that inevitably lurk within every human helps an employer consider if they are judging potential or current employees fairly.[13]

Exploring the possible punishments for false weights and measures, the Talmud explains that false measures are worse than ordinary robbery, because the robbers can always find and repay their victims, but "who could ever track down all the victims of false measures?" (BT *Bava Batra* 88b). The Talmud recognizes the pervading impact of false weights and the impossibility of restoring justice after a seller uses them in daily commerce. The text, in fact, goes on to say that communities must appoint inspectors to ensure not only fair weights and measures but also fair pricing (BT *Bava Batra* 89a). Rabbi Arthur Waskow points out the importance of this law, emphasizing that "almost all autonomous Jewish communities since then have appointed inspectors of weights and measures to make sure that these laws were communally enforced, not left to individual ethical decision alone."[14] Gender pay inequality also has lasting effects, impacting the standard of living for female employees and their families. Like false weights and measures, it is impossible to completely repair the damage done by the wage gap, for it affects the access the employee and her family has to quality food, health care, childcare, education, and retirement. The Talmud also teaches, "When a person robs his fellow even the value of a [penny], it is as though he had taken his life away from him" (BT *Bava Kama* 119a). The institutionalized *oshek* (oppression) of female workers, through the deliberate or inadvertent undervaluing of their contribution to the workplace, impacts their finances and their sense of self-worth. Professional and industrial organizations must strive to narrow the wage gap by educating both employers and employees. Offering ethics training to employers and regularly producing salary studies to track the gender wage gap need to be part of the solution.

In the well-known narrative of women demanding fair treatment under biblical law, the daughters of Zelophehad (Numbers 27) petition Moses, Eleazar the priest, the chieftains, and the whole assembly for their right to inherit their deceased father's property holdings, since there are no male heirs. Standing at the entrance of the Tent of Meeting, the five daughters, Mahlah, Noah, Hoglah, Milcah, and Tirzah, plead their case, ending with this pointed argument: "Let not our father's name be lost to his clan just because he had no son! Give us a holding among our father's kinsmen!" (Numbers 27:4). The daughters ask that inheritance rights be extended to women, when male heirs are not present, to protect their father's legacy within his own clan. In ancient times, asking for women's equal rights would not have been a compelling argument, and therefore the five daughters ask for their inheritance by claiming the dead man's right to be remembered and continuously linked to the clan. Yet this biblical model of women, standing up to power and making the moral claim for their rights to be protected, resonates with the independent moral gravitas of contemporary feminist demands for equality.

The modern feminist argument is augmented by the truism discussed earlier that underpaying women affects men, as women often contribute to joint household income. The underpayment of women impacts their husbands, partners, and children, too. The nonprofit National Committee on Pay Equity urges:

In 2009, the number of women in the workforce exceeded the number of men, and more men than women lost jobs. With more families relying on women's paychecks for their livelihood, the US must address the wage gap for the sake of American families and their financial stability.[15]

The voices of the daughters of Zelophehad echo in these lines.

The narrative of the five daughters provides a groundbreaking legal argument for several reasons. First, the women speak out for themselves, directly petitioning the leaders of their community, confronting those with power, authority, and control over the reins of justice. Modern women can learn from these role models and make sure they are educated in the advocacy and negotiation skills to argue for fair wages. Male allies are essential to advancing gender pay equity, but women must be advocates for themselves on the frontlines of the workplace. The result of the petition of the daughters of Zelophehad is they were given the rights to their father's property in the absence of male heirs. This was a win for five specific women, but it also created a legal precedent for future cases. This is an important reminder for each woman who demands equal pay. Every cent that a female employee's salary moves closer to her male colleagues' earnings not only helps that individual woman, but also raises the expectation of equal pay for all women. The daughters of Zelophehad also illustrate a much more important lesson than just securing property rights for women. It shows that even in Torah, the law can evolve, addressing injustices as they are raised within the community. Jewish law can and has evolved over our existence as a people. Women's rights, within both Jewish and secular law, continually strengthen as well.

The true story of gender pay inequality, which opened this essay, happened not after graduation at an American business school, but at a rabbinical seminary. The friends were two recently ordained Reform rabbis. Unfortunately, the Reform Movement's consistent commitment to *tikkun olam* and to economic justice does not make it immune to ethical challenges within its own congregations and institutions. The wage gap persists within the Reform Movement, as it does within the greater American Jewish community.[16] A comparison of salary surveys and studies of the rabbis, cantors, executive directors, and educators of the Reform Movement reveal that on average Jewish women professionals earn roughly 85 percent of what their male counterparts earn.[17] It is even more troubling that gender pay equality eludes the women Jewish professionals of the Reform Movement since it is this branch of Judaism that touts gender equality and social justice as foundational values. The movement's commitment to social justice can surely lead the way to more ethical employment practices. This injustice must be addressed firmly and consistently, taking it out of the shadows and discussing it openly. The Reform Jewish community must be willing to admit that a wage gap exists throughout the Reform Movement and that it is utterly unacceptable. Then, through widespread education of both employers and employees, the Movement can work to narrow the wage gap. With over one million people affiliating with its congregations[18] and up to another million identifying with the movement,[19] Reform Judaism has the power to raise consciousness about the gender wage gap and teach the religious and ethical imperative to correct it. The result of such targeted efforts should not only be the steady narrowing of the gap within the Reform Movement, but also the empowerment of Reform Jews to raise this issue within their workplaces and the greater American society.

The Women's Rabbinic Network and the Women of Reform Judaism, funded by a grant from the Jewish Women's Foundation of New York, have joined to lead the Reform Pay Equity Initiative to bring together every affiliate organization of the Reform Movement to work on the wage gap. By sharing salary studies and surveys, aligning the method of tracking such regularly collected data, teaching negotiation skills to the women Jewish professionals of the movement, and educating employers, Reform congregations and institutions, about ethical employment practices and the Jewish teachings that inspire *tikkun*, "repair," of this troubling ethical shortfall, the Reform Movement has the possibility of effecting significant and meaningful change for many. And in the process of correcting the movement's own employment ethics, Reform Judaism can become a role model for other communities to move toward pay equity for women.

NOTES

1. Kevin Miller, "The Simple Truth about the Gender Pay Gap," AAUW, 2017, http://www.aauw.org/research/the-simple-truth-about-the-gender-pay-gap/.

2. Ibid.

3. Ibid.

4. Catherine Rampell, "U.S. Women on the Rise as Family Breadwinner," *New York Times*, May 29, 2013, http://www.nytimes.com/2013/05/30/business/economy/women-as-family-breadwinner-on-the-rise-study-says.html.

5. *Report on the Economic Well-Being of U.S. Households in 2015* (Washington, DC: Board of Governors of the Federal Reserve System, May 2016), https://www.federalreserve.gov/2015-report-economic-well-being-us-households-201605.pdf.

6. Minimum wage is not included in this discussion, since there should be no gender gap when minimum wage is offered. It is, however, important to note many women are employed in work in which minimum wage requirements are ignored or not applicable (housekeepers, waitresses), which exacerbates pay disparity injustices.

7. A dry measure, equivalent to about a half a bushel or eighteen liters. W. Gunther Plaut, ed., *The Torah: A Modern Commentary*, rev. ed. (New York: CCAR Press, 2005) 803, comm. 35–36.

8. A liquid measure, equivalent to about an American gallon or four liters. Ibid.

9. Abraham Ben Isaiah and Benjamin Sharfman, *The Pentateuch and Rashi's Commentary* (Brooklyn: S.S. & R., 1977), 3:197.

10. Ibid., 3:197–98.

11. *Workplace Justice: Advancing Equal Pay; Innovative Employer Approaches* (Washington, DC: National Women's Law Center, June 2016), https://nwlc.org/wp-content/uploads/2016/06/Advancing-Equal-Pay-Innovative-Employer-Approaches-1.pdf.

12. The most widely used implicit bias inventory is Project Implicit. https://implicit.harvard.edu.

13. Project Implicit, https://implicit.harvard.edu/implicit/education.html.

14. Arthur Waskow, *Down-to-Earth Judaism: Food, Money, Sex, and the Rest of Life* (New York: William Morrow, 1995), 178.

15. "Equal Pay Day Op-Ed," National Committee on Pay Equity, accessed December 20, 2107, https://www.pay-equity.org/day-kit-oped.html.

16. Jane Eisner, "How Much Are Jewish Non-Profit Leaders Making?," *Forward*, December 13, 2015, http://forward.com/news/325847/salary-survey-2015/.

17. Based on salary studies and surveys shared at the October 20, 2016, convening of leaders of the affiliate groups of the Reform Movement in New York City. The salary studies and surveys included published and unpublished data.

18. "The Reform Movement," Union for Reform Judaism, 2017, http://urj.org/reform-movement.

19. *A Portrait of Jewish Americans: Findings from a Pew Research Center Survey of U.S. Jews* (Washington, DC: Pew Research Center Religion and Public Life Project, 2013), http://www.pewforum.org/2013/10/01/jewish-american-beliefs-attitudes-culture-survey/.

WHEN GOOD ISN'T ENOUGH

Understanding Racial Privilege
and Challenging Racial Injustice

ILANA KAUFMAN AND RABBI REBEKAH P. STERN

We all like to think of ourselves as "good" people. As Jews, we tell ourselves the stories of our people's social justice heroes and point to our tradition's prophetic calls for justice, which reinforce beliefs in our own righteousness. And it's not untrue. In our synagogues we heed the Torah's repeated call to welcome the stranger by providing meals and shelter to our homeless neighbors, creating networks of support for refugees and undocumented immigrant families, and myriad other efforts to provide care for those most in need. Many of us work in helping professions, as teachers and counselors for at-risk youth, as doctors, nurses, and attorneys in community clinics. We are rightfully proud of our efforts to pursue justice and to lift up the divine image in all people.

So long as we chip away at the injustices in our world a little each day, we are affirmed and can comfort ourselves with Rabbi Tarfon's famous quote that "it is not upon you to finish the work" (*Pirkei Avot* 2:21). As Jews, we hold the notion of justice at the highest level, and we feel good about ourselves when we live out our tradition in our actions. But the truth is that because of our privilege many of us also miss significant opportunities each day to act as reliable allies and make a real difference in the lives of people who are members of our own communities and beyond.

While there are many different kinds of social privilege at work in our American culture, the focus here is the privilege that comes with having white skin. According to one source, "privilege" is defined as follows:

> Unearned social power accorded by the formal and informal institutions of society to ALL members of a dominant group (e.g., white privilege, male privilege, etc.). Privilege is usually invisible to those who have it because we're taught not to see it, but nevertheless it puts them at an advantage over those who do not have it.[1]

Within the Jewish community, many of us move through the world with the privilege accorded to those with white skin, and some of us do not.

Though we may often think otherwise, the Jewish community's racial and ethnic identity is anything but all white. Our stories of justice that pass from one generation to the next, waxing poetic about lifting up those who are down, don't reveal all of the dimensions of our own struggle to act with and embody racial justice. What does racial justice really look like for U.S. Jews? Our usual answers are often informed by emphatically referencing the Torah's story of the creation of the first human beings *b'tzelem Elohim* (in God's image; Genesis 1:27) or by reciting a narrative that reflects only the voices of Jews with white skin. We are more diverse than the way we depict ourselves in our own stories. Our ability as U.S. Jews to push back against racial injustice is strengthened when we better understand the diversity of our domestic Jewish community, which, like the rest of the United States, is steadily becoming more racially and ethnically diverse.

The Jews who came to the United States from Europe in the nineteenth and early twentieth centuries did not think of themselves as white. Nor were they treated as such. Upon arrival to the United States Jews fell into the U.S. systems of social stratification that marginalized those who were not identified as Anglo-Saxon Protestant. American Jews in the early twentieth century were treated similarly to

African Americans in experiencing systemic discrimination that limited employment opportunities[2] and barred them from unrestricted access into universities.[3] As the twentieth and now early twenty-first centuries have unfolded, in the aftermath of the Holocaust, the civil rights movement of the 1960s, and the Black Lives Matter movement of the 2010s, Jews of European descent in the United States have enjoyed, relative to other ethnic groups, a disproportionate amount of upward mobility and success. Karen Brodkin argues that it is a "myth that Jews pulled themselves up by their own bootstraps."[4] Systemic racism is built into the infrastructure of this nation. Ethnic groups with mostly lighter skin, including European Jews, have benefited from not only a can-do attitude but a history of programs that have allowed Jews "to float on a rising economic tide," while African Americans continue to endure "the cement boots of segregation, redlining, urban renewal, and discrimination."[5]

As we work to actively dismantle structures of racism and understand how Jewish whiteness plays into perpetuating or resisting that racism, we enter the work of being true allies to people of color, including Jews of color. This means we move from being aware of racism to engaging in the actual, hands-on work of racial justice. To do so requires identifying the moments of transformation and action, taking real risks, and redistributing and transferring power.

The transfer of power happens in actual, most often awkward, if not very difficult, moments. In those moments, power manifests as concrete—who has decision-making authority, which voice gets heard, and who benefits from opportunities, access to networks, and community. There is risk involved in these moments when power differentials are made visible. People of color are often deeply terrified by the idea of how a white person will react when their power is challenged. We know all too well the hateful word or look that is intended to minimize, punish, or further marginalize us for speaking out.

White people who call attention to white privilege and dominance risk upsetting our white friends and family members, as well as those who have power over us. We risk admitting to ourselves and to others that we care more about our roles of esteem and our relationships than about what is ethical and right. We risk having to admit to ourselves that we are not only racist, but that we benefit from and feel the need to maintain those systems. We risk having to move from a space of doing all we can to maintain the fictive narrative of our own goodness as *rodfei tzedek* (pursuers of justice), to one that is much more honest and therefore much more unattractive. Ta-Nehesi Coates, in his book *Between the World and Me*, writes:

> My experience in this world has been that the people who believe themselves to be white are obsessed with the politics of personal exoneration. . . . There are no racists in America, or at least none that the people who need to be white know personally.[6]

Failing to embody a deep and multidimensional understanding of the racial diversity of our Jewish community, and of real justice, has tangible, and possibly catastrophic, consequences for us as individuals, for our communities, and for our larger society. This includes the denial, willful or otherwise, of our own power and privilege based on skin color. The Rabbis of the Talmud make the point that even seemingly small misuses of power can have significant effects—not only on the individuals involved in a particular incident, but on the whole community:

> The destruction of Jerusalem came through a Kamza and a Bar Kamza in this way. A certain man had a friend Kamza and an enemy Bar Kamza. He once made a party and said to his servant, "Go and bring Kamza." The man went and brought Bar Kamza. When the man [who gave the party] found him there, he said, "See, you tell tales about me; what are you doing here? Get out." Said the other, "Since I am here, let me stay, and I will pay you for whatever I eat and drink." He said, "I won't." "Then let me give you half the cost of the party." "No," said the other. "Then let me pay for the whole party." He still said, "No," and he took him by the hand and put him out. Said the other, "Since the rabbis were sitting there and did not stop him, this shows that they agreed with him. I will go and inform against them, to the government." He

went and said to the emperor, "The Jews are rebelling against you."
(Babylonian Talmud, *Gittin* 55b–56a)

In this episode, the man who threw the party and the rabbis, who were
there as powerful witnesses and ultimately silent bystanders, held all
of the privilege and power. Both privileged and powerful parties were
indicted for their misuse of power. The entire Jewish community suffered as a result of the party-thrower's abuse of and the rabbis' refusal
to use their power. Elsewhere in Jewish text the pain and suffering
that result from the siege of Jerusalem are described in vivid detail.
This story of Bar Kamza's public shaming falls into the broader category of *sinat chinam*, "free hatred," as one example of many found in
the Rabbinic literature. The Rabbis say *sinat chinam* was common in
the period leading up to the destruction of the Second Temple, and
they claim that it was the cause for the destruction. In this case *sinat
chinam* is equated with the abuse or misuse of the power that is born
of privilege (BT *Yoma* 9b).

Elsewhere in the Rabbinic literature we find the following:

> Why was the first building [the Temple] of Jerusalem destroyed?
> Because of the idolatry, sexual immorality, and spilling of blood
> that was in its midst. But we know that in the later one [Second
> Temple] they labored in Torah and were careful with tithes, so why
> were they exiled? Because they loved money and each one hated his
> fellow. This comes to teach you that hating one's fellow is difficult
> in God's eyes, and the Torah considered it equivalent to idolatry,
> sexual immorality, and the spilling of blood. (*Tosefta*, *M'nachot* 13:4)

We have much in common with the Jews of the Second Temple period
who "labored in Torah and were careful with tithes." We study our
texts and work for justice. We give *tzedakah*, feeling and acting responsible for both Jewish and universal causes. But many of us are also
guilty of *sinat chinam*, free hatred, in the same way that the host of the
party and the rabbis in the story of Bar Kamza were also guilty. We
American Jews of European descent in the early twenty-first century
wield tremendous power, as we have come to be seen by others and

(although often reluctantly) by ourselves as white. Even though we are not seen as white in some contexts, we benefit from white privilege in most social settings here in the United States. We may not often see ourselves as having power and privilege in the national civic context, but if we are going to truly identify as *rodfei tzedek* (pursuers of justice), we have to better understand the contemporary contexts and expressions of our power. We must learn how to use it to support both our own Jewish community in all of its diversity *and* our American neighbors who are not Jewish, who, over the next two decades will become a majority people of color.[7] As we read these texts from the Rabbinic literature, we are reminded that the whole community suffers when we misunderstand, ignore, or misuse the power that is born of our skin color privilege in a time when, in the United States, race really matters.

A few years ago, Ilana came to the synagogue to meet with Rebekah to prepare to co-teach a learning session on Yom Kippur afternoon titled "Finding My Voice—A Conversation about Racial Justice." While Ilana was a congregant, religious school parent, and Jewish community professional, she and Rebekah had previously met only in passing once or twice. They'd never worked together; they didn't even really know each other. Outside of the synagogue offices, where they met, there was a waiting area with a few comfortable chairs, a bulletin board with event announcements, and the synagogue gift shop. Rebekah came out of her office to greet Ilana and to fill up a pitcher of water at the nearby drinking fountain. Ilana was distracted, quickly moving from pleasantries to alarmedly pointing out a small handwritten sign above the nearby gift shop's cookbook section that read to Rebekah, "Kozy Kitchen Korner," but to Ilana, "Kozy Kitchen Korner."

Rebekah had looked at that sign many times as she stood filling her office water pitcher. Ilana's concern surprised Rebekah, as Rebekah's sensitivity had always been tuned to the incorrect spelling in the words "kozy" and "korner." But the sign author's effort at being cute was lost on Ilana, since it reminded her of the small Northern California towns near her undergraduate college that proudly sported shop signs like the Kozy Kar Klub where you could find the local mechanic by day, grand dragon (that is, the leader of the local Ku Klux Klan organization) by night.

As a Jew of European descent, Rebekah too feels threatened by the KKK, but since this sign was posted inside their synagogue, she was certain that there was no such terrorizing intent. And that was part of Rebekah's response to Ilana that day. Rebekah said she would mention Ilana's concern to the gift shop volunteers. Rebekah did not take down the sign.

After Ilana and Rebekah's initial, brief, and, at least for Ilana, very awkward interaction, they went into their meeting. And while the moment had passed, the irony was not lost on Ilana. Ilana sat in the waiting room next to a sign that read "Kozy Kitchen Korner" that wasn't immediately removed when pointed out to her rabbi and colleague as racist. Then they went to go work together work on a session about racial justice.

On that day, Rebekah had an opportunity to use her power, not only as a white-skinned Jew, but her positional power as a rabbi, to be an ally not only to the people of color who are members of and visitors to the synagogue, but specifically to her colleague and someone with whom she was starting a relationship related to grappling with racial justice. She missed it. And though certainly the KKK has no love for Rebekah as a white-skinned Jew, in many settings her white skin allows her to "pass" in a way that isn't possible for people of color. After a lifetime of passing, those with privilege can become blind to the way the world around them is experienced by those who do not share in both the bounty and basic safety that are provided by skin color privilege. We suffer from inattentional blindness,[8] that is, how people with more privilege perceive so little when we are not paying attention. Those of us who live more privileged lives, whether due to skin color, sexual orientation, gender identity, able-bodiedness, and so on, just simply miss the challenges faced by people with less privilege. Ilana had shared with Rebekah that as a Jew and as a person of color, that sign inside of her home synagogue made her uncomfortable, and Rebekah had hedged. She had never noticed the sign's reference to the KKK and was blinded by her own more privileged perspective. While absent of any malicious intent, Rebekah did not act. Rebekah's behavior in that moment was much like that of the rabbis in the story of Bar Kamza, though the circumstances were perhaps less egregious. Looking back, Rebekah realizes the better choice would have been to respond compassionately to Ilana's discomfort by taking immediate action—taking the sign down first and then going to talk with the volunteers who run the gift shop. Doing so would have been an example of being an ally: using power to bring some justice to an unjust moment.

Addressing inattentional blindness is critical in the work of racial justice. When those of us with more privilege begin to truly see and understand our experiences with privilege and the experiences of people with less privilege, we can more effectively use our power to become allies and make meaningful change. And we have so much to gain, though using our power in this way may also feel risky for white-skinned Jews, as mentioned above. In Genesis 1:27 we learn that human beings are created *b'tzelem Elohim*, "in the image of God." We value that sense of universal humanity. Yet we are all so different. Perhaps each person, like a single tile in a mosaic, holds only one piece of God's image, and it is only when we come together in our differences that we begin to see a fuller picture of the Divine. As individuals, we are limited in our understanding by the lenses through which we view the world—lenses that have been shaped exclusively by our own experiences. When we who live lives of privilege really open ourselves, through the honest building of meaningful relationships, to the experiences of those with less privilege, we gain new lenses through which to understand the world. This opens doors to new possibilities for many different kinds of connections.

Obviously, we do not have the full answer to the question of how to fix the problem of racial injustice in our American culture. But we do believe that part of the answer lies in the work of both personal responsibility and public advocacy. As Debby Irving wrote in her book *Waking Up White and Finding Myself in the Story of Race*:

> Making visible the privilege of white skin is key to racism's undoing. . . . Privilege is a strange thing in that you notice it least when you have it most. . . . As a white person, whether or not I know it, whether or not I admit it, I've got white privilege, an advantage that both is born of and has fed into white dominance.[9]

When Jews of European descent who benefit from white skin privilege and the power that comes with it get into meaningful relationships with people of color—whether in our own Jewish communities or beyond—we have an opportunity to open ourselves to a perspective that is different from our own. We can cast off some of our own blindness to the ways that our upward mobility comes at the cost of pushing down our friends, family, and community members of color, and we can start to become meaningful allies in creating spaces that feel safer and more just.

We also must continue our work to advocate personally for racial justice in public and visible spaces. If we do it well, we will have opportunities to acknowledge and then redistribute our own power and privilege in moments of both personal responsibility and public advocacy. Doing so will not only serve to increase our empathy, but, if the Rabbinic tradition is right, it just may keep the whole of our American society from collapsing under the weight of *sinat chinam*, free hate. We all want to think of ourselves as good people. In Debby Irving's words, "At this point, the only thing needed for racism to continue is for good people to do nothing."[10]

NOTES

1. "Glossary," Racial Equity Tools, accessed December 20, 2017, http://racialequitytools.org/glossary#.

2. Lois Waldman, "Employment Discrimination against Jews in the United States—1955," *Jewish Social Studies* 18, no. 3 (July 1956): 208–16, https://www.jstor.org/stable/4465458?seq=1#page_scan_tab_contents.

3. Peter Jacobs, "Harvard Is Being Accused of Treating Asians the Same Way It Used to Treat Jews," December 4, 2014, *Business Insider*, http://www.businessinsider .com/the-ivy-leagues-history-of-discriminating-against-jews-2014-12.

4. Karen Brodkin, *How Jews Became White Folks and What That Says about Race in America* (New Brunswick, NJ: Rutgers University Press, 1998), 281.

5. Ibid., 282.

6. Ta-Nehisi Coates, *Between the World and Me* (New York: Spiegel & Grau, 2015), 97.

7. "New Census Bureau Report Analyzes U.S. Population Projections," United States Census Bureau, March 3, 2015, https://www.census.gov/newsroom/press-releases/2015/cb15-tps16.html.

8. Siri Carpenter, "Sights Unseen," *Monitor on Psychology* 32, no. 4 (April 2001): 54, http://www.apa.org/monitor/apr01/blindness.aspx.

9. Debby Irving, *Waking Up White and Finding Myself in the Story of Race* (Cambridge, MA: Elephant Room Press, 2014), 70–72.

10. Ibid., 60.

ADVOCACY IN ACTION

Working toward Immigration Reform

Rabbi John A. Linder

America's immigration system is broken and long in need of reform. The current system drives undocumented immigrants into the shadows, gives organized crime a constituency of the disenfranchised and most vulnerable, hamstrings law enforcement from developing trust in underserved neighborhoods, and erodes the foundation of respect and diversity upon which our country was founded. As articulated earlier in this volume, one of the cornerstone obligations in Judaism is to treat the stranger, the alien—that is, the undocumented—in our midst just as we would treat our own citizens. We are reminded of this obligation thirty-six times in Torah, more than any other commandment. If, as Jews, we are commanded to stand with the undocumented in our communities, the question then is: What does this look like and how can we make a difference?

As senior rabbi of Temple Solel in Phoenix, Arizona, for the past ten years, I serve in a state that is on the front lines of our broken immigration system. We in Arizona know that the system will *not* change itself—that people of principle need to advocate and work for change. Speaking truth to power, learning the details of legislation, and especially utilizing the model of congregation-based community organizing (CBCO) have been powerful ways to unite our brothers and

194 MORAL RESISTANCE AND SPIRITUAL AUTHORITY

sisters in the interfaith community around immigration reform. We stand, after all, on a common foundation of compassion for the most vulnerable—in this case, for the undocumented in our midst. And we knew we needed to lift our voices together to advocate for those so often silenced.

Our work started long before Arizona passed its regressive, notorious immigration law known as Senate Bill (SB) 1070. The story of our communal fight against that law didn't begin in the corridors of power, but instead in sacred spaces. The model of CBCO is grounded in listening campaigns. Listening campaigns, typically held in people's homes and facilitated by temple members, are centered around common questions. In our case we asked people to consider, "What keeps you up at night, and what gets you up in the morning?" We began our listening campaign, which we called "Ties That Bind," months before Arizona enacted SB 1070. With hostility toward the immigrant community already in the air, it was not surprising that the treatment of the undocumented was one of the issues our members spoke about— one that kept them up at night, one they felt motivated to get up in the morning and do something about. Given the plight of Jews over thousands of years and our biblical Exodus story, we in the Jewish community are no strangers to being the stranger. For most of us, the American Jewish immigration journey to America occurred within the most recent three generations of our families. Immigration is an issue that resonates with Jews. Being part of a broad-based organization, the Valley Interfaith Project (VIP), whose other members shared many of the same concerns about immigration, gave us a vehicle through we could educate, act, and have an impact. Ultimately, we were able to have impact on leaders local and national and to keep our commitment to work on the ground that would continue to feed our ability to advocate effectively.

In Phoenix, we were able to have impact by advocating directly to city officials with regard to how anti-immigrant measures were enforced. It was well known, before the passing of SB 1070, that the Maricopa County Sheriff's Department, under the direction of Sheriff

Joe Arpaio, was violating people's civil rights through intimidation and profiling. Members of Temple Solel were part of a delegation of VIP leaders to bring the real-life stories of these illegal intimidation tactics to Phoenix mayor Greg Stanton and Phoenix police chief Jack Harris (as well as the Department of Justice [DOJ] in Washington, DC). VIP organized meetings of five hundred to a thousand people for Mayor Stanton and Chief Harris, in which we raised voices and elevated stories of citizen profiling and the plight of the undocumented who were being driven into the shadows for fear of losing their families.

At a time when statewide support for stricter immigration enforcement intensified—support that culminated in Governor Jan Brewer signing SB 1070 into law—Police Chief Harris had the backbone to resist jumping on the bandwagon. Moved in part by the stories he heard, Chief Harris went on public record at our meetings, stating that his officers were not going to participate in routine immigration checks. Chief Harris made it clear that the priorities of his department, with his already scarce resources, would be used to pursue violent criminals—smugglers, drug dealers, murderers, rapists, and burglars—not spend time picking up landscapers and busboys and turning them over to U.S. Immigration and Customs Enforcement. Mayor Stanton, too, standing in front of our members, publicly decried both the civil rights implications of SB 1070 and Sheriff Arpaio's blatant disregard for people's civil rights. While the actions of Chief Harris had the most immediate impact, the public statements of the mayor made a major difference as well.

But our work combatting anti-immigrant sentiment and law was not limited only to local action in Phoenix and Arizona. Once SB 1070 was signed into law, an interfaith clergy delegation organized by VIP—in which I was honored to participate—traveled to Washington, DC, to meet with the Civil Rights Division of the DOJ and Arizona's congressional representatives around the increasingly urgent need to pass comprehensive immigration reform. Our group consisted of Tucson Diocese Bishop Gerald Karcanas, vice president of the U.S. Conference of Catholic Bishops; Yuma's Monsignor

Richard O'Keefe; Bishop Minerva Carcaño of the Desert Southwest United Methodist Church; Lutheran Reverend Jan Flaaten, executive director of the Arizona Ecumenical Council; Reverend Gary Kinnaman, national Evangelical leader; and Joe Rubio, lead organizer for VIP. I include this list to make an important point about advocacy: individually, the voice of even the most influential clergy member in our delegation could not carry the weight of the collective group, speaking truth to power together, as part of the same organization. Organizing reinforces that the whole is greater than the sum of its parts, and that greater sum makes all the difference in arguing with elected officials about legislative change.

Organizing and advocacy do not always have immediate impact or lead directly to immediate gratification and desired outcomes. As the Reverend Martin Luther King Jr. reminds us, "The arc of the moral universe is long, but it bends toward justice."[1] The VIP delegation to Washington did not experience the "success" of having its voice persuasively change the minds of elected officials. Our meeting with Senator John McCain (of blessed memory) was particularly difficult. The senator's once impassioned voice and leadership around comprehensive immigration reform, his reputation of being a maverick, was being muffled and distorted by the pressure of political challengers on the right. In response, Senator McCain publicly cast a broad net over the whole of the undocumented community as criminals. In that political context, our decision to remind the senator of his past bipartisan leadership, co-sponsoring with Senator Ted Kennedy (of blessed memory) comprehensive immigration reform, was not what the senator wanted to hear. It is safe to say that our meeting did not go well. However, as our clergy team was boarding the plane to return to Phoenix, Senator McCain—reflecting on his abrasive, defensive demeanor during our session—personally called members of our delegation and expressed the desire to keep the door open for further dialogue.

Another session that day in Washington also led to an outcome, although not necessarily the one we imagined. Our clergy delegation met with the Department of Justice assistant attorney general, Tom

Perez, along with his staff at the Civil Rights Division. We spent an hour sharing stories from our members of abuse and violations many people had experienced at the hands of Sheriff Joe Arpaio. While no immediate change happened after that meeting, years later, when an Arizona judge ordered an investigation of Sheriff Arpaio, the stories and contacts from VIP served as meaningful evidence. Eventually, Sheriff Arpaio was convicted of criminal contempt for abusive tactics that exceeded his legal power.

We learned three things in Washington. The first is that a shared religious voice speaking truth to power does make a difference. The second is that the change we seek may not immediately occur or even be the precise change that takes place. Lastly, we were reminded of the power of personal stories not only to bring a community together, but also to express that community's values and impress them strongly in the minds of people who push the levers of political power.

Over the past few years, caught between the lack of political will on Capitol Hill for immigration reform and aggressive anti-immigration measures from the White House, we have focused our energy on local efforts that—most importantly—make a difference in the real lives of real people. We also continue to sustain our organizing and advocacy work by uniting our community around relationships and stories. Much of our focus has shifted to the hands-on work of supporting new refugees arriving in Phoenix and volunteering at a humanitarian shelter for migrants deported back across the Mexican border. This work has fueled our ongoing commitment to advocacy, as we continue to speak out for the Dreamers, those eight hundred thousand undocumented immigrants who arrived in the United States as children, to gain a pathway to permanent legal status (contingent upon meeting certain conditions).

The Syrian refugee crisis, in which some eleven million people fled for their lives from the murderous regime of President Bashar al-Assad, had a profound effect on members of Temple Solel. While there is a need to speak out against the international wave of nationalism and xenophobia, a wave that includes America, we felt we also were required to do something more tangible, something where we could serve others in need. Building upon the relationships we had developed in the interfaith community through our organizing work with VIP, our lay leaders reached out to our brothers and sisters at Ascension Lutheran Church and the Islamic Center of the East Valley. We formed what we called the Abrahamic Coalition to Welcome the Stranger. Working with a federally qualified agency called Refugee Focus, we made arrangements to welcome and support a Syrian family arriving in Phoenix in August of 2016. The young parents of our Syrian family, Ahmad and Anoud, had spent six years in a Jordanian refugee camp, where their two sons, Mohammed and Abdul, were born. Members of Solel, as well as the church and mosque, were at the airport to greet our family, welcoming them to America. Now, some eighteen months later, we continue to be engaged in helping the family integrate into our society. As meaningful as our support has been for Ahmad, Anoud, and the boys, it's been equally as important for the three faith communities to be of service.

Around the same time, and also through our relationships within the interfaith community, I was introduced to Father Sean Carroll, a Jesuit priest who is the executive director of the Kino Border Initiative (KBI). KBI promotes U.S./Mexico border and immigration policies that affirm the dignity of the human person and promotes binational solidarity. Members of Temple Solel traveled to the border to serve a meal in their *comedor*/aid center for the migrant men, women, and children who are deported to Nogales, Sonora, Mexico, or arrive in the city fleeing from Central America. They often arrive with only the clothes on their backs and a small plastic bag that contains their belongings. They often do not know where to turn to receive a meal, find shelter, and make a phone call. They also arrive emotionally and psychologically devastated, due to separation from their family members or the inability to work legally in the United States. There is no better way to understand the plight of immigrants than to spend time with them, serve them, and listen to their stories. The experience is transformative in and of itself; the experience also serves as an important step for people to want to fight for immigration laws that represent the best of American and Jewish values.

Our direct work with immigrants and refugees did not put a halt to our organizing and advocacy efforts; in fact, they strengthened our resolve. In early September of 2017, the White House announced an end to the Deferred Action of Childhood Arrivals. DACA was put in place to protect the eight hundred thousand Dreamers, those undocumented immigrants who arrived in America as children, their average age at six and a half. At the time of drafting this essay, the fate of the Dreamers is still in the balance. Working closely with the national staff at the Religious Action Center, rabbis and lay leaders of Phoenix Reform synagogues met at the local offices of Senator McCain and Congressman Schweikert; we sought their support and co-sponsorship of legislation, in the Senate and the House respectively, for the Dream Act. The process of readying for these sessions, preparing ourselves for advocacy with the help of the RAC, and having each member of our clergy/lay leader delegations speak in the meeting was a great model of civic engagement. It was a good reminder that our elected officials are accountable to us, their constituents. It is up to us to make our voices heard in an organized, thoughtful way.

My colleague Rabbi Emily Langowitz and I sent a special Shabbat message over Labor Day weekend 2017, urging members of Temple Solel to get involved in the work of organizing and advocacy by calling their respective representatives on Capitol Hill to support the Dream Act legislation. We ended our message saying, "The promise that these 800,000 young people bring to America, as well as our own humanity, depend upon it [our advocacy]. These Dreamers may not be our sons and daughters, but they are surely our brothers and sisters." At the end of the day, that's what drives us as Americans and as Jews to be on the front lines of comprehensive immigration reform. We are bound together by our common humanity to lead with compassion. America has always been a land of immigrants. Our future success depends on welcoming immigrants to our shores, with security and the welfare of our country always in the forefront. Being immigrant friendly and ensuring responsible security measures are not mutually exclusive. As our siddur *Mishkan T'filah* creatively offers in the *Amidah*'s *Hodaah* blessing, "We pray that we may live not by our fears but by our hopes, not by our words but by our deeds."[2] May our engagement, through organizing initiatives around immigration reform, opportunities to serve the vulnerable immigrant and refugee communities, and advocacy efforts to speak moral truths to power, reflect our highest hopes and most heartfelt deeds.

NOTES

1. From Dr. King's "Where Do We Go from Here?" speech, delivered August 16, 1967, to the Southern Christian Leadership Conference in Atlanta.

2. *Mishkan T'filah: A Reform Siddur*, ed. Elyse D. Frishman (New York: CCAR Press, 2007), 257.

STUCK ON THE SHORES
OF THE PARTED SEA

Mass Incarceration through a Jewish Lens

HILLY HABER

During my third year of rabbinical school, I had the privilege of co-teaching two college classes at New York City's main jail complex, Rikers Island. The students I worked with in the class were either serving out a sentence or detained and awaiting trial or sentencing. Every Friday, I rode the city bus from Queens across the bridge onto Rikers Island, surrounded by men, women, and children visiting their parents, children, loved ones, and friends who were detained on the island. I would pass through security, then wait in the classroom for my students as one by one each man was escorted by the corrections officers from his housing unit to the facility's educational wing, then frisked before being allowed to enter the room—readings, notebook, and pencils in hand.

As soon as the last student entered, I closed the door. During our time together, we learned about and discussed the historical origins of the prison system, debated various philosophies of punishment, and armed ourselves with knowledge about today's criminal justice system. These men were members of what Professor Andrew Skotnicki calls "the Rikers Island Campus of Manhattan College." After finishing their semester-long course, the Rikers students received acceptance letters to Manhattan College from Professor Skotnicki on behalf of the admissions office.

In the spring of second semester, I missed a class to celebrate Passover with my family. Later, as I explained the story of Passover and the Exodus from Egypt to the students, I was overcome with the realization that these men, some of whom were being detained for crimes for which they had not yet been found guilty, were living, and would go on living, in a perpetual Egypt—a perpetual state of non-freedom.

According to the Pew Charitable Trusts, nearly one in every thirty-one Americans lives either under correctional control in prison or jail or on probation or parole for nonviolent offenses.[1] This shocking statistic does not even take into account the thousands of men and women who live with the permanent scar of a felony incarceration on their record or the family members of those who have been incarcerated. Across the country, a felony incarceration can lead to legalized forms of discrimination, including but not limited to denying men and women employment, housing, public benefits, the right to vote, the ability to serve on a jury, and public accommodations, all of which affect not only the person being discriminated against, but his or her family members as well. As Michelle Alexander argues in *The New Jim Crow*, mass incarceration in the United States has led to the creation of a caste system in which men and women who live or have lived under the control of the criminal justice system are permanently subjected to legalized discrimination for the rest of their lives.[2]

The Exodus narrative is an inspiring story in which the Israelites move from slavery to freedom; the statistics on mass incarceration, on the other hand, tell the dispiriting story of a people who have moved from one form of enslavement to another. While incarceration rates differ from state to state, on average, one in eleven African American adults compared with one in forty-five white adults live under correctional control.[3] As Professor Jonathan Simon so aptly writes in *Governing Through Crime*:

> For the first time since the abolition of slavery, a definable group
> of Americans lives, on a more or less permanent basis, in a state of
> legal nonfreedom . . . a shocking percentage of them descendants
> of those freed slaves.[4]

The cycle of incarceration and recidivism fueled by racism and poverty within the United States is the Egypt in our midst.

In contrast to today's criminal justice system, biblical and Rabbinic legal structures did not utilize incarceration as a means of punishment or a way of forcing someone to remain in a permanent state of nonfreedom or exile from the community. Indeed, rather than isolate and oppress members of the community who were found guilty of committing a crime, systems of punishment outlined by the Bible and refined by the Rabbis actually sought the opposite outcome. The absence of incarceration as a form of punishment in biblical and Rabbinic texts speaks volumes. Punishment in Jewish tradition, with the exception of capital cases, functioned as a way of bringing about *t'shuvah* and full return to the community.

Imprisonment as the sole form of punishment is a foreign concept to both biblical and Rabbinic notions of justice. While there are instances in the Bible and in Rabbinic law in which a person is detained for a crime, the period of detention lasts only as long as it takes to determine the person's guilt or innocence and the exact nature of his or her punishment. Citing the story of the blasphemer who was detained for his crime in Leviticus 24, for example, the Rabbis argue that incarceration may be used when waiting to hear if the accused will be put to death or not (Babylonian Talmud, *Sanhedrin* 78b). Similarly, citing the example of the man who "illegally" gathered wood on Shabbat and was kept under guard even though it was clear he would be sentenced to death (Numbers 15:34), the Rabbis assert that a person may be incarcerated until the exact nature of the punishment (e.g., stoning, burning) is determined (BT *Sanhedrin* 78b).

Other instances of incarceration cited in the Talmud include cases of murder in which the accused is either a repeat offender or there were no witnesses to the crime. Incarceration in these cases, however, is understood as a means of bringing about a quick death through depriving the accused of food and other basic necessities (*Mishnah Sanhedrin* 9:5; BT *Sanhedrin* 81b). It should also be noted here that sentences of capital punishment were not handled lightly by the courts. Even in cases in which someone was sentenced to death, the court engaged in an elaborate system of communication in which a rider on horseback waited within sight of the courthouse and the site of execution just in case new evidence emerged that would exonerate the convicted (BT *Sanhedrin* 42b).

Other legal mechanisms within biblical and Rabbinic notions of justice existed to ensure both the safety of one who commits certain crimes and his or her eventual return from a state of exile. Biblical texts document the existence of six cities of refuge, towns to which those who had accidentally committed manslaughter could flee and live their lives in safety (Joshua 20:7–9). Following the death of the High Priest, these accidental manslayers could return home, forever pardoned for their crime (BT *Makot* 11b).

The Gemara also displays a certain empathy for those who have been imprisoned and is aware of our social responsibility toward the incarcerated, teaching that "prisoners cannot free themselves from their shackles" (BT *B'rachot* 5b). Today's shackles are not limited to the walls of a prison. Once released from prison, most people are still bound by both the force of law and by stigma, forces that keep the walls of the sea from parting for millions of men, women, and children. Stanford Law professor Joan Petersilia writes:

> Parole departments in most large urban areas have developed a prevailing culture that emphasizes surveillance over services. . . . Not surprisingly, most released prisoners are rearrested and returned to prison. The Bureau of Justice Statistics recently released the most comprehensive study ever conducted in the United States of prisoner recidivism (i.e., an offender's return to crime). The study found that 30 percent—or nearly one in three—released prisoners were rearrested in the first six months, 44 percent within the first

year, and 67.5 percent within three years of release from prison (Langan and Levin 2002). . . . Ex-convicts appear to be doing less well than their counterparts released a decade earlier.[5]

In the *Mishneh Torah*, Maimonides writes that *t'shuvah* atones for all sins.[6] Maimonides's conception of *t'shuvah* involves repentance, atonement, and return. Once a person has repented for his or her sins, forgiveness and reintegration into society must follow. Today's criminal justice system, one that emphasizes punishment and surveillance over rehabilitation and reintegration, offers few opportunities for true *t'shuvah*—true return for those permanently sentenced to states of non-freedom.

In a modern midrash by Howard Schwartz, Rabbi Yochanan asked his students what they thought the parted walls of the Red Sea looked like as the Israelites crossed from slavery into freedom. When no one answered, Rabbi Yochanan told them that the walls of the sea resembled a window lattice. Suddenly, there came a voice from the back of the *beit midrash*. The voice was that of Serach bat Asher, Serach the daughter of Asher, granddaughter of Jacob. Serach called out, "I know exactly what the walls resembled. I was there, I crossed the Red Sea—and they resembled shining mirrors, mirrors in which every man, woman, and child was reflected, so that it seemed like an even greater multitude crossed there, not only those of the present, but also those of the past and future as well." When Serach finished, no one questioned her, for she had been there.[7]

Every year during the holiday of Passover we read the story of the Exodus from Egypt. We retell and relive our journey from slavery to freedom. Every year we remind ourselves that we too know oppression, hardship, and alienation. Every year we return to Egypt, and every year we leave again. If we were to look at the reflection staring back at us from the walls of the parted sea, we should wonder who would be with us on this march to freedom. And who would be missing. And who in our midst still suffers from oppression, hardship, and alienation. If we today were to look into the mirrors of the sea as we walk out of Egypt, we would notice that a significant number of our fellow citizens are not walking with us. If our Reform Jewish community takes seriously our commitment to both social justice and Jewish tradition, we must work to open new pathways for people who remain shackled in narrow places.

I offer four questions for all of us who treasure freedom: How can we help build new pathways out of Egypt? How can we look in the mirrors of the parted sea, notice who is missing, and bring even more people into our mixed multitude (Exodus 12:38)? How can we emphasize and model compassion and *t'shuvah* within our communities? What are the ways in which Judaism can inspire change in our criminal justice system today?

NOTES

1. "One in 31 U.S. Adults Are Behind Bars, on Parole or Probation," Pew Charitable Trusts, accessed 1/2/2018, http://www.pewtrusts.org/en/about/news-room/press-releases/0001/01/01/one-in-31-us-adults-are-behind-bars-on-parole-or-probation.

2. Michelle Alexander, *The New Jim Crow: Mass Incarceration in the Age of Colorblindness* (New York: New Press, 2012).

3. Ibid., 99

4. Jonathan Simon, *Governing through Crime: How the War on Crime Transformed American Democracy and Created a Culture of Fear* (New York: Oxford University Press, 2007), 6.

5. Joan Petersilia, *When Prisoners Return Home: Parole and Prisoner Reentry* (New York: Oxford University Press, 2003), 11.

6. Maimonides, *Mishneh Torah, Hilchot T'shuvah* 1:3.

7. Howard Schwartz, *Tree of Souls: The Mythology of Judaism* (New York: Oxford University Press, 2004), 381.

THE PLANET IN PERIL

Rabbi Rachel Greengrass

2100 BCE:

The room was pitch black. Naamah couldn't even see her hands, although she could feel them shaking with fear. The air was thick with moisture, fear, and the smell of animal feces, even her own. The sounds were deafening. Who could tell if anyone spoke? All she could hear was the pounding of the rain, the sloshing of the ocean.

Naamah was afraid.

Hope was not on her mind, talk of sunshine and rainbows was beyond anything she could imagine in that moment. Only one thought crossed her mind, a prayer. "Please, God, make this stop; please, God I want to live." Her prayers left her mouth and vanished into the deafening void.

We all know the story of Noah. Perhaps you even sang songs about him and his "arky-arky" in Sunday school. He is a good ecological role model, working hard to ensure that each species of animal survives.[1] Although they are very familiar characters, we don't often discuss what life was like on the ark for Noah, his wife Naamah, and their family. The eight humans on the ark prefigured today's tsunami of environmental migrants (as the International Organization for Migration recognizes them),[2] people forced to move because of environmental change.

All over our warming world, people are, or soon will be, on the move. In the Middle East and North Africa, this movement is largely due to drought; in Asia, floods. According to Foresight, a UK government research body, by 2060 there could be hundreds of millions environmental migrants, with the number of people living in vulnerable urban coastal floodplains, primarily in Asia and Africa, increasing by as many as 192 million.[3]

In the twenty-first century, natural disasters, such as floods, hurricanes, mudslides, and droughts, are increasing in intensity and frequency, largely due to climate change. None of the existing tools of international and regional refugee law specifically addresses the plight of such people. The acceleration of drought, desertification, and salinization of groundwater and soil due to rising sea levels has led to climate change contributing to the displacement of people across international frontiers.[4]

> When the Eternal saw how great was the wickedness of human beings in the earth, that the direction of their thoughts was nothing but wickedness all the time, the Eternal regretted having made human beings on earth, and was heartsick. So the Eternal thought: "I will wipe the humans who I created off the face of the earth—the humans [and with them] the beasts, the reptiles, the birds of the sky—for I rue the day I made them." But Noah found favor in the Eternal's sight. (Genesis 6:5–8)

According to *B'reishit Rabbah* 30:7, Noah spent 120 years trying to convince the people that a flood was coming and that they had to change their way of life.[5] Their retort is imagined by Rava (Babylonian Talmud, *Sanhedrin* 108b):

> When Noah rebuked them and spoke words to them that were as hard as fiery flints, they scorned him! They said to him, "Old man, what is this ark for?" He replied, "The Holy One, blessed be God, will bring a flood upon you." "A flood of what?" they jeered. "If a flood of fire, we have a substance called *alita* [to put out the fire]; and if God should bring a flood of water, then, if God brings it up from the earth, we have iron plates with which we can cover the

earth [and prevent the water from coming up]; and if [the water comes] from heaven, we have a substance called *akob* [which can ward it off]."

Does this sound familiar? In this retelling, Noah warns the people of the oncoming flood, that they need to change how they're living—but the people believe that their tools and technology will protect them from the coming flood. They will be okay. No change is necessary. Noah is an alarmist.

Right now, we have not just one Noah, but many knowledgeable individuals who are warning us of changing conditions. They include 97 percent of the scientific community.[6]

Many are responding to these warnings with scorn. They claim that those who predict dire consequences to the planet are fear-mongering, while insisting that we have, or will have, technologies to protect us from any oncoming climate crisis. Sadly, technology is, at best, a stop-gap measure. Eventually, if we don't change how we are living today, the flood *will* come. With the rainbow, God promised never again to destroy our world (Genesis 9:11)—but if we don't change our ways, we may end up destroying ourselves.

As Rabbi Tarfon taught, "You are not obligated to complete the work, but neither are you free to desist from it" (*Pirkei Avot* 2:21). Judaism calls on us to step forward, to do all we can. There is no such thing in Judaism as an "innocent bystander." We are obligated to act, and never to stand idly by.[7] In fact, according to the midrash, we were created for the purpose of protecting God's creation.

> Upon creating the first human beings, God guided them around the Garden of Eden, saying; "Look at My creations! See how beautiful and perfect they are! I created everything for you. Make sure you don't ruin or destroy My world. If you do, there will be no one after you to fix it." (*Kohelet Rabbah* 7:13)

If we destroy God's world, we destroy ourselves. If we act now, we have the potential to save millions of lives (as well as billions of dollars).[8]

Such action would include retooling our economy and society toward sustainability. It would entail attainable but serious changes to our diet and agriculture, our travel, our land use, and our sources of energy. Long ago, the Torah bade us to do just that through the radical notions of the Sabbatical and Jubilee years. Maharat Rori Picker Neiss writes:

> The laws of the Jubilee year, as well as the laws of the Sabbatical year, teach us that property and employment are not rights, but responsibilities. As the Torah teaches us, "For the land is [God's]; you are but strangers resident with [God]" (Leviticus 25:23). As residents of the land, we have an obligation to care for the land. And as human beings, we have a responsibility to care for our fellow brothers and sisters. And lest we forget and presume for ourselves that we have control, power, or even ownership over a piece of land or a fellow human, in the Jubilee year we are commanded to stop, to let the land lie fallow, to return all land that we had acquired, and to let all people go free—ourselves included.[9]

Our modern prophets echo the ancient, as the prophet Isaiah taught, "God did not create it [the earth] a wasteland, but formed it for habitation" (Isaiah 45:18). And yet, in opposition to our prophetic call to make deserts bloom (Isaiah 35:1), humanity is taking lush greenery and transforming it into deserts.

Trees produce the air we breathe and absorb carbon dioxide; their roots prevent soil erosion and absorb and filter water; trees produce needed shade and humidity, along with fruit; they provide homes for animals, insects, and other flora and fauna. In economic terms, one in four people depend directly on forests for their livelihoods. More than 120 prescription drugs derive directly from plants found in forests. Despite all this, the world has lost nearly half its forests to agriculture, development, or resource extraction just in the past century—on top of which, deforestation accounts for 11 percent of human-caused greenhouse gas emissions.

This is a concern not just for nature, but for humanity as well.[10] The livestock industry pollutes our air, earth, and water by releasing harmful chemicals such as ammonia, carbon monoxide, cyanide, phosphorus, nitrates, heavy metals, and methane (a potent greenhouse gas) into our environment. Animal waste breeds microbial pathogens including salmonella, cryptosporidium, streptococci, and giardia.[11] The U.S. Environmental Protection Agency has estimated that thirty-five thousand miles of rivers in twenty-two states are severely polluted by animal excrement. And residents breathe the fecal mists, causing a 50 percent increase in asthma, as well as sore throats, headaches, diarrhea, depression, fatigue, and more. The story is even worse in South America, east Asia, and other regions where meat is grown—often for export to the United States—on recently deforested land.[12]

As we read in *Kohelet*, "The advantage of land is supreme; even the king is subject to the soil" (Ecclesiastes 5:8). The time to act is now; we must all do the work of *tikkun*, of repairing the damage we have done. Planting is key, as Rabbi Yochanan ben Zakkai taught: "If you have a sapling in your hand and are told that the Messiah has come, first plant the sapling, and then go welcome the Messiah" (*Avot D'Rabbi Natan* 31b). We cannot wait for heavenly messengers; it's up to us to consume responsibly, reduce our footprint, and protect vital ecosystems, species, and people, now.

Why did God insist that Noah preserve every species, not just one kind of each animal? Couldn't we have spared ourselves by leaving behind mosquitoes? Perhaps because there is a danger in having a lack of biodiversity.

Our planet is now experiencing the worst spate of species die-offs since the loss of the dinosaurs sixty-five million years ago. Although extinction is a natural phenomenon, it occurs at a natural "background" rate of about one to five species per year. Scientists estimate we're now losing species at one thousand to ten thousand times the background rate, with literally dozens going extinct every day.[13]

Commenting on the biblical command not to take a mother bird and her young (to eat) at the same time (Deuteronomy 22:6), Nachmanides explains that this mitzvah has nothing to do with compassion, but everything to do with species preservation. "Scripture does not allow us to destroy a species altogether, although it permits slaughter for food from that species. Someone who kills a mother and her children in one day . . . it is considered as if he has destroyed the species."

Judaism gives us laws to protect against the purposeful or accidental elimination of a species. And yet that is what we have done; 99 percent of currently threatened species are at risk as a result of human activities, primarily those driving habitat loss, introduction of exotic species, and global warming.[14] Because the rate of change in our biosphere is increasing, and because every species' extinction potentially leads to the extinction of others bound to that species in an ecological train, numbers of extinctions are likely to increase in the coming decades as ecosystems are derailed.[15]

In Leviticus 19:19, God commands, "You shall observe My laws. You shall not let your cattle mate with a different kind; you shall not sow your field with two kinds of seed; you shall not put on cloth from a mixture of two kinds of material." This biblical command has been understood by the Jewish people for countless generations as a prohibition against the blending of fabrics (*shaatnez*) and the interbreeding of species (*kilayim*). Today, we may also understand this commandment to address issues of genetic engineering.[16] When we look at how scientists have engineered our crops to produce what the market deems to be the most valuable, resulting in less variety, and therefore posing a threat to nature's ability to adapt to new bugs, climates, and strains, we uncover a deep wisdom found in this passage.

Too often, we try to "out-tech" nature. Don't like seeds in your watermelon? No problem! Don't like where that river is flowing? No problem! Think that dog would be cute if only it had shorter legs? No problem! What results? A whole host of problems, including plants that cannot reproduce naturally (this is happening with some varieties of farm animals as well), loss of habitat, erosion of soil, and dogs that require hip replacement surgery.

Science is a beautiful thing. Understanding our world is how Maimonides believed we could draw closer to God.[17] The problem is when we use science to alter nature without understanding the consequences for our actions. As we are taught in the Talmud:

> In all that God created in this world, the Holy One did not create a single thing without purpose: thus the snail is a remedy for the scab, the fly is an antidote for the hornet's sting, the mosquito (crushed up) for a snake bite, the snake can cure certain types of boils, and the spider as a remedy for a scorpion (sting).[18]

Perhaps the most definitive verse from the Torah on the prohibition against destruction is found in the laws against cutting down fruit trees. In Deuteronomy we are told:

> When in your war against a city you have to besiege it a long time in order to capture it, you must not destroy its trees, wielding the ax against them. You may eat of them, but you must not cut them down. Are trees of the field human to withdraw before you into the besieged city? (Deuteronomy 20:19)

Maimonides expands this ruling, "This law does not only apply to trees. Whoever breaks vessels, rips up garments, destroys a building, stops up a fountain, or ruins food is guilty of violating the prohibition of *bal tashchit* [do not destroy]."[19]

From this passage, our ancestors codified laws against waste or destruction. *Sefer HaChinuch*, the thirteenth-century text designed, among other goals, to provide the ethical significance to the 613 traditional commandments of the Bible, connects this behavior to our virtue:

> This is the way of the righteous and those who improve society, who love peace and rejoice in the good in people and bring them close to Torah: that nothing, not even a grain of mustard, should be lost to the world, that they should regret any loss or destruction that they see, and if possible they will prevent any destruction that they can. Not so are the wicked, who are like demons, who rejoice in the destruction of the world, and they are destroying themselves.[20]

Again, Maimonides applies this teaching with specificity even to the most significant moments of life, suggesting that such mitzvot, such regulations, are important not just for their own sake but as a means of conditioning Jews to be sensitive to important Jewish values such as not wasting. In his "Laws on Mourning" he teaches:

> One should be trained not to be destructive. When you bury a person, do not waste garments by burying them in the grave. It is better to give them to the poor than to cast them to worms and moths. Anyone who buries the dead in an expensive garment violates the negative mitzvah of *bal tashchit*.[21]

This may seem extreme to our standards, but the amount of waste we currently produce is extreme. Waste has been a profitable manufacturing philosophy since the 1920s; it's called "planned obsolescence." Vance Packard, author of *The Waste Makers*, published in 1960, warned: "This course appears to be taking the people of the United States toward more and more force feeding, more and more manipulation, more and more fast-fading or deteriorating products, more and more self-indulgence, more and more depletion of irreplaceable resources."[22] When we purchase a new cell phone, computer, television, or car, the product very quickly feels outdated. This leads to a cycle of waste and high replacement needs. Each new product quickly becomes old when innovations are produced before the initial invention has even finished its life cycle.

This materialistic waste machine is harming not only our happiness levels but also the planet. All waste is terrible for the planet. Electronic waste, containing toxic heavy metals such as mercury, lead, beryllium, and cadmium, as well as hazardous chemicals such as brominated flame retardants, is particularly corrosive. Toxic pollution affects more than two hundred million people worldwide. In some of the world's worst polluted places, babies are born with birth defects, children can lose thirty to forty IQ points, and life expectancy may be as low as forty-five years because of cancers and other diseases.[23]

We often feel that our choices affect only us or maybe our immediate surroundings. But the truth is that we live in a global economy of an interconnected world. The first question a person asks God is, "Am

I my brother's keeper?" (Genesis 4:9). The answer is yes. We are all in this together. The point is beautifully illustrated in *Vayikra Rabbah* 4:6:

> If one Jew sins, all of Israel feels it. . . . This can be compared to the case of men on a ship, one of whom took a drill and began drilling beneath his own place. His fellow travelers to said to him, "What are you doing?" He replied, "What does that matter to you? I am drilling only under my own place!" They continued, "We care because the water will come up and flood the ship for us all."

We can no longer pretend that what we do, as an individual, a company, or a nation, does not affect others. This is codified in the *Shulchan Aruch*, a widely accepted code of Jewish law: "One who does something at a distance and it causes damage to his fellow, it has disturbed [the peace]; he must pay and he is liable."[24]

We are all sustained by the environment and are therefore responsible for protecting this precious and irreplaceable resource. Too often we believe that we can own something that only belongs to God. We do not own the earth. We rely on her for our lives. So, let's conclude with a story:

> Rav Yerucham tells of a dispute brought before Rav Chayim Volozhin[25] where two people were fighting over a piece of land. They were both stubborn, and neither one was willing to listen to any compromise.
>
> Rav Chayim then turned his ear down to the ground as if he were listening to what the ground was saying. He then turned to the disputants and said, "After hearing both your arguments, I wanted to hear what the land in dispute has to say. And do you know what it said? It said, 'Why are they both fighting who owns me? In the end, the two of them both belong to me!'"

NOTES

1. The Coalition on the Environment and Jewish Life, in the late 1990s, ran "Operation Noah," to help raise awareness about endangered species. The tagline,

based on Genesis 6:9, was "Noah was a righteous upstanding man in his generation. Shouldn't we be in ours?"

2. According to the IOM, "Environmental migrants are persons or groups of persons who, for compelling reasons of sudden or progressive changes in the environment that adversely affect their lives or living conditions, are obliged to leave their habitual homes, or choose to do so, either temporarily or permanently, and who move either within their country or abroad." "Migration, Climate Change and the Environment," International Organization for Migration, accessed June 1, 2017, https://www.iom.int/definitional-issues.

3. Poppy McPherson, "Dhaka: The City Where Climate Refugees Are Already a Reality," *Guardian*, December 1, 2015, https://www.theguardian.com/cities/2015/dec/01/dhaka-city-climate-refugees-reality.

4. "Refugees," United Nations, accessed May 18, 2017, http://www.un.org/en/sections/issues-depth/refugees/index.html.

5. Rashi's commentary: "Many ways to bring relief and rescue are available to God; why, then, did God burden Noah with this construction? In order that the people of the generation of the Flood should see him occupying himself with it for 120 years and ask him, 'For what do you need this?' And he would say to them, 'The Holy One, blessed be God, is destined to bring a flood upon the world.' Perhaps they would repent" (*Aggadat B'reishit* 1:2; *Tanchuma, Noach* 5; *Tanchuma Buber, B'reishit* 37; *B'reishit Rabbah* 30:7).

6. Authors of seven climate consensus studies—including Naomi Oreskes, Peter Doran, William Anderegg, Bart Verheggen, Ed Maibach, J. Stuart Carlton, and John Cook—co-authored a paper to settle the expert climate consensus question once and for all. The two key conclusions from the paper are as follows: (1) Depending on exactly how the expert consensus is measured, somewhere between 90 percent and 100 percent agree that humans are responsible for climate change, with most of the studies finding 97 percent consensus among publishing climate scientists; and (2) the greater the climate expertise among those surveyed, the higher the consensus on human-caused global warming. J. Cook et al., "Consensus on Consensus: A Synthesis of Consensus Estimates on Human-Caused Global Warming," *Environmental Research Letters* 11, no. 4 (April 13, 2016), https://doi.org/10.1088/1748-9326/11/4/048002.

7. "*Do not stand idly by* while your neighbor's blood is shed" (Leviticus 19:16).

8. In 2016, the Risky Business Project (https://riskybusiness.org/) led by former New York City mayor Michael Bloomberg and U.S. Treasury secretary Henry Paulson placed the value of Florida property at risk from climate change first in the nation. By 2030, they estimated some $69 billion will be at risk, with sea rise alone expected to threaten $15 billion in property.

9. Rori Picker Neiss, "Behar-Bechukotai," *Limmud on One Leg*, 5773 (May 2013), https://limmud.org/publications/limmudononeleg/5773/behar-bechukotai/.

10. In addition to the health effects of pollution that follows, according to the World Wildlife Federation, "in the expanding soy plantations of Brazil, poor people are lured from villages and deprived neighborhoods to remote soy estates where they are put to work in barbaric conditions, sometimes at gunpoint, with no chance of escape. Worker abuse is especially prevalent where there is strong agricultural expansion, such as in the Amazon states of Pará and Mato Grosso." "Forest Conversion,"

WWF Global, accessed May 18, 2017, http://wwf.panda.org/about_our_earth/deforestation/deforestation_causes/forest_conversion/.

11. Jeff Tietz, "Boss Hog," *Rolling Stone*, July 8, 2008. Accessed May 19, 2017. https://www.rollingstone.com/culture/news/boss-hog-the-dark-side-of-americas-top-pork-producer-20061214.

12. Sergio Margulis, *Causes of Deforestation of the Brazilian Amazon*, World Bank Working Paper 22 (Washington DC: World Bank, 2004).

13. E. Chivian and A. Bernstein, eds., *Sustaining Life: How Human Health Depends on Biodiversity* (New York: Oxford University Press, 2008).

14. Holly Dublin, "Endangered Species," *Encyclopaedia Britannica Online* (2009), http://www.britannica.com/EBchecked/topic/186738/endangered-species.

15. "The Extinction Crisis," Center for Biological Diversity, accessed May 19, 2017, http://www.biologicaldiversity.org/programs/biodiversity/elements_of_biodiversity/extinction_crisis/.

16. For a thorough discussion of Jewish sources and issues of genetic engineering, see Rabbi Daniel S. Nevins, "Halakhic Perspectives on Genetically Modified Organisms," Rabbinic Assembly, November 10, 2015, http://www.rabbinicalassembly.org/sites/default/files/public/halakhah/teshuvot/2011-2020/nevins-gmos.pdf.

17. Maimonides, *Guide of the Perplexed, Part III, Chapter XVIII*. "Every individual member of humankind enjoys the influence of Divine providence in proportion to his intellectual perfection. . ." One of many passages that suggest that the more knowledge one acquires, the closer the relationship with the Creator.

18. Babylonian Talmud, *Shabbat* 77b. A similar teaching is found in *B'reishit Rabbah* 10:7, "The Rabbis said: Even though you may think superfluous in the world things such as fleas, gnats, and flies, even they are included in the creation of the world. The Holy One has a purpose for everything including the snakes, scorpions, gnats, and frogs."

19. Maimonides, *Mishneh Torah, Hilchot M'lachim* 6:9–10.

20. *Sefer HaChinuch* 530.

21. Maimonides, *Mishneh Torah, Hilchot Eivel* 14:24.

22. Vance Packard, *The Waste Makers* (New York, NY: David McKay, 1960), p. 213.

23. Alina Bradford, "Pollution Facts & Types of Pollution," *Live Science*, March 10, 2015, https://www.livescience.com/22728-pollution-facts.html.

24. *Shulchan Aruch, Choshen Mishpat* 155:33. Another compelling example of this kind of law is given by Maimonides in his *Mishneh Torah, Hilchot Nizkei Mamon* 13, where it describes liability.

25. This is based upon his understanding of BT *Bava Batra* 37a–b, which discusses conflicts in ownership of land during the Sabbatical year.

SEEK PEACE AND PURSUE IT

RABBI JOEL MOSBACHER

Don't stop after beating the swords
into plowshares, don't stop! Go on beating
and make musical instruments out of them.
Whoever wants to make war again
will have to turn them into plowshares first.[1]

—Yehuda Amichai, *Tosefet Lachazon Hashalom*

One of the earliest stories in our most sacred text recounts the events of
Cain killing his brother, and then callously asking, "Am I my brother's
keeper?" (Genesis 4:9). This seemingly rhetorical question conveys one
of the most profound moral responsibilities for all humankind, including for us as Jews. The answer to the question "Do I have a responsibility to keep my fellow human beings safe?" is an unequivocal "yes."

We have further evidence of this obligation for Jews to prevent
harm from befalling other people in the Book of Deuteronomy, as we
are taught, "When you build a new house, you shall make a parapet for
your roof, so that you do not bring bloodguilt on your house if anyone should fall from it" (Deuteronomy 22:8). One might legitimately
think: if someone else puts themselves in harm's way (e.g., by walking
on another person's roof), surely we do not have any responsibility for

them. But this text affirms that we do, indeed, need to do more than not harm another person; we must actively prevent harm from happening whenever possible.

On the other hand, so often in human history, people have used religion as a pretext for cruelty, baseless hatred, violence, and murder. Many have used it as a basis to supposedly bring peace to God's world by waging aggressive war. Within the Hebrew Bible, we have examples of God seeking to redress the wrongs in God's own creation with violence and examples of God's explicit instructions to the Israelites to destroy other nations they encounter. We see from some of the earliest verses of the Torah's history of humanity that God's creatures, just ten generations removed from the Garden of Eden, are resorting to "wickedness" and "that the direction of their thoughts was nothing but wicked all the time" (Genesis 6:5). In this moment, God decides, with regret for having created humanity in the first place, that the way forward is to begin again with Noah and his family, destroying nearly all life in God's world. For those who read the text of Creation and note that we humans are created in God's image, can the message truly be that we are to destroy just as God destroys?

In modern times, our own Reform responsa wrestle with the idea of violence. While more recently responsa have acknowledged that war is sometimes obligatory,[2] the Columbus Platform of 1947 teaches that "Judaism from the days of the prophets, has proclaimed to [hu]mankind the ideal of universal peace, striving for the spiritual and physical disarmament of all nations. Judaism rejects violence and relies upon moral education, love, and sympathy."

So how shall we as people of faith respond from a place of faith to the violence in our world? When we look all around us, within our own country and across the world, we see people claim religious values as the basis for forceful, threatening, and violent acts. Can we indeed claim, as Rabbi Lord Jonathan Sacks argues in his recent volume, that "God speaks, sometimes in a still, small voice almost inaudible beneath the clamour of those claiming to speak on His behalf. What we say in those times [of violence] is: *Not in My Name*"?[3] Can we authentically assert that our motto as Jews is to "depart from evil and do good" (Psalm 34:15)?

I imagine that we aspire for this to be the case. At times of uncertainty and violence in our neighborhoods, our country, and our world, we want to hold on to the saying in the midrash, "Great is peace, for all blessings are contained in it. . . . Great is peace, for God's name is peace" (*B'midbar Rabbah* 11:7).

But so often, when we are guiding studies of the Hebrew Bible, students will note the incredible amount of violence present in our sacred text, much of it sanctioned, even commanded, by God.

The Book of Deuteronomy contains numerous examples of seeming wanton destruction of life:

> So the Eternal our God also delivered into our power King Og of Bashan, with all his troops, and we dealt them such a blow that no survivor was left. . . . We doomed them as we had done in the case of King Sihon of Heshbon; we doomed every town—men, women, and children. . . . And [when] the Eternal your God delivers them to you and you defeat them, you must doom them to destruction: grant them no terms and give them no quarter. (Deuteronomy 3:3, 3:6, 7:2)

The ancient Israelites lived in a time that seemed to have no concept of peaceful coexistence; there was often little or no option in those days for negotiated settlements.

As I wrestle with passages like these, seeking to respond to both my own heartache and that of my fellow students of these texts, I return time and again to the idea that we live in a different place and time. As Dr. Reuven Firestone writes:

> Historically the Hebrew Bible emerged out of a real-life environment in which there was no universal legal system for arbitrating disputes and aggression. Violence between peoples was a common and normal fact of life. All the evidence suggests that at least at certain times, the biblical people of Israel had to fight, perhaps even to the death, simply in order to survive as a distinct religious community. Fighting is therefore required at times in the Hebrew Bible

because the alternative was perceived as destruction and therefore the inability to carry out the divine will.[4]

And yet, even in those very different times, the Torah's command is to begin by offering terms of peace, as Deuteronomy teaches, "When you approach a town to attack it, you shall offer it terms of peace" (Deuteronomy 20:10).

Maimonides goes even further to teach that in the event that a nation that the Israelites faced chose not to make a treaty, the Israelites were still commanded to fight mercifully. For example, when besieging a city to conquer it, the Israelites were never to surround it on all sides. This way, one side was always left open to allow anyone who wanted to escape.[5]

The Talmud teaches about the place of self-defense when it comes to violence:

> **As it is taught** in a *baraita* that **Rabbi Yonatan ben Shaul says**: If a **person pursues another to kill him, and** the one being pursued **can save himself by injuring one of the limbs of** the pursuer, **but he does not save** himself in this manner and instead kills the pursuer, he **is executed for** killing **him** even though he acted in self-defense. (Babylonian Talmud, *Sanhedrin* 57a–57b)[6]

Although Jewish tradition permits violence in the case of self-defense, here, too, there are limits. The eighteenth-century commentary *Ikar Siftei Chachamim* notes that "if it is possible to stop [an attacker] with a non-lethal injury and one kills the pursuer anyway, the one who kills can be executed by the court for murder."[7]

And while the Bible makes a distinction between an optional war— *milchemet r'shut*—and an obligatory war—*milchemet mitzvah*—Maimonides teaches, "You may not wage war on anyone until you make peace overtures, whether it is an optional or obligatory war."[8]

Ecclesiastes seems to accept violence as a part of the human experience: "To everything there is a season, and a time to every purpose under heaven . . . a time to kill and a time to heal . . . a time for war and a time for peace" (Ecclesiastes 3:1, 3:3, 3:8).

The Talmud, in a discussion around the laws of what a person may carry on Shabbat, makes it clear how the rabbis feel about weapons in general. On the one hand, war is sometimes necessary, but on the other, it is never the Judaic ideal. On the one hand, a Jew might have to carry a sword, but on the other hand, it should never be what we strive for:

> A man may not go out [on Shabbat] with a sword, nor with a bow, nor with a shield, nor with a round shield, nor with a spear. If he has gone out [with any of these] he is liable for a *chatat* [sacrificial offering]. Rabbi Eliezer says, "They are ornaments for him." But the Sages say, "They are nothing but an indignity, for it is said, 'They shall beat their swords into plowshares, and their spears into pruning hooks; nation shall not lift up sword against nation, neither shall they learn war any more' (Isaiah 2:4)." (BT *Shabbat* 63a)[9]

Indeed, King David is denied the privilege of building the Temple in Jerusalem because he engaged in violence:

> Then David the king stood up upon his feet, and said, "Hear me, my brethren, and my people; as for me, it was in my heart to build a house of rest for the Ark of the Covenant of the Eternal, and for the footstool of our God; and I had made ready for the building. But God said to me, 'You shall not build a house for My name, because you are a man of war, and have shed blood.'" (I Chronicles 28:2–3)

What seems clear from the biblical ethic is that Judaism is not at its root a purely pacifistic religion; there is such a thing as obligatory self-defense and justified war. That said, the preponderance of Jewish textual sources call us, as in the words of the Psalmist, "to seek peace and pursue it" (Psalm 34:15). The Rabbis of our tradition conclude that it is the responsibility of each individual to respect and protect the life of other human beings, based on the commandment in Leviticus 18:5, "You shall live by them," and the teaching that the saving of a single life is attributed to a person as if he or she saved an entire world (*Mishnah Sanhedrin* 4:5).

And further, we find so many texts that call us to envision the world as it should be. It is the audacity of religion that demands we not accept the world as it is, but aspire to a more perfect world, and to work to bring that world into reality, even against all odds.

The prophet Micah asserts his vision for the future—it is the one that inspired Yehuda Amichai's poem at this chapter's beginning. Micah's is a vision of a world without violence:

> And they shall beat their swords into plowshares
> and their spears into pruning hooks.
> Nation shall not lift up
> sword against nation;
> neither shall they learn war any more.
> But they shall sit every person
> under their vine and under their fig tree,
> and none shall make them afraid.
> For the mouth of the Eternal of Hosts has spoken.

(Micah 4:3–4)

We have an affirmative commandment to save lives, stemming from the law in Leviticus 19:16, "You shall not stand idly by the blood of your neighbor." About this text, Rashi teaches:

> This means: You may not simply stand there and watch a person die if there is a possibility that you might be able to save his or her life—for example, if you see a person drowning in a river or being chased by a wild animal or bandits.

Regarding the next line in Leviticus, "You shall not hate your kinsfolk in your heart. Reprove your kinsman but incur no guilt because of him." (Lev. 19:17), Rabbi Tamar Grimm notes:

> Perhaps it is no coincidence that this text juxtaposes the obligation to save a life with the prohibition against vengeance…. Unfortunately, we are not just faced with external calamities, such as Rashi's examples of drowning or being chased by an animal. The

obligation to save a life precedes a statement about the very real danger of human volatility.[10]

Rabbi Hezkiah, in Midrash *Vayikra Rabbah*, teaches the importance of pursuing peace by reminding us that the Torah itself makes a distinction between the command to make peace and all the other commandments:

> The law does not order you to run after or pursue [*rodeif*] the other commandments, but only to fulfill them on the appropriate occasion. But peace you must run after in your place and pursue it even to another place as well. (*Vaykira Rabbah* 9:9)

The Rabbis helps us understand that peace and justice are inexorably linked—that when we overcome violence and make peace, justice will follow, and vice versa:

> Rabban Shimon ben Gamliel says that the world stands on three things: On justice, on truth, and on peace. Rabbi Muna said, "Those three are really one thing! If justice is served, truth is served, and peace will be made. [The proof is that] all three are mentioned in one verse, where it is written, 'You shall judge truth and a judgment of peace in your dwellings' (Zechariah 8:16). In any place that there is peace, there will be justice."[11]

Rabbi Jonathan Sacks teaches a profound lesson about Abraham:

> Abraham himself, the man revered by 2.4 billion Christians, 1.6 billion Muslims, and 13 million Jews, ruled no empire, commanded no army, conquered no territory, performed no miracles and delivered no prophecies. Though he lived differently from his neighbours, he fought for them and prayed for them in some of the most audacious language ever uttered by a human to God—"Shall the Judge of all the earth not do justice?"[12]

Ultimately the words of the prophet Zechariah echo in our ears as we wrestle with the violence we see in our world and ask ourselves if such violence is built into human nature—that is, if it is something insurmountable and eternal. The prophet teaches, "Not by might nor by strength shall you prevail, but only through My spirit, says the Eternal of Hosts" (Zechariah 4:6). We have an affirmative obligation not only to prevent violence, we must also seek peace and pursue it. Created in the divine image, we have an obligation to see that image in others, even when it can seem hard to find. We have an obligation to partner with them to reduce violence in the world, even in the face of adversity. We seek peace because it is the highest of Jewish values. And we pursue it even when it seems an uphill battle, for when we bring peace into the world, we bring justice.

NOTES

1. Yehuda Amichai, "*Tosefet Lachazon Hashalom/*An Appendix to the Vision of Peace," in *The Great Tranquility*, trans. Glenda Abramson and Tudorarfitt (New York: HarperCollins Publishers, 1983). Copyright © 1983 by Yehuda Amichai.

2. Reform Responsa 5762.8, "Preventive War," in *Reform Responsa for the Twenty-First Century*, ed. Mark Washofsky (New York: CCAR Press, 2010), 2:366–379. See also Rabbi Edwin Goldberg's chapter in this volume, "Justified? The Moral Burden of Launching a Preemptive War, 235–246."

3. Jonathan Sacks, *Not in God's Name: Confronting Religious Violence* (New York: Schocken Books, 2015), 3.

4. Reuven Firestone, "Judaism on Violence and Reconciliation," in *Beyond Violence: Religious Sources of Social Transformation* (James Heft, ed.; New York: Fordham University, 2004), 77.

5. Maimonides, *Mishneh Torah, Hilchot M'lachim* 6:7.

6. English translation from The William Davidson digital edition of the Koren Noé Talmud, with interpolated explanatory commentary by Rabbi Adin Steinsaltz Even-Israel. https://www.sefaria.org/Sanhedrin.57a. Literal translation of the text appears in bold; commentary appears in plain type.

7. *Ikar Siftei Chachamim* on Genesis 32:8.

8. Maimonides, *Mishneh Torah, Hilchot M'lachim* 6:1.

9. Adapted from the William Davidson Talmud, with interpolated explanatory commentary by Rabbi Adin Steinsaltz Even-Israel. https://www.sefaria.org/Shabbat.63a

10. Tamar Grimm, "Vigil against Gun Violence" (source sheet), https://www.sefaria.org/sheets/21956.

11. *Derech Eretz Zuta, Perek Shalom, halachah* 2.

12. Sacks, *Not in God's Name*, 4.

MORAL OUTRAGE

Reform Jews and Guns

Rabbi Eric H. Yoffie

Americans in general may be divided about gun violence, but Jewish Americans are not. They have been among the most enthusiastic advocates of legislation that would regulate gun ownership in a reasonable way.

There are a variety of reasons for this phenomenon. Jews are mostly an urban people who lack a culture of hunting and gun ownership. According to one study, Jews have the lowest rate of gun ownership of any religious group.[1] In addition, most Jews are still Democrats, and gun violence prevention is more of a Democratic issue than a Republican one.

It is true that American Jews are modestly more conservative on economic and foreign policy than they were a generation ago. But this shift has not led to a change in Jewish views on guns.

The likely reason is that whether they are Democrats or Republicans, Jews support the forces of stability and security in American politics. Oppressed and persecuted for nearly two millennia before making their way to America, most Jews are classical, small "L" liberals. They have more experience than most other Americans with dictators and demagogues, and they understand precisely how fragile modern democratic governments can be. Therefore, they favor established, mainstream politicians, who balance centrist nationalism with individual rights, oppose radical populism and extremism in all forms, and close yawning gaps between rich and poor. For American Jews, moderate, justice-oriented politics are consistent with what they perceive to be their values and their interests as a small, still-vulnerable minority.

And for the last half century, and particularly the last few decades, there has been no more extreme force in mainstream American politics than the pro-gun faction, led by the National Rifle Association (NRA). In the positions it has advocated and the language it has used, the NRA has embraced a brand of radical fanaticism that has frightened Jews and from which they instinctively recoil. If it supported a reasonable system for Americans to acquire firearms, consistent with the Constitution but with appropriate limitations, its actions would be unobjectionable. But in fact what it supports is the right of virtually anyone—including terrorist suspects, wife beaters, and criminals—to buy almost any weapon at any time, no questions asked.

The advocacy of the NRA is well-known for its bullying, belligerence, and sheer virulence. And such an approach gets results: almost half of the civilian-owned firearms in the world are now to be found in the United States, which has less than 5 percent of the world's population.[2] This mass ownership of guns has led, in turn, to an American gun homicide rate—and gun suicide rate—that far exceeds that of any developed country. America also has a rate of mass shootings that is much, much higher than any other developed country.

While gun enthusiasts have attempted to attribute these gun deaths to other factors, such as racial divisions, higher crime rates, violent video games, and lack of proper mental health care, these claims have been proved false. An ample body of research has demonstrated that there is a direct correlation between American gun ownership and the sky-high number of American gun deaths.[3]

And American Jews, like most Americans, find the slaughter to be both unacceptable and inexplicable. The climbing death rate from firearms is a direct challenge to the cautious, middle-of-the-road approach to politics of the organized Jewish community. And recently, as disturbed individuals have again and again opened fire in our children's schools, Jewish leaders across the communal and religious spectrum have been among the first to assert the commonsense proposition that these individuals simply could not have injured and killed so many people if they had not had guns.

Nonetheless, efforts have been made by pro-gun forces and the modest number of pro-gun Jews to overcome Jewish aversion to firearms. Three arguments specifically tailored to Jews have been put forward.

First is the claim that if Jews in Germany and Europe had had greater access to guns in the 1930s, there would have never been a Holocaust, or many fewer Jews would have perished. This was a point made twenty-five years ago by NRA head Wayne LaPierre and heard regularly since, including from Dr. Ben Carson, now Secretary of Housing and Urban Development, during his recent presidential campaign. But as every responsible historian has pointed out, the German military forces that devastated Europe, sweeping aside the armies of Norway, Belgium, the Netherlands, and France, would not have been slowed by a few guns in the hands of local Jews. And in Eastern Europe, if the Jews had been armed, the local collaborators who played a major role in the murder of Jews would have been armed as well, speeding up rather than delaying the extermination.[4]

Second is the claim that the experience of Israel, where armed soldiers and security guards are to be found everywhere and where many settlers carry guns, argues for easy gun access as a guarantee of security. But the situation in Israel, which has hostile neighbors on its borders and faces the constant threat of organized terror, is very different from the political and cultural realities in America. And more to the point, private gun ownership is far lower in Israel than in America, and gun laws are exceedingly strict. Israel mandates registration of guns, ongoing firearms training, and extensive background checks, and Israeli law requires that guns be securely stored. An Israeli whose gun is misplaced or stolen is likely to be prosecuted and jailed.

Third is the claim that growing alt-right politics, antisemitism, and neo-Nazism in America make it imperative to loosen rather than tighten gun laws so that Jews can be properly prepared for self-defense. But in an already over-armed America, allowing armed thugs and hooligans to acquire even more massive quantities of firearms would threaten communal stability and pose a special threat to minorities, Jews included.

These arguments, in short, are ludicrous. And Jewish Americans, unmoved and unconvinced, have paid no heed. Instead, they have thrown themselves into various national efforts to limit gun access in America. As noted, Jewish communal and religious groups have virtually all spoken out on guns, and the Reform Movement in particular has involved itself in gun violence prevention advocacy. The first resolution passed by the Reform Movement calling for greater regulation of guns was adopted by the North American Board of the Union of American Hebrew Congregations (now the Union for Reform Judaism, or URJ) in 1968, and a dozen resolutions and innumerable statements by lay and rabbinic Reform leaders have been issued since.

The language used by the Reform Movement has, appropriately, been largely framed in religious terms. In my presidential sermon to the Biennial Assembly of the URJ in 1999, drawing on three decades of URJ activism, I summed up the movement's message in these words: "We need to see the control of guns not as a political problem but as a solemn religious obligation. Our gun-flooded society has turned guns into idols, and the worship of idols must be recognized for what it is—blasphemy. The only appropriate religious response to idolatry is sustained moral outrage." Then and later, building on this message and reflecting what leaders of our movement had long proclaimed, I went on to call for a knock-down, drag-out, no-holds-barred battle against the NRA, which, I said, is "the real criminals' lobby in this country, and which is drenched in the blood of murdered children."[5]

Are such sentiments, admittedly raw and graphic, appropriate for use by religious organizations and leaders? One need only think of the ever-growing list of dead and injured children. Think of Columbine and Virginia Tech. Think of Sandy Hook Elementary School in Newtown, Connecticut, and Marjory Stoneman Douglas High School in

Parkland, Florida. Think of the words of former senator Bill Bradley, who referred to the NRA as "the sickest major lobbying organization in American life." Think of the intent of the gun fanatics to deplete us morally as a nation.

When considered in this light, the answer is clearly "yes"; such words are both accurate and necessary. And religious leaders, resolute in their belief that human life is sacred and that justice is a supreme value, have an absolute obligation to affirm them.

In reviewing statements of Jewish religious bodies of all denominations, one finds that two strands of the tradition are most frequently used as the religious foundation for restrictions on guns. First is the generally negative view of weapons that one finds in the sources, drawing on the principle in Isaiah 2:4: "They shall beat their swords into ploughshares and their spears into pruning-knives; nation shall not lift up sword against nation, neither shall they learn war anymore." Commenting on this verse, most Rabbinic sages in the Talmud thought it a "disgrace" to carry weapons on the Sabbath (see BT *Shabbat* 63a). The Talmud also notes that it is forbidden to keep dangerous animals and objects in one's home—a prohibition that would appear to apply to a gun, which is obviously a dangerous object, designed to kill (see BT *Bava Kama* 46a). As Rabbi Shlomo Yaffe has written, the tradition suggests that "weapons and their possession are a reproach to mankind—and not anything desirable."[6]

A second strand of tradition used to support restrictions on guns consists of broad principles drawn from Torah that promote a general sense of communal well-being and moral obligation. Guns threaten life, endanger relationships and families, and disrupt the normal workings of society. Therefore, principles that maintain the foundations of civilization—"You shall not . . . place a stumbling block before the blind" (Leviticus 19:14); "Do not stand idly by while your neighbor's blood is shed" (Leviticus 19:16); and "the dignity of the individual" (*k'vod habriyot*; see BT *B'rachot* 19b)—are often cited as support from Jewish teachings for adopting gun violence prevention measures.

Also helpful in understanding the character of the tradition are the words of Professor Mira Morgenstern, author of *Reframing Politics in the Hebrew Bible*. The so-called militarism of the Hebrew Bible is sometimes invoked as a religious justification for widespread gun ownership. But as Dr. Morgenstern notes, while "the Israelites do fight against other nations . . . they do not fetishize the act of war, and they do not view military prowess as central either to the expression of leadership, or to their identity as a people."[7]

While Jewish tradition is surely not pacifist and does not oppose guns under all circumstances (more on this below), it is fair to say that not a single word of Jewish teachings, or of Christian or Islamic teachings either, opposes commonsensical gun violence prevention. And neither does it offer support for the idea of some God-given right to automatic weapons that fire one hundred shots in a single minute.

Jewish tradition, after all, does affirm the legitimacy of the right of self-defense. The Talmudic principle is "If one comes to kill you, kill him first" (see BT *B'rachot* 58a). The usual interpretation of this passage and its parallels is that the ability to protect oneself can reasonably be seen to include possessing the weapons necessary to safeguard your person and your family, guns included. Such an interpretation does not lead to a general ban on firearms but to a consideration of what is a reasonable system of gun regulation; and "reasonable" here is today thought to refer to measures that will minimize gun violence, suicides, and school killings, while preserving access to firearms for legitimate purposes such as hunting, target shooting, and self-protection.

This then should be the American Jewish agenda on gun regulation in the months and years ahead: joining with allies in the religious and general community, American Jews will advocate for a legislative agenda that will regulate firearms in a sensible way, putting an end to the boomerang of bullets and the senseless slaughter now afflicting America.

We Jews will involve ourselves in anti-violence coalitions to make our communities whole.

We will insist on serious background checks for every gun sale.

We will go on the moral offensive against the NRA, matching their resources with resources of our own, and with deep anti-gun passion.

We will say "no more" to the guns that wreak havoc in our cities, disproportionately among minority communities, and allow a child to be killed every few hours.

And we will do all these things guided by a tradition that does not prohibit guns, but never celebrates them, and that demands that their use be subject to common decency, common sense, and an abiding awareness of the holiness of God's Creation.

NOTES

1. "Jews and Guns," My Jewish Learning, https://www.myjewishlearning.com/article/hunting-in-judaism/.

2. "School Shootings: How Many More?," *Economist*, February 17, 2018, https://www.economist.com/news/united-states/21737061-there-nothing-surprising-article-unfortunately-america-seems-unable-solve.

3. Max Fisher and Josh Keller, "What Explains U.S. Mass Shootings? International Comparisons Suggest an Answer," *New York Times*, November 7, 2017, https://mobile.nytimes.com/2017/11/07/world/americas/mass-shootings-us-international.html?referer=.

4. Alex Seitz-Wald, "The Hitler Gun Control Lie," *Salon*, January 11, 2013, https://www.salon.com/2013/01/11/stop_talking_about_hitler/.

5. Eric Yoffie, "Million Mom March for Gun Control," https://ericyoffie.com/gun-control-march/.

6. Shlomo Yaffe, "What Does Judaism Say About Gun Control?," Chabad.org, https://www.chabad.org/library/article_cdo/aid/507002/jewish/What-Does-Judaism-Say-About-Gun-Control.htm.

7. Mira Morgenstern, *Reframing Politics in the Hebrew Bible* (Indianapolis: Hackett, 2017), 200.

JUSTIFIED?

The Moral Burden of Launching a Preemptive War

RABBI EDWIN GOLDBERG, DHL

Jewish tradition, as represented in the Bible and Rabbinic literature, treats the subject of war and peace from a theological perspective. On the one hand, we are expected to follow God's commandments concerning making war with certain peoples and in defense of our property and lives. We are also permitted, within explicit boundaries, to launch a war to amass property and possessions. In the moral environment of today, neither required wars against certain peoples or optional wars (both categories were barred centuries ago by the Rabbis) are relevant or acceptable. A war of self-defense, on the other hand, is not only permitted; it is a *milchemet mitzvah*, a commanded war. Preservation of life in Jewish tradition cannot be overestimated. There is, however, one other type of war suggested by classic Jewish texts: *a preemptive war*. The Six-Day War of 1967 appears to have been an example of such a fight, irrespective of the moral complications that followed its conclusion.[1]

In our time, is it morally permissible to launch a war of preemption? To discern this, we will examine the difficulty of determining whether the war *is* preemptive and how such a war is classified by the Rabbinic texts—that is, is it a discretionary war or a war of self-defense?

While ancient and medieval Jewish texts may not have anticipated today's scenarios, nor is the U.S. government or the Israeli government bound to Rabbinic reasoning, the moral perspective and spiritual authority of the Sages offer some important directions for our uncertain future. For those of us who remember Vietnam and the Lebanon War and have lived through the recent wars in the Middle East—not to mention the fragile nuclear deal with Iran, and most recently, the growing tension with North Korea—we know that the difference between launching a justified war and engaging in a war of opportunity means more than soldiers dying needlessly and governmental resources wasted. The picture is even worse. It all goes back to the dire prediction usually attributed to Harry S. Truman, our first "nuclear president": "I do not know with what weapons World War III will be fought, but World War IV will be fought with sticks and stones."

In short, for a war to be justified, it must be a war of justice. In an age of thermonuclear bombs, chemical weapons, drones, ICBMs, and bunker busting missiles, the price is so high that any other kind of war is an abomination. What constitutes just reasons to go to war? In this essay, we will explore classic Jewish sources that, sadly enough, could not be timelier.[2]

Background: Jewish Views of War and Peace

The classic Jewish texts cite three types of wars. We briefly will explore each kind.

Milchemet Chovah: Required Wars

A "required war" refers to a war fought against enemies specifically designated by God in the Bible. This list is as short as it is nonnegotiable. Included are the seven Canaanite nations who were dwelling in the Land of Israel when Joshua led the Israelites into the Promised Land. The other nation on the list is the Amalekites, who attacked the Israelites from behind shortly after they left Egypt. The two most relevant texts are as follows:

> When the Eternal your God brings you to the land that you are about to enter and possess, and [God] dislodges many nations before you—the Hittites, Girgashites, Amorites, Canaanites, Perizzites, Hivites, and Jebusites . . . and the Eternal your God delivers them to you and you defeat them, you must doom them to destruction: grant them no terms and give them no quarter. (Deuteronomy 7:1–2)

> Remember what Amalek did to you on your journey, after you left Egypt—how, undeterred by fear of God, he surprised you on the march, when you were famished and weary, and cut down all the stragglers in your rear. Therefore, when the Eternal your God grants you safety from all your enemies around you, in the land that the Eternal your God is giving you as a hereditary portion, you shall blot out the memory of Amalek from under heaven. Do not forget! (Deuteronomy 25:17–19)

Required war implies there is no choice but to fight. As a religious tradition, the lack of choice in Israelite history was due both to pragmatic and religious concerns. Pragmatically, the Israelites had to fight to win land for themselves after entering the Promised Land. Religiously, they were following the command of God. Later Jewish tradition, while not in any way casting doubt on the legitimacy of the Jewish right to the Promised Land, became far less comfortable with the violence described in the Bible. In fact, Rabbinic tradition declares that there can no longer be required wars since the enemies no longer exist.[3]

Milchemet R'shut: Optional Wars

A second type of war suggested by the Bible is not obligatory, but rather a war of choice, and therefore must be authorized by a legislative/judicial body. The Babylonian Talmud includes the following statement regarding the difference between required and optional wars:

> Mishnah: He [the king] may lead forth [the army] to a voluntary war on the decision of a court of seventy-one. He may force a way through private property and none may oppose him. There is no limitation to the king's way. The plunder taken by the people [in war] must be given to him. And he receives the first choice [when it is divided]. (*Mishnah Sanhedrin* 2:4)

The Rabbinic view toward optional wars was summarized by Moses Maimonides in his classic code of Jewish law, the *Mishneh Torah*:

> The only time a king can initiate a war is when it is an obligatory war. What war is considered obligatory? The war against the seven Canaanite nations (when the Land of Israel was first captured in the time of Joshua), the war against Amalek, and a war to help Israel from the hand of a siege that came upon them. Afterward he can wage an authorized war, which is a war that can be fought with any nation to enlarge the borders of Israel and to enhance its greatness and reputation. He does not have to receive permission from the court to wage an obligatory war, but he can wage it by himself at any time and he can compel the nation to go out [to war]. He cannot, however, force the nation to wage an authorized war unless he has the approval of the court of seventy-one judges.[4]

Optional wars in Jewish tradition are understood as containing complications not found in the other biblical types of war. They are at times necessary because it is natural for kings—even Israelite kings—to wish for more land, but they are considered complicated because such violence is not absolutely required for the safety and security of the people. To fight an optional war, the king must present his argument for a war before the Sanhedrin, the court of seventy-one judges, which also had a legislative function. This check is important because the violence is going to be more difficult to morally support.

According to some authorities,[5] the protocol for conducting an optional war included seeking permission from not only the Sanhedrin but also the *Kohein Gadol* (the High Priest) and the *Urim* and *Thummim*, the oracular devices used to ascertain the will of God. Since none of these institutions existed after the destruction of the Second Temple in 70 CE, the question of waging an optional war became moot.

Milchemet Mitzvah: **Defensive Wars**

As Jewish tradition developed, required wars became obsolete because the seven Canaanite nations and the Amalekites no longer existed. Optional wars also became impossible to wage, since conditions necessary to authorize such wars were no longer extant. A third type of war was still necessary to consider: defensive wars. The term for such a war is not "obligatory" (*chovah*) since this implied God commanded the war against a specific people. Rather, the term is "commanded" (*mitzvah*) because self-defense is considered a commandment of God.

It is logical to understand that, of all types of war, this category is the least controversial. Jewish tradition never adopted the view that peace is preferable at all costs. Violence is a last resort, but at times the only way to fight aggressive violence is with violence. *Mishnah Sotah* 8:7 quotes Rabbi Y'hudah as saying that, in contrast to categories of people exempt from serving in an optional war, "In a defensive war (i.e., commanded) all go out, even a bridegroom from his chamber and a bride from her canopy." When the homestead is under attack, everyone fights.

Indeed, the right to self-defense is well established within Jewish law as reflected by the law of *rodeif* (the pursuer). The Sages contended that the verse "You shall not stand idly by the blood of your neighbor" (Leviticus 19:16) not only demands saving a friend from drowning or other dangerous situations but further commands that one stop an assailant from committing murder (BT *Sanhedrin* 73a). This right was extended to both onlookers and threatened victims. The status of *rodeif* was even applied to a fetus whose mother is endangered by the pregnancy, thereby allowing for abortion, even as the fetus certainly had no intentional malicious intent.[6]

Launching a Preemptive War

Since two of the three categories of war discussed above are no longer applicable—obligatory wars, that is, those mandated in the Bible against specific enemies no longer in existence; and optional wars, meaning aggressive wars of Jewish kings—the only relevant option left are wars of self-defense, waged when the enemy has invaded your land.

A fourth category of war, however, and its moral justification are the most difficult to assess: the preemptive war. Neither the Bible nor the Mishnah mentions preemptive strikes as a possibility. It is brought up for the first time in the Babylonian Talmud, centuries later. The issue concerns an enemy that has yet to attack but clearly is preparing to do so. Is this considered a war that must be fought, may be fought, or should not be fought?

A complicating problem with such questions is the interpretation of the enemy's preparations. Today we would ask, "Are they building a bomb factory that may be ready in ten years, or are their troops already amassed on the borders? Is a weapon of mass destruction days away from being unleashed? Or what if it is years away from being used, but you conclude your defensive needs prevent it from being developed? Are we preventing a possible strike or facing a clear and present danger?" A war deterring or eliminating a long-term threat in modern "just war" discussion is often referred to as a "preventive war" as opposed to eliminating an imminent threat ("preemptive war"). Preventive wars are not legal under current international law.

Here, then, is the classic Rabbinic text on this thorny question:

> Rava said: Everyone agrees that the wars Joshua fought to conquer [the Land of Israel] were obligatory [*chovah*]. Everyone agrees the expansionist wars of King David had to be authorized [*r'shut*]. They argue about a strike against gentiles in order to weaken them from a future attack. One party considers it commanded [mitzvah] [in self-defense] and one requires it be authorized [*r'shut*]. (BT *Sotah* 44b)

When deciding to engage in a preemptive attack, the Talmud does not create a new category per se. Instead there is a debate about whether the war fits into one of two preexisting categories. Is it a war of self-defense or an optional war, requiring the usual confirmation process involving the High Priest, Sanhedrin, and *Urim* and *Thummim*? Since such a confirmation process was impossible by the time of the Talmud, labeling a war as optional is basically calling it invalid. Therefore, only wars of self-defense (i.e., commanded) can be waged.

Isaac ben Moses of Vienna (1180–1250), in his commentary, *Or Zarua*, argues that if there has been no enemy attack, a preemptive war can be waged only if the enemy has announced its intention to attack. In other words, if a hostile government declares its intention, this is like an actual attack, and defensive measures can be taken. This description basing justification on intent rather than on military preparations conveying imminent attack would seem to include the preventive war situation.

Offensive war cannot be subsumed under the inalienable right of self-defense, but the moral status of preemptive attacks is not as clear. Is the moral category of self-defense limited to an already launched attack? Or can it cover a future attack?

If preemption is self-defense, then the classic text appears in the Babylonian Talmud (*B'rachot* 58a, among other places): "The Torah [thereby] says: If someone comes to kill you, get up early in the morning [or preempt] to kill him first."[7] Clearly, self-preservation is a Jewish value. And yet, the line between self-defense and preemption is often fuzzy. On the one hand, we want to protect our own lives and health as well as the lives of our families and community. On the other hand, we do not engage in war lightly. Indeed, we are to seek peace and pursue it.

As Prof. Reuven Kimelman has discussed:

> The major clash among the commentators occurs between the 11-century Franco-German scholar Rashi and the 13th-century Franco-Provencal scholar Meiri. According to Rashi, the majority position in the Talmud deems preemptive action to be *discretionary* while the minority opinion expounded by Rabbi Judah considers it to be *mandatory*.
>
> According to Meiri, a preemptive strike (which he describes as a military move against an enemy who, it is feared, might attack or who is already known to be preparing for war) is judged to be *mandatory* by the majority of rabbis, but only deemed discretionary by

Rabbi Judah. According to this reading, Rabbi Judah defines mandatory wars only as those responding to an already launched attack.[8]

With this distinction between mandatory and discretionary wars in mind, we should be able to investigate the Jewish concerns with the problematics of war by focusing on preemptive strikes and declarations of war. Must any legitimate attack be a counterattack? The majority opinion is yes. The minority position of Rabbi Y'hudah, according to Rashi, and the majority position, according to Meiri, however, hold that a preemptive strike against an enemy amassing for attack is close enough to a defensive counterattack to be categorized as mandatory. This position holds that to wait for an actual attack might so jeopardize national security as to make resistance impossible.

This understanding of anticipatory defense allows for a counterattack before the initial blow falls. Under the terms of modern warfare, for example, if an enemy were to launch a missile attack, the target country could legitimately retaliate even if the enemy's missiles were still inside their borders. The doctrine of anticipatory defense allows for a preemptive strike even if the missiles are still on their launching pads if the order has been issued for their launching.

The various distinctions between the different types of war can be seen in real-life challenges that Israel has faced in various decisions of when it needed to use military actions. The War for Independence when Israel, surrounded by nations who had announced their intention to destroy Israel, and then attacked, is a classic example of a war of self-defense.

To use the Six-Day War as an example, we can argue that the decision to launch the preemptive strike was justified due to the vocal belligerence of the enemy, not to mention some threatening military and political acts that were executed before hostilities commenced (such as the closing of the Straits of Tiran). Michael Oren's *Six Days of War* well documents the stresses of the time. By these standards, the Six-Day war was clearly more than prevention from a later threat. It was clearly preemptive.

Far be it for us to Monday-morning quarterback the Israeli leaders of fifty years ago. Such a notion is like judging President Truman's decision to use atomic bombs against Japan. This side of history is a high perch from which to judge decisions made with uncertainty long ago.

The perception of risk was much higher than, say, the 1982 Lebanon War, which was clearly also a war of choice. The war in 1967, unlike 1982, was waged from a perception of existential threat as opposed to an opportunity to create a more favorable political reality. I was studying at Hebrew University in June 1982, right before the war in Lebanon commenced, and I asked my political science professor, Meron Medzini, why Israel was planning to invade Lebanon. "Because we can," he told me. This answer was very different from the rationale for fighting in 1948, and some would argue in 1967: "*Ein b'reirah*—We have no choice."

Finally, there was Israel's destruction in 1981 of the Iraqi reactor in Osiraq. Israel struck before the reactor went on line and clearly years before it might have been used to develop a military capability. This is a classic "preventive war" scenario. Yet, we need to ask whether new technologies require a reassessment of just war standards and how to apply them. If Israel had allowed an avowed enemy, still technically in a state of war against Israel (Iraq was one of the countries that never accepted the 1949 armistice agreement), to put the reactor on line, if Israel had waited and attacked years later, the damage to innocent civilian life and damage to the surrounding environment—both of which are important criteria in Jewish standards of how a war must be fought—would have been far, far greater. And the possibility of damage to a nuclear attack on Israel would have been astronomically more devastating. These are considerations that the rabbis of the past could not have fully anticipated. The *Or Zarua* standard discussed above suggests, however, that the Osiraq reactor could have passed muster under the war of defense standard for a preemptive or even preventive war.

Nevertheless, Israel continues to wrestle with preemptive war as a clear and present possibility (consider its approach to potential threats from Iran, or its policy of targeted assassination of terrorists who might engage in actions against Israel), as does the United States of America.

There are two important points to consider: (1) Talmudic and medieval debate on these matters do not reflect realpolitik in waging war, since there was no sovereign Jewish state during the composition of those texts. It is all theoretical and thus tends toward the morally idealistic. (2) Since we do not yet live in an age envisioned by Philip K. Dick's *Minority Report*, when we can know in advance the consequences of our actions, we cannot reasonably expect a decision to wage a preemptive war to be predicated on secure knowledge of the consequences, intended or otherwise. All we can do, morally, is determine whether the actions are justified from the point of view of self-defense. If the action is going to prevent a future, but not imminent threat, then the moral voice of our tradition counsels us to wait. If there is a clear and present danger, then the self-defense argument holds sway.

Conclusion

Iran. Syria. North Korea. Hamas. Hezbollah. ISIS. Who will be the next enemy that will challenge those who want peace but also need to protect their people, to make a terrible choice? And what will be the criterion for striking if the other side has yet to launch their attack? How will the action be justified? As a preventive measure? As self-defense? As a preemptive measure? And how can any act of war be initiated when we cannot possibly know the consequences of such an act? The biblical and Rabbinic texts are clear on the reasons for war, but our age is not theirs and our burden is heavier, our options cloudier. We want our wars justified, and we also want our people safe. Ironically, borders are not merely lines on maps these days. Missiles and airplanes are much quicker than standing armies. Hence, interpretations of enemy moves are fraught with misconceptions and prejudices. Do we believe the rhetoric? Or do we hope for the best?

In this maze of possible choices, traditional Jewish wisdom offers helpful guideposts. A war of self-defense is justifiable. A war of prevention from some future nightmare has a far higher bar to justify. A war of preemption falls somewhere in between.

As the fiftieth anniversary of the Six-Day War has been observed now with ceremony and intellectual debate, we are offered a spectrum of accusations and justifications for the war. Michael Oren's *Six Days of War* argues that Israel had no choice but to preemptively attack Egypt and Syria.[9] More recently Guy Laron has suggested that the war was not at all justified, rather, the *casus belli* (the "just cause for war") created by Israeli junior officers to assert their authority over the older generation.[10]

As we face a frightening future, at home and abroad, one in which borders are porous and threats come from within as well as from far away, the collective wisdom of Jewish tradition about preemptive war holds us accountable to great and pressing questions:

> *Are we doing all we can to defend ourselves?*
> *Are we remembering that every human being is created in the image of God?*
> *Do we have strong checks and balances that prevent our leaders from waging unjustified attacks?*
> *Have we done all we can to seek peace and pursue it?*

How we address these questions will lead to real-life consequences, whether we are dealing with Iran, North Korea, ISIS, or so many other hot spots. For a people who have not waged war for most of the last two millennia (but were continually victims of violence), we have a great deal to say on the subject.

Let our voices be heard.

NOTES

1. A recent listing of these moral complications is found in Micah Goodman, *Catch 67: The Left, the Right, and the Legacy of the Six Day War* [in Hebrew] (Kinneret: Dvir, 2017). An English version, by Yale University Press and translatd by Elyon Levy, is due out in September 2018.

2. Many of the classic sources in this essay can be found in my book *Swords and Plowshares: Jewish Views of War and Peace* (New York: URJ Press, 2006).

3. Cf. Shalom Carmy, "The Origin of Nations and the Shadow of Violence: Theological Perspectives on Canaan and Amalek," in *Tradition* 39, no. 4 (2006): 65–66. Carmy admits that some sources in recent decades, such as Yosef Dov Soloveitchik, have argued that the designation Amalekite can apply to new enemies such as Hitler.

4. Maimonides, *Mishneh Torah, Hilchot M'lachim* 5:1–2.

5. Cf. David S. Shapiro, "The Jewish Attitude towards War and Peace," in *Israel of Tomorrow*, ed. Leo Jung (New York: Herald Square Press, 1946), 237.

6. Cf. Mishnah *Oholot* 7:6: "If a woman is in hard travail, one cuts up the offspring in her womb and brings it forth member by member, because her life comes before the life of her fetus. But if the greater part has proceeded forth, one may not set aside one person for the sake of saving another."

7. This text is the source of the title for the recent book on extra-legal killings by the Israeli secret services, Ronen Bergman, *Rise and Kill First: The Secret History of Israel's Targeted Assassinations* (New York: Random House, 2018).

8. Reuven Kimelman, "Judaism and the Ethics of War," *Proceedings of the 1987 Rabbinical Assembly Convention*, 9.

9. Michael Oren, *Six Days of War: June 1967 and the Making of the Middle East* (New York: Random House, 2002).

10. Guy Laron, *The Six-Day War: The Breaking of the Middle East* (New Haven, CT: Yale University Press, 2017).

THE JEWISH STAKE IN THE STRUGGLE FOR INTERNATIONAL RELIGIOUS FREEDOM

RABBI DAVID SAPERSTEIN

In 2018, the Chinese government engaged in a massive crackdown on Uighur Muslims, a more than thousand-year-old community in Xinjiang province, with large-scale arrests, internment camps, and harassment of Muslim religious life—while it also continued its efforts to culturally eviscerate Tibetan Buddhist life. In 2017–18, the government of Myanmar ethnically cleansed hundreds of thousands of Rohingya Muslims. Russia has cracked down this past year on many religious groups it had heretofore tolerated, banning Jehovah's Witnesses and prosecuting Scientologists and other "nontraditional groups" for extremism. In Scandinavia, we are seeing efforts to curtail kosher slaughtering, and Iceland and Denmark face serious challenges regarding Jewish and Muslim male circumcision.[1] Hate crimes against Jews and Muslims have escalated in many Western countries (including the United States). There are escalating tensions between Muslims and Christians in the Middle Belt of Nigeria and in the Central Africa Republic. In Pakistan, the country's strict blasphemy laws and increased extremist activity continue to threaten already marginalized minority communities, including Ahmadis, Christians, Hindus, Sikhs, and Shia Muslims; from 1987 to 2014, over thirteen hundred

247

people were accused of blasphemy, and over forty remain on death row.[2] The annual Pew study on global religious freedom trends finds that 83 percent of the world's population lives in countries with serious restrictions on religious freedom—whether caused by government policies or the hostile acts of individuals, organizations, or societal groups.[3]

For over two years, I was honored to serve as the United States Ambassador-at-Large for International Religious Freedom,[4] America's chief diplomat on religious freedom issues. It required leaving the Religious Action Center of Reform Judaism (RAC)—the passion of my heart for forty years. At the RAC, I had been blessed to represent the extraordinary social justice mission of the Reform Movement and its rabbis in making real the prophetic values, ideals, and dreams of the Jewish people in this country—a country that has given the Jewish people more rights, more freedoms, and more opportunities than we have ever known. I left the RAC in the hands of my inspiring successor, Rabbi Jonah Dov Pesner, and focused on the urgent and daunting new task at hand, at a time when religious freedom was under enormous pressure across the globe.

Religious freedom was essential to America from its start. Many early colonists fled religious persecution. Religious freedom was the first freedom enshrined in our Bill of Rights, and on that foundation, over the past two centuries, we have built a system that protects the rights of religious believers and nonbelievers to worship, practice, share, change, and express their beliefs freely. The Constitution's Article VI ban on a religious test for office, together with the First Amendment's ban on establishment of religion and its guarantee of free exercise of religion, promulgated a radically new vision of the implications of religious freedom as a national value, creating, for the first time in human history, a state in which a person's rights as a citizen would not depend on religious identity, religious practices, or religious beliefs. As Uriah Levy, the head of the Jewish family that, out of respect for Thomas Jefferson, bought and preserved Monticello for ninety years, said in 1832 of Jefferson's contribution to this concept, "He did much to mold our Republic in a form in which a man's religion does not make him ineligible for political or governmental life."

As with so many other promised rights, they were not realized immediately. But, by the mid-twentieth century, the Supreme Court, robustly interpreting the free exercise and establishment clauses, helped make the promise a reality. This concept had significant impact on the Universal Declaration on Human Rights and on the International Covenant on Civil and Political Rights (ICCPR), which made religious freedom an international norm.

So too religious freedom is a vital component of our foreign policy today. Religious discrimination and marginalization across the globe make every foreign policy job we do harder: from fighting terror to keeping the peace, to building economic opportunity and upholding democratic values. We cannot succeed in counter-terrorism, conflict resolution, democracy stabilization efforts, economic development, and human rights efforts if societies are torn apart by sectarian strife. And if segments of society are subject to the kind of persecution and discrimination that isolates entire groups, drives religious life underground, and generates frustration, despair, and hopelessness, this will create fertile ground for extremist answers to their plight.

I am convinced that we as Americans, but especially as American Jews, are the heirs of a unique vision, and of a special responsibility, to do whatever we can to ensure that the value of religious freedom is established and respected globally.

I have always been inspired in my work not only by the family stories of my great-grandparents, all of whom came as refugees to these shores seeking safety and the opportunity to live freely as Jews, but by the schema of Jewish values possessing proto-democratic and proto–human rights resonance, and especially with those values directly connected to the concepts of religious pluralism and religious freedom.[5] Our tradition long recognized that there could be validity in different religions: "The righteous of all nations have a share in the world-to-come" (*Tosefta, Sanhedrin* 13:2); "Justice and righteousness [God] does not withhold; God does not withhold from a non-Jew who does mitzvot" (Jerusalem Talmud, *Pei-ah* 2b). Maimonides explains that "those who accept upon themselves the fulfillment of these seven mitzvot and are careful in their observance are considered one of 'the righteous of the nations' and will merit a share in the world-to-come" (*Mishneh Torah, Hilchot M'lachim* 8:11). Moses Mendelssohn observed:

> We believe that the other nations of the earth are directed by God to observe (only) the law of nature and the religion of the Patriarchs. Those who conduct their lives in accordance with this religion of nature and of reason, are known as "righteous gentiles" and are "children of everlasting salvation."[6]

Even more ancient than the Rabbinic voices are the biblical notions that seem to resonate with our modern ideas of international law. Consider, in this context, what is arguably the prophets' most eloquent call for international peace. From Micah 4:1–3, expanding upon the words of Isaiah:

> In the end of days, it shall come to pass,
> That the mountain of the Eternal's house shall be established on
>   the top of the mountains,
> And it shall be exalted above the hills.
> Peoples shall flow unto it,
> And many nations shall come and say,
> "Come, let us go up to the mountain of the Eternal,
> To the house of the God of Jacob;
> So that God may teach us of God's ways,
> And we will walk in God's paths;
> For the law shall go forth from Zion,
> And the word of the Eternal from Jerusalem."
> And God shall judge among many peoples,
> And rebuke strong nations afar off.

Dr. Robert Gordis, the esteemed Conservative Movement scholar of the mid-twentieth century, illuminates a number of relevant themes. First, the phrase *acharit hayamim*, the "end of days," is not, in the Hebrew Bible, understood the way it is understood in other religious traditions. Repeatedly, the Bible uses the term to refer to goals that are within the foreseeable future, such as the conquest of Canaan described in Genesis or the anticipated early restoration of the Kingdom of Ephraim in Hosea.[7]

Second, the passage presumes the existence of "nation-states," of separate entities working cooperatively and justly together.

Third, this vision calls for the creation of a law applicable to all nations: "For out of Zion shall go forth the Law. . . . And God shall judge among many peoples and rebuke strong nations afar off" (Isaiah 2:3–4). In other words, before peace can come, this model suggests there must be a law accepted by all nations, with mechanisms to enforce that law and a process to judge the disputes that will inevitably arise. The United Nations, international human rights norms, and international adjudication of disputes—all these are modern representations of this strand of our religious values.

In addition to the values transmitted by our biblical and Rabbinic traditions, we must remember the lessons of Jewish history. Like most Jews, I know all too well that over the centuries, the Jewish people have been the quintessential victim of religious persecution, ethnic cleansing, and demonization.

We have learned, firsthand, the costs to the universal rights, security, and well-being of religious communities when good people remain silent in the face of such persecution. This is just one key reason why we cannot remain silent today, when we see historic Christian, Yezidi, and other communities in Iraq and Syria being devastated; when we see Bahais in Iran; Tibetan Buddhists and Uighur Muslims in China; Shia Muslims in Saudi Arabia, Pakistan, and Bahrain; Rohingya Muslims in Burma—all victims of governmental or societal discrimination, harassment, persecution, or physical attacks. Even in Western Europe, we are witnessing a steady increase in anti-Muslim acts and rhetoric, antisemitic discourse, and acts of desecrations and violence against Jewish individuals, synagogues, schools, and communal institutions. Sadly, this list is far from exhaustive, but it shows the broad range of very serious threats to religious freedom and religious communities in nearly every corner of the globe.

We have also learned that if any minority group is subject to religious discrimination or persecution, then every minority group (and often segments of the majority community as well) is endangered.

We who have condemned the conscience of the world for remaining silent in the face of the Holocaust and of so much persecution that afflicted the Jewish people, can we now stand by idly when we see persecution aimed at others?

Can we remain silent when Christians, Yezidis, Bahais, Tibetan Buddhists, and Muslims in Burma and China face ethnic cleansing or cultural or physical genocide? Candidly, the Jewish community is too often on the sidelines of such battles, often not part of coalitions that stood with us during the Soviet Jewry struggles. The recent exception—a badge of honor for the Jewish community—was the role the community played in mobilizing U.S. and global attention to the urgent need to staunch genocide in Darfur. We need to assume such leadership on behalf of those suffering religious discrimination and persecution, more assertively and more consistently than we have until now.

So where do we have to look in order to live up to the values and lessons we inherited?

Fortunately, in many countries, religious freedom flourishes; people are free to choose their faith, change their faith, speak about their faith to others, teach their faith to their children, dissent from religion, build places of worship, worship alone or in fellowship with others. In such societies, denominations and faith groups organize as their leaders and members see fit. In these countries, religious communities contribute significantly to the social welfare of their fellow citizens; they serve as a moral compass to their nations, and interfaith cooperation flourishes. Indeed, it is worth noting that we are witnessing today interfaith cooperation at a level unprecedented in all of human history. When religious groups work together for common goals, they manifest a power and influence none of them could exert alone. In working together, they powerfully model the very pluralism, tolerance, and freedom that they are seeking to create in their society. Those are the societies in which minority communities (including Jewish communities) flourish.

Yet in too many other countries, far too many people face daunting, alarming, growing, too often deadly, challenges on account of their beliefs.

Non-state actors and terrorist groups have merged as among the most brutal enemies of religious freedom in recent years. Even in countries where religious minorities have contributed to their national societies in relative comity for decades, centuries, or millennia, we continue to witness violent upheavals—some of historic proportions, in which entire communities are in danger of being driven out of their homelands based on their religious and ethnic identity. ISIL has targeted Iraqi and Syrian religious minorities, other Muslims, people perceived to be LGBTQ, journalists, and professional women. The captured men are often beheaded; captured women are tortured, raped, enslaved, or forced to convert and marry. The genocidal effort against the Yezidis, Christians, and Shia Muslims was mitigated only by U.S. and international intervention. Boko Haram in northern Nigeria and the Lakes region, Al Shabbab in Somalia and northern Kenya, militant Buddhists in Myanmar, Christian militias in Central Africa Republic—all represent devastating forces who, in the name of religion, target religious populations that differ from their particular views.

Blasphemy and apostasy laws pose particularly acute threats to religious pluralism and freedom. Just to orient ourselves, when we talk about "blasphemy laws," we're talking about legislation punishing irreverence or disrespect toward religious, holy personages, religious artifacts, customs, or beliefs. "Apostasy laws" are those that criminalize the abandonment or renunciation of a religious belief. Roughly a quarter of the world's countries have blasphemy laws, and more than one in ten have laws or policies penalizing apostasy. These laws have been used by governments in too many cases to limit the exercise of freedoms of religion and expression and to target minority religions. These "crimes" are sometimes punishable by death (as is the case in twelve countries throughout the world) or life imprisonment.

Understand what blasphemy is. It is a crime that often punishes people for the simple expression of the core values or beliefs of their faith, and it punishes people for engaging in sincere criticism of or dissent from the religious views held by those with power. Since such restrictions almost always reflect the views of the majority, the effect is to repress and intimidate minority religions.

These laws have a cascading effect that goes far beyond infringing on an individual's exercise of the freedoms of religion or expression. Laws contribute to shaping societal norms. In numerous instances, mere accusations of blasphemy have sparked vigilante mob violence and killings, with few steps taken afterward to hold those responsible to account, as the world saw when two years ago a Jordanian writer was murdered outside the court where he was standing trial on charges of blasphemy and inciting sectarian strife following his posting on social media a satirical cartoon that many believed to be insulting to Islam, or the Pakistani Christian couple burned alive in a brick kiln by a mob for alleged blasphemy. When governments fail to deter violence bred by blasphemy laws or fail to take steps to hold perpetrators of violence accountable—whether as a product of institutional weaknesses, negligence, or willful inaction—it breeds an atmosphere of impunity and undermines the rule of law, which destabilizes communities and leaves members of minority groups ever more vulnerable. And we must never forget brave individuals like my friend the Pakistani minister of minority affairs, Shahbaz Bhatti, whom I had hosted at the Religious Action Center, and the governor of Punjab Province, Salman Taseer, political leaders who were assassinated for their commitment to religious freedom and their outspoken criticism of blasphemy laws.

Often when I would meet with officials of governments that had blasphemy laws, to encourage them to seek non-criminalized ways to address religious speech that others might find offensive, I heard, "Why do you single us out when *six* of your own states continue to hold blasphemy laws on the books?" While the U.S. Supreme Court has held blasphemy laws unenforceable, Massachusetts, Michigan, Oklahoma, South Carolina, Wyoming, and Pennsylvania still have blasphemy laws on the books and thereby give cover for those who actually enforce their own laws. It is time for every one of those states to rescind these embarrassing laws and thereby strengthen our efforts to protect the victims of such laws across the globe.

One of the most common threats to religious pluralism and freedom flows from repressive laws and regulations that too many governments impose on religious life. Frightened of any way that their citizens organize their lives around ideas and ideologies they cannot control, they respond by trying to impose control on the religious leaders and institutions that represent and inculcate those ideas. Fears of terrorism exacerbate this tendency. Such nations try to control the religious schools, the houses of worship, the sermons, the public presence of their religious communities. And where this also involves the entanglement of a majority religion with the government, it is the minority communities (particularly when they are an ethnic as well as a religious minority) that often suffer the most under special repressive and discriminatory restrictions.

These, then, are some of the alarming trends that should compel us to stand up and speak out on behalf of the religiously oppressed worldwide.

One painfully vivid example of this, which has galvanized the moral conscience of the world, has been the humanitarian and human rights crisis in Rakhine State, rooted in historic discrimination against members of Rohingya Muslims spurred by xenophobic, militant Buddhist groups—a problem about which the United States has long voiced grave concerns. When Aung San Suu Kyi's election resulted in the easing of U.S. sanctions, the religious freedom sanctions remained in place. But things have dramatically worsened. According to various UN bodies, in 2017–18, many thousands were killed by government forces or militias; between 700,000 and 900,000 Rohingya have been forced to flee their Rakhine State homes; scores of thousands of Rohingya and other Muslims continue to be confined in Rakhine State in camps; and thousands of others have been trapped by human traffickers in the northern Kachin State in Burma, forced to work in wretched conditions in the mineral mines there. I visited the massive refugee camps over the border in Bangladesh in December 2016 and then again in the winter of 2018, when the most recent flood of Rohingya refugees threatened to overwhelm the camps just across the border in Bangladesh. The stories I heard of the destruction of makeshift mosques and whole villages, the burning of holy books, the widespread reports of rape and murders by both government forces and militias, parents slaughtered in front of their children, and children torn from their mothers' arms and thrown into fires were profoundly disturbing. The international community has urged the Myanmar government, in the strongest terms, to allow humanitarian groups and media into Rakhine province, take forceful steps to provide accountability for the substantiated abuses of human rights, and begin to resolve the underlying issues in that region that threaten continuing violence, abuses, and destabilization. Only by addressing the underlying problems can there be any realistic prospect of the safe return of those driven out. Until then, the international community must ensure that the refugees in Bangladesh are provided for.

We should feel great pride that the U.S. government has played a lead role in the fight for international religious freedom.

Consider:

- Our Annual Report on International Religious Freedom covering 199 countries is used by local media and civil society organizations as an advocacy tool and by other governments as a blueprint for their own human rights efforts.
- This is a cause enjoying bipartisan support on Capitol Hill, and as a result, today the United States expends over $20 million a year to support civil society's efforts to enhance religious freedom, build interfaith coalitions, and train human rights lawyers and advocates.
- The United States has played a lead role organizing an international contact group now approaching forty in number—all committed to working more closely on behalf of our religious freedom efforts.
- In July 2018, the Trump Administration, whose problematic policies in many areas run counter to the positions of mainstream Jewish

organizations, on this issue has been quite strong. In the summer of 2018, Secretary of State Mike Pompeo and my successor, Ambassador Sam Brownback, hosted the first ever foreign-minister-level gathering of eighty nations seeking ways to strengthen our efforts on behalf of religious freedom. Every speaker emphasized the universal commitment required of the international community gathered there to secure religious freedom for all.

Allow me to conclude with a personal story. In the summer of 1939, my father traveled throughout Poland and Palestine. He was one of the last to see the glory of European Jewry in full bloom before the nightmare of Nazism enveloped and destroyed it. He visited Danzig, now Gdansk, just days after the Nazis had been elected in the May elections. He went with enthusiasm to see the magnificent historic main synagogue of this vibrant Jewish community. To his utter dismay; it lay in ruins, only the portal over what had been the beautiful entrance front doors was still intact. On the front lawn, there was a sign that had been erected during the election campaign by the Nazis, which said, *Komm lieber Mai und mache von Juden uns jetzt frei*, "Come dear month of May and free us from the Jews." With a chilling sense of the impending disaster embodied by this scene, his glance gazed upward and then he saw the words of the ancient vision of Malachi still inscribed over the remaining doorway: *Halo Av echad l'chulanu; halo eil echad b'raanu*, "Have we all not one Father? Has not one God created us?" (Malachi 2:10). Two visions: one of hatred and tyranny, the other of brotherhood and sisterhood, of unity and peace; one of oppression, the other of freedom; one of darkness and despair, the other of light and hope. This is the choice we face today with a sense of great urgency.

During my tenure, I traveled to thirty-five countries and eighty-two cities. Across the world, America is seen as the gold standard of religious freedom. In every corner of the world where religious persecution or other human rights violations prevail, Jefferson's words "All men are created equal" were a cherished talisman of hope in the face of despair. I saw firsthand the power of these words to nourish, to sustain, to inspire dreams of freedom throughout the world. As Muhtar Kent, an immigrant to the United States himself, and later the head of the Coca-Cola Company, observed in a speech given at Monticello, Jefferson's home, "There is no containing these words. No mere border, no barrier of language can stop them. No dictator, no army, no secret police can silence them. Not now and not ever."

So that must be our task as Jews and as Americans. To the religiously oppressed in every land who live in fear, afraid to speak of their beliefs; who worship in underground churches, mosques, or temples; who languish in prisons, bodies broken, spirits too often disfigured, simply because they love God in their own way or question the existence of God; who feel so desperate that they flee their homes to avoid persecution or being killed because of their faith—to all of them, we must be a beacon of light and hope.

NOTES

1. Nathan Guttman, "Why Does Scandinavia Want to Ban Circumscision and Kosher Slaughter?," *Forward*, March 18, 2018, https://forward.com/news/world/395213/why-does-scandinavia-want-to-ban-circumcision-and-kosher-slaughter/.

2. See generally 2018 Report of the United States Commission on International Religious Freedom, http://www.uscirf.gov/reports-briefs/annual-report/2018-annual-report, and the 2017 State Department Report on International Religious Freedom, https://www.state.gov/j/drl/rls/irf/religiousfreedom/index.htm#wrapper.

3. Pew Research Center, "Global Uptick in Government Restrictions on Religion in 2016," June 21, 2018, http://www.pewforum.org/2018/06/21/global-uptick-in-government-restrictions-on-religion-in-2016/.

4. The term "ambassador-at-large" refers to an ambassador with global rather than country-specific responsibilities. Each such ambassador has responsibilities in a specific policy area.

5. See David Saperstein's introduction to this volume, where these universal principles are discussed in greater detail. Among these values are the fundamental dignity of every human being based on the notion that we are created in the image of the Divine; the midrashic stories about the equality of all people; the rule of law to which even the highest rulers were held accountable; the idea of judicial review; rabbinic leadership accessible to all, rich and poor alike, based on merit (at least for all males, until recent times); the idea of the right to dissent embodied in the Talmudic dictum of *Eilu v'eilu divrei Elohim chayim*, "These and these are the words of

the living God" (Babylonian Talmud, *Eiruvin* 13b), a concept that applied to debates over religious ideas as well as other topics; and protection against self-incrimination. So too the Noachide law requiring of all nations creating and maintaining courts of justice. See also Milton Konvitz, *Judaism and the American Idea* (Ithaca, NY: Cornell University Press, 1978); and Harold Schulweis, *Conscience: The Duty to Obey and the Duty to Disobey* (Woodstock, VT: Jewish Lights, 2008).

6. As cited in Norman Solomon, *Judaism: A Very Short Introduction* (Oxford: Oxford University Press, 2014).

7. Robert Gordis, *Judaism for the Modern Age* (New York: Farrar, Strauss, and Cudahy, 1955), 319–30. What is distinctive in Micah's words, as Gordis points out, is that there is no indication that he envisioned the establishment of a new world order as a result of a great cataclysm or of a special divine intervention. It will happen as an outgrowth of history. In other words, the bringing of peace and justice is our responsibility and, the Bible reminds us, ours to actually achieve.

ON GLOBAL JEWISH RESPONSIBILITY

Putting the *Olam* in *Tikkun Olam*

RUTH W. MESSINGER AND RABBI RICK JACOBS

B'reishit bara Elohim, in the beginning, God didn't create the Land of Israel or the Jewish people. No, God created a wondrous universe, teeming with beauty, complexity, and possibility. Within this incomplete world, God created human beings to partner with God in shaping a world of justice and compassion. The sphere of divine concern includes not only the triumphs and trials of our people. Its reach is global, extending to all who inhabit the planet.

And even when Abraham and Sarah are called upon to begin Jewish history by setting out on a radical new journey, to a new land, and they enter a new covenantal relationship with the Holy One, God promises them that "through you all the families of the earth shall be blessed" (Genesis 12:3). The blessing they receive will extend beyond themselves.

The fundamental question for this chapter has in many ways already been asked and answered, debated by Rabbinic sages and subjected to further discussion by contemporary writers. We ask it anew today as Jews work to find themselves in a rapidly changing twenty-first-century landscape. Are Jews responsible only to other Jews and only for their well-being, or do we have a responsibility to the other and the stranger, whether they live in our community or across the globe? Although scholars and leaders—and the members of the Jewish community more broadly—have had differing answers and differing priorities, if we take the texts at their word, if we take seriously our responsibility to the *ger*, "the stranger," and define that notion broadly, recognizing the many strangers among whom we live and who live among us, then we have our answer. As Jews, we have a foundational responsibility, a moral obligation, to act not only for ourselves, our families, and our people, but also for the global community.

In Genesis, we read that the progenitors of all humanity were created in the image of the Divine—an insight that has proved to be one of our most important sources for the evolution of human rights in modern times. In the story of the Flood, we are warned that when evil and suffering pervade the world, then all of humanity and all of creation risk devastating consequences—a message that directly addresses the global impact of the climate change crisis we face today.

Similarly, when Abraham challenges God to protect the non-Jewish innocents of Sodom and Gomorrah, we see a model of what we must do to protect the Jewish and non-Jewish innocents of our time. When Shiphrah and Puah as midwives refuse to kill babies born to Jewish women, we see that civil disobedience is a strategy that can be employed to save lives. When Joseph uses his God-given wisdom and insight to prevent famine from devastating all of Egypt and the whole region, we recognize our responsibility to use our wisdom to help the nations of the world in which we dwell—including, among many other challenges, the responsibility to act in the world, these three millennia later, to prevent famines in our own time.

And the prophets, including Isaiah, Malachi, and Micah, among others, remind us, time and again, of a promise of a day of universal peace and justice:

- "They shall beat their swords into plowshares and their spears into pruning hooks; nation shall not lift up sword against nation; neither shall they learn war anymore" (Isaiah 2:4; Micah 4:3).

- Malachi's powerful query: "Have we not all one Father? Has not one God created us?" (Malachi 2:10).
- Joel's conveyance of God's promise: "I shall pour out My spirit on all flesh" (Joel 3:1).
- Jonah's mission to bring God's word of justice to Nineveh, the symbol of Israel's bitterest enemies: "And should I not care about Nineveh, that great city, in which there are more than 120,000 persons who do not know their right hand from their left, and many beasts as well!" (Jonah 4:11).
- "In the end of days it shall come to pass . . . For the law shall go forth from Zion, and the word of the Eternal from Jerusalem. And God shall judge among many peoples, and rebuke strong nations afar off" (Isaiah 2:2–4; Micah 4:1–4).

Many of the teachings from our prophets seem to call for the creation of an international law by which God will judge the nations. In other words, before peace can come, there must be a law accepted by all nations, with mechanisms to enforce that law and a process to judge the disputes that inevitably will arise. Hence, the role that the United Nations, international human rights norms, and international adjudication of disputes can play represents one strand of our religious values. So too, the Rabbis, with their concept of universal moral values embodied in their understanding of the Noachide Laws, which we might think of as the first Geneva Convention in world history, convey a set of moral norms to which all nations should adhere.

All these provisions from the Bible through the Rabbinic period provide the foundation, the rationale, the "how-to manual" of the Rabbinic decree that we must be an *or lagoyim*, "a light unto the nations," a call that animates much of Jewish life yet today.

And it is not only from text that we derive this global perspective, but also from Jewish history. When Deborah the judge calls her people to action and Esther the queen lobbies the king on behalf of her people, we see the prototype for the indispensable role that women must be afforded and must play in the pursuit of Jewish values and interests—and also in transforming the world. In the Exodus, we have the paradigmatic story of freedom that has inspired non-Jews and Jews for centuries in their own pursuit of freedom. Our recasting of Chanukah, in our own time, as a holiday of religious freedom has captured the imagination of many across the globe seeking just that goal. And, of course, the lessons of the Holocaust animate so much moral questing in the world today, particularly in those urgent situations in which we see incipient genocidal activity that demands that people step forward no matter who is being persecuted.

All these prophecies and stories testify to the global responsibilities our tradition and our history call upon the Jewish people to own. And each one has helped to shape the destiny of nations across the globe.

Then the next sets of questions loom: Why do we have this responsibility, and how has it played out over time? How broadly must we take this charge? What kinds of actions are we compelled to take?

Leviticus 19:33–34 gives us a series of obligations regarding the *ger*, the stranger. First, we are forbidden from oppressing the stranger. Then the text stretches further, requiring that we treat the stranger as an equal within our communities. Our final obligation is to love the stranger, for we should know from our own experiences of oppression and persecution the pain the stranger has endured.

> When strangers reside with you in your land, you shall not wrong them. The strangers who reside with you shall be to you as your citizens; you shall love each one as yourself, for you were strangers in the land of Egypt: I the Eternal am your God. (Leviticus 19:33–34)

As we have a broad vision of Jewish responsibility, we must also look within, heeding periodic reminders to reach out beyond the insular walls of our own community. As we learn from the nineteenth-century Polish Chasidic master, the first Gerer Rebbe, Rabbi Yitzchak Meir Alter:

> A stork is not kosher because it only helps out its own kind, limiting its kindness to its fellow birds. Given this behavior, the stork cannot be considered kosher, because it does not recognize the

fundamental truth that goodness and kindness are meaningless if they are limited to ourselves; they must be extended to the many circles of influence in our lives. (*Maayanah Shel Torah, Parashat Sh'mini*)

This is the idea as well in Hillel's well-known dictum "If I am not for myself, who should be for me; if I am for myself alone, what am I?" (*Pirkei Avot* 1:14). But in Hebrew the two phrases are linked by a conjunction, *uch'she*, which connects the idea that we are responsible for ourselves *and* for others.

Being told that being there for others is our responsibility raises several questions we cannot definitively answer. Do we have this responsibility because we know what it means to be the stranger and because we know we would have wanted more people to help us when we were the other? Are we referring here to the biblical text and the horrific indignities our ancestors suffered in Egypt and in the wilderness? And how does this question refer to our more contemporary experience during the Shoah, recognizing both the power of those who risked death and acted to save Jewish lives, as well as how many others might have acted to save many more of our people? Rabbinic literature characterized this challenge of considering the needs of others as our obligation to care for urgent needs of non-Jews alongside those of Jews.

> Our Rabbis taught: We sustain the non-Jewish poor with the Jewish poor, visit the non-Jewish sick with the Jewish sick, and bury the non-Jewish dead with the Jewish dead, for the sake of peace. (BT *Gittin* 61a)

Or as a more modern commentator, Rabbi Jacob Emden, taught about obligations to non-Jews in eighteenth-century Germany:

> A Jew with political responsibility (*adam chashuv*) has the obligation to rescue the oppressed from the hands of the oppressor by all means available to him, whether by direct action or through political effort, regardless of whether the oppressed is Jewish. So Job praised himself by saying, "I have broken the teeth of evil," and the Torah says of Moses that "he arose and championed them,"

referring to the daughters of Jethro, even though they were the daughters of an idolatrous priest. (Responsa, *Sh'eilat Yaavetz* 2:51)

When we are instructed to care for non-Jews as well as Jews for the sake of peace, do we understand that it is incumbent upon us to reach out across lines of difference and division because that is our moral obligation or because it will allow us to live more safely in the world?

Where can this caring, this assumption of responsibility, occur in our own communities, where we live side by side with people of diverse backgrounds? In our country, where the Constitution protects individual rights, yet we know that we do not always live up to its precepts, and there are times and places when we need to be present for those whose rights are being denied? In Israel, where the struggle of different populations to live side by side raises these issues at practical, humanitarian, and geopolitical levels?

Or, most significantly for this chapter, building on what has gone before, are we to understand that we need to extend our care and our concern to the rest of the world? Do we have a responsibility, a moral obligation to respond also to victims of hunger in East Africa or of oppression in Sri Lanka? For whom and how far do we extend ourselves?

Anyone who is able to protest against the transgressions of one's household and does not is punished for the actions of the members of the household; anyone who is able to protest against the transgressions of one's townspeople and does not is punished for the transgressions of the townspeople; anyone who is able to protest against the transgressions of the entire world and does not is punished for the transgressions of the entire world. (BT *Shabbat* 54b)

Be a force for good in the world: *any* time we fail to act, for *any* persons, whatever their relationships to us, when we know that they are in need, we are to be held accountable for whatever goes wrong.

And, whether we are responding locally or globally, there is the question of what response we are asked to make.

> Rabbi Tarfon and some elders were hanging out on the roof of Nit-
> za's house in Lod when this question arose: Which is greater, study
> or action? Rabbi Tarfon answered and said, "Action is greater."
> Rabbi Akiva answered and said, "Study is greater." The others
> responded, "Study is greater because it leads to action." (BT *Kid-
> dushin* 40b)

Study is necessary but not sufficient. Action is required, and protest is
often an appropriate response. It is not enough to learn that people are
starving in East Africa or that climate change literally will drown some
island nations. Once we know the facts, we need to act. Even though
we alone cannot feed a nation or stop climate change, we need to act
because there is always *something* we can do.

There are two sources for the oft-quoted teaching that to save one
life is to save the world. In the Babylonian Talmud, *Sanhedrin* 37a, only
by saving a Jewish life do we save the world, but in the Jerusalem Talmud, *Sanhedrin* 4:1, we find the more universal expression that saving
any human being is as if one has saved the world. The power of what
we do or don't do can affect the entire world.

> Whoever destroys a soul from Israel, the Scripture considers it
> as if he destroyed an entire world. And whoever saves a life from
> Israel, the Scripture considers it as if he saved an entire world. (BT
> *Sanhedrin* 37a)

> Whoever destroys a soul, it is considered as if he destroyed an
> entire world. And whoever saves a life, it is considered as if he saved
> an entire world. (JT *Sanhedrin* 4:1 [22a])

As Rabbi Abraham Joshua Heschel observed:

> We meet as human beings who have much in common: a heart, a
> face, a voice, the presence of a soul, fears, hope, the ability to trust,
> a capacity for compassion and understanding, the kinship of being
> human. . . . A person is not just a specimen of the species called
> *Homo sapiens*. He is all of humanity in one, and whenever one man
> is hurt, we are all injured. The human is a disclosure of the divine,
> and all men are one in God's care for man. Many things on earth
> are precious, some are holy, humanity is holy of holies.[1]

No one among us can solve the world's wrongs alone. But we can make a difference, and our obligation is to do what we can, to intervene for one person, but also to speak out against what is wrong—in the hope that enough people will do this to save even more lives, to make a greater difference, but understanding that it is not acceptable to do nothing. We are reminded, in a more contemporary text, from Adlai Stevenson's memorial tribute to Eleanor Roosevelt, that "it is better to light a candle than to curse the darkness."

Rabbi Abraham Joshua Heschel, born of a particular Jewish tradition, was steeped in learning from text. It infused his life, but that was never enough for him. He persistently focused on what meaning these various ancient texts and traditions had for the world, how they were to be interpreted in the twentieth century. He observed powerfully that there was "no time for neutrality,"[2] that it was incumbent on us to tackle problems head-on. He became a key ally of Dr. Martin Luther King in exposing the racism in American society and in demonstrating against it in ways that were designed for maximum visibility.

And then, even more dramatically, Rabbi Heschel joined with Dr. King in speaking out against the Vietnam War—although each was criticized for taking that step, for diluting his moral leadership of the vital domestic civil rights issue by becoming involved with such a contentious, international one that, at that time, even divided proponents of civil rights.

In explaining his reasons for taking this step Heschel wrote:

> Morally speaking, there is no limit to the concern one must feel for the suffering of human beings, that indifference to evil is worse than evil itself, that in a free society, some are guilty, but all are responsible.[3]

These arguments, capped by Heschel's demand that we take responsibility for the world's transgressions, provide the argument for the work that Jews have done in the world in the last century. The range of international issues in which Jews and Jewish organizations have played, and continue to play, is legion. Focusing solely on the work of the organizations with which the authors of this essay are affiliated, the Reform Jewish Movement (the Union for Reform Judaism and the Religious Action Center) and American Jewish World Service (AJWS), consider these endeavors:

The Union for Reform Judaism

- The role of URJ president Rabbi Maurice Eisendrath and Jane Evans, founding director of Women of Reform Judaism, in establishing Religions for Peace, a UN-affiliated interfaith cooperative effort that has worked in ninety-two countries.
- Jane Evans's role in the crafting of the UN charter in San Francisco.
- Raphael Lemkin's drafting of the International Convention on the Prevention and Punishment of the Crime of Genocide, and the URJ's decision to provide him with office space as he launched the efforts for U.S. ratification of the convention.
- The URJ as the first major Jewish organization to oppose the war in Vietnam in 1965; subsequently, almost every major national Jewish organization opposed the war.
- Beginning in the 1950s, the active role of the URJ in shaping efforts at nonproliferation of nuclear weapons, as well as a leadership role in the religious community around the nuclear freeze campaign.
- The URJ's vigorous effort to establish the National Religious Partnership on the Environment.
- A lead role in advocating for international intervention in Bosnia and Kosovo, as well as shaping the Sudan Peace Act.

The American Jewish World Service

- AJWS emerged over thirty years ago when members of the Jewish community recognized that its rhetoric on global responsibility fell short of the reality.

- AJWS was created explicitly to advance human rights and end poverty for marginalized people in the developing world, using a Jewish lens for its work.
- Since its founding, AJWS has worked in some fifty countries and made grants of $320 million to support grassroots organizations committed to land and water rights, sexual health and rights, ending early and forced child marriage, and civil and political rights.
- Among its particular successes AJWS has supported peacemakers in Liberia, aided LGBT rights battles throughout the developing world, done thoughtful relief and development work following earthquakes and tsunamis, and helped indigenous farmers fight to retain their land and their water access.
- AJWS maintains a policy advocacy staff in Washington, DC, and has been critical to battles to improve the delivery of foreign aid, appoint a special secretary for LGBT rights, and stop the genocide in Darfur and the looming genocide against the Rohingya people in Burma (Myanmar).

Consider an issue on which the two of us worked especially closely both as individuals and through our organizations: the dramatic response of so many in the Jewish community to the genocide in Darfur. Several Jewish organizations came together in 2004 to urge stronger U.S. action against the government of Sudan. Spurred on by what was happening in Darfur, which was denounced as a genocide, congregations and community relations councils got involved, day schools and Hebrew schools participated, all joining in a major Washington, DC, demonstration at which they believed they were, indeed, to use Heschel's image, "praying with their feet."

Today Jewish groups, small and large, are responding to the earthquake in Nepal, fighting for the rights of Muslim travelers, supporting migrants across the globe, providing sanctuary and assistance to those arriving at our own shores, and demanding attention from the U.S. government on myriad issues, including global warming and the incipient famine looming in South Sudan, Somalia, and Yemen, threatening up to twenty million lives.

Again, Jewish values and the lessons of our history animate our response to each of these crises: we cannot stand idly by the blood of our global neighbors, neither in Nepal in an earthquake nor among the sixty-three million migrants cast adrift in a world seemingly unable or unwilling to provide for them. We, who have been the quintessential refugee community—banished, forced to flee, seeking safety and freedom—*must* do what we can to help. We know all too well that if any minority group can be victimized simply because of who they are, none will be safe. If the climate of the earth is changed, with devastating consequences, there will be no Noah's ark for the Jewish people. With ample warning of the impending famine and too little action being taken to avoid it, let the true cause of death be written on every death certificate of those who will die in that famine: we just didn't care enough; they were too far away; we didn't recognize the Divine within them.

There will be—in fact, there already are—those who argue that these global concerns might have been acceptable at other times, but now that so much is at stake in our own communities in the United States and in Israel, all our attention must be focused closer to home. This position claims that until we address American racism or challenge the president on health care, or secure Israel's safety, we cannot look beyond our own borders in Israel and the United States.

It is an understandable argument, but our Rabbis and our texts and our history would have it otherwise. We are responsible for the victims of the transgressions of the world—and here in the United States we might argue that we are in fact responsible for some of these transgressions directly, that our failure to support the Paris Accords, for example, will hasten climate crises around the world, that the increase in hate crimes here sends a signal to people in other countries that indeed ethnic violence is acceptable.

So, we are called upon to act, to do what we can, both at home and abroad, to be that light unto the nations even—or perhaps, particularly—in hard times. We must pursue justice at home, in our own communities, in our own country, in Israel, and throughout the world. Before millions starve in East Africa or new violence erupts in Sudan, we, as Jews, motivated by text, by tradition, and by history, must heed the call to accept responsibility, to act, and to protest these transgressions. Only in these ways can we take up fully our intended role on this planet, helping to create a world in which we toil for equity and fairness and hope that encourages others so that more and more of us each day are working for the good of the entire globe.

NOTES

1. Abraham Joshua Heschel, "No Religion Is an Island" (1965), in *Moral Grandeur and Spiritual Audacity*, ed. Susannah Heschel (New York: Farrar, Straus and Giroux, 1996), 238.

2. Heschel, "No Time for Neutrality," in *Moral Grandeur and Spiritual Audacity*, 75.

3. Heschel, "The Reasons for My Involvement in the Peace Movement" (1972), in *Moral Grandeur and Spiritual Audacity*, 224.

· Part Two ·

Moral Resistance

Section B
Tools of Resistance

"TWO ARE BETTER THAN ONE"

Community Organizing and the Art of Building Power to Repair the World

RABBI STEPHANIE KOLIN

"It broke my heart when Prop 8 passed in California," Rabbi Don Goor told me. Same-sex marriage had previously been a constitutionally protected right in that state until 2008, when Proposition 8, an attempt to limit marriage to between a man and a woman, was placed on the ballot. When the measure passed, Rabbi Goor and his husband, Cantor Evan Kent, were among so many Reform Jews in the state to mourn this attack on our values of love, equality, and the belief that every human being is created in the image of God. Many rabbis and lay leaders had worked tirelessly on LGBTQ issues and specifically to defeat Prop 8, activating their congregations and exercising courageous leadership. Rabbi Goor lamented to me that he wished he had had a way to gather our movement together so we could have acted as one. Nothing like that existed then. But his broken heart whispered into existence a new kind of community organizing initiative. After that, our clergy and lay leaders wondered: what could we do so that we could stand up together for what we believed in—not just on same-sex marriage, but on so many issues of justice and compassion that touched our families' and our neighbors' lives?

Reform CA was born as this budding team of California rabbis and lay leaders spread out in their communities and began having deep conversations, each beginning with this question: What is the California that you dream of? They shared stories with each other about a school system that was once first in the country and was now forty-ninth, by some measures. They spoke of frightened undocumented immigrants, a lacking transportation system, not enough affordable housing, and more. They spoke of their desires to connect with people of other faiths and races to create a more just and compassionate California. And so the first statewide organizing campaign of the Reform Movement, Reform CA, came into being.

We worked to figure out what issue we might take on first. We listened to our members and clergy and learned from experts in the field, ultimately drawing on our own sacred narrative as perpetual strangers who are called on to care for the stranger and on our political analysis in order to make our decision—we would join the interfaith TRUST Act coalition to address the suffering faced by immigrants without documents in our state.

Immigrant rights coalitions in California were asking their elected state leaders to pass the TRUST Act. The TRUST Act was a bill that would protect immigrants without documents from unjust deportation by separating law enforcement from the U.S. Department of Homeland Security's U.S. Immigration and Customs Enforcement (ICE). This was designed to protect witnesses and victims of crimes, victims of domestic abuse, laborers, families, and more and to rebuild trust between immigrants and local police. The bill had been introduced several times before in the California legislature, but Governor Jerry Brown vetoed it every time it appeared. There was reason to believe he would veto it again that year. As California's Reform congregations joined Reform CA, excited to work on this campaign, we believed we could make a difference by joining the highly strategic and talented coalition.

We employed various tactics as part of this campaign, including bringing planeloads of Reform Jews to Sacramento to meet with their elected officials and with Governor Brown's staff. Rabbis and lay leaders also met with elected officials in their districts. For example, Rabbi David Frank of Cardiff by the Sea spoke with his assembly member, Rocky Chavez, on behalf of Reform CA, and the two shared their common religious commitment to caring for the stranger as well as their own family immigrant narratives. This conversation resonated deeply with Assembly Member Chavez. He became the only Republican to abstain from the vote rather than voting "no" when the bill came to the floor of the California State Assembly.

Our final campaign strategy was tailored to the High Holy Days. Rabbis throughout the state signed on to preach their Rosh HaShanah sermons on immigration, asking their congregants to break the governor's switchboard and let him know that Reform Jews of California wanted him to sign the TRUST Act into law. The Ten Days of Awe became Ten Days of Action as more than one thousand congregants answered the call to make their voice heard as one. Meanwhile, an influential individual, a congregant of Leo Baeck Temple in Los Angeles, heard Rabbi Ken Chasen powerfully call the community to action. He was appalled to learn how immigrants were being treated in his own state. Within minutes, he had secured a meeting with the governor—a meeting that had previously been elusive. That relationship, in conjunction with the thousand phone calls, our trip to Sacramento, negotiations with the district attorney's office, in-district meetings, and the deeply strategic years of work of the interfaith coalition, led to a Saturday morning that changed millions of lives.

On October 5, 2013, I received a call from coalition leader Chris Newman from the National Day Laborer Organizing Network. Chris said five words that I will never forget: "He signed it this morning." I felt the tears running down my cheeks. Reform Jews of California had helped to protect millions of immigrants in our state. Reform CA would go on to victories in affordable housing, racial injustice, criminal justice, and more. Other states would soon begin to build their own statewide campaigns.

Victories such as these are inspiring—but not unique. They are examples of countless successful campaigns that have been conducted by faith communities across the world and over decades in an approach called congregation-based community organizing. In this chapter, we will explore some of the processes and tools that advance this model and the challenges as well as the successes we've seen employing it in our congregations.

Congregation-based community organizing (CBCO) has been the Reform Movement's predominant model of systemic change work in the public square for more than a decade. This model of local activism, pioneered in the 1930s by Saul Alinsky, is the foundation of the Industrial Areas Foundation, PICO, and several other organizing entities, which build broad-based organizations and continue to bring CBCO to cities across the United States. CBCO is designed to bring together members of diverse religious institutions and community groups to build relationships across lines of faith, race, and class; identify shared concerns; develop strategies and campaigns on identified issues; build collective power; and hold each other accountable to act together to make change. By the late 1990s, a handful of synagogues were engaged in local CBCO groups. Through CBCO they discovered the transformative power of this work in strengthening relationships within the congregation and achieving victories for social justice in community across lines of faith, class, and race.

In 2006, Rabbi Jonah Dov Pesner founded Just Congregations as an initiative of the Union for Reform Judaism. Just Congregations promoted the engagement of Reform congregations in local congregation-based community organizing efforts. This initiative trained thousands of Reform Movement clergy and lay leaders throughout the country, partnered with the Hebrew Union College–Jewish Institute of Religion to train hundreds of rabbinical students in the art and skills of community organizing, and built a network of spiritual leaders who learned from one another and brought congregational community organizing to the forefront of Reform synagogue life. These leaders achieved significant victories on a broad range of issues including immigrant rights, improvements in public education, racial justice, LGBTQ rights, affordable housing, gun safety, the environment, criminal justice reform, and more. Alongside congregational engagement in direct service and the Religious Action Center's leadership in national advocacy, Just Congregations served as a platform for congregations to enact solutions to the root causes of problems in their own towns, cities, and states, bringing Jewish values into the public square. In 2016 the work of Just Congregations merged with the RAC to create one integrated, aligned, and growing Reform Movement social justice organization that reflects *our heart*, engages *our souls*, and harnesses *our might* to pursue a world of compassion, wholeness, and justice.

The premise of community organizing is fairly simple: we are more powerful together than we are alone. The premise is simple, and as they say, God is in the details.

Why We Organize

While people and congregations organize for many different reasons, I want to suggest that there are three primary motivations that drive the strategy and focus of the Reform Movement's organizing: to repair injustice, to deepen connections inside our communities, and to build relationships across lines of difference.

First, we organize so that we can have as large and enduring an impact on our broken world as possible. As many have written throughout the chapters of this book, the Jewish people are called to repair that which is broken in our world, addressing inequality and suffering, and protecting the vulnerable. In order to deliver on these values, not only do we need to be able to respond to urgent need, but we must also address the systemic injustices and imbalances that determine how individuals and families will fare in this society. Applying the tools of community organizing allows us to have an impact "upstream" in the political process. By pinpointing unjust or inhumane laws, policies, budgets, and systems that are in place, we shine a light on structures that put the most vulnerable at risk. By understanding who controls the levers of power, we can determine on whom we need to apply pressure or with whom we need to work to change the status quo. While some models of justice work call on us to feed the hungry, this model guides us to ask why there are hungry people to begin with, who is benefitting from that reality, and how we might work toward a system that is more compassionate and equitable. Understanding the political landscape of our day and participating in the public square through the lens of Torah can afford us a seat at the table in shaping this moment in history.

Second, we organize because it is a model of change work that leads to deeper relationship with others in our congregations, helping our congregations become places where each person is known and joined to others in a sacred web of connection. At a time when people feel more isolated than ever, the tools of community organizing deliberately weave us together by creating a context for conversations in which we come to learn one another's interests, obstacles, pain, and dreams. As community members' hearts are open to one another through an exchange of story, we can find ourselves inspired to be accountable to each other and feel less alone in the world. It enables us to ask ourselves and one another what we are willing to do to build the world we want, and it offers real opportunities to act together.

For example, I witnessed the power of the relational culture of organizing while I was working with a talented leader in Los Angeles, Rachel Kennison. Rachel was a leader in her synagogue's "listening campaign," a tool we use to build relationships and learn what truly matters to a community. She went to the home of a new member and asked her about her life. The woman responded, "I appreciate that you've come to my home, but I don't want to be part of this." Rachel was taken aback, but recalled her training and so instead of thanking the woman and leaving, she said, "I hear you and I respect that. Can you tell me why you don't want to get involved?" (The magic word of organizing: Why?) This woman shared that when she was younger, she, along with many others, had opposed the Vietnam war and fought against poverty. They thought they had won, she explained. But now she looks at her world and sees that in many ways they lost. Her own child couldn't afford to live near her, and her pension had been wiped out by the 2008 economic crash. Rachel listened hard and then shared her own story about her son's struggle with a broken public education system. His overcrowded classroom and a lack of resources were threatening his education and his love for learning. Each day, she felt at a greater loss for how to help him. As they finished their conversation, the woman surprised Rachel, saying, "If more people are going to be having conversations like this one, I think I'd like to be a part of that."

Developing our sense of curiosity about one another transforms lives and strengthens our communities. It can feel risky in that it is surely countercultural to speak so honestly with another person, but it has also contributed to our congregations being places where people can feel truly heard, seen, and known in ways that epitomize what is sacred about a faith community.

And finally, we organize so we can build sacred relationships across lines of race, faith, and economic position. While it is certainly true that we are more powerful when we act in partnership with others, it is also deeply in our values to see the divine spark in the other, to get close to stories that are different from ours, and to come to more fully understand how our lives and happiness are intertwined with those of other communities and faiths.

So how do we do it? While community organizing employs many tools of change, four of the most foundational are story, leadership, power, and action. When leaders employ these tools, they are well positioned to craft effective strategies and bring about measurable change that will heal suffering and build community. Over the years, we have found that the better we know how to use our tools, the more creative we can be with them.

Story and the Relational Meeting

Rabbi Asher Knight describes a transformational meeting that took place at Temple Emanuel of Dallas, Texas. As community members gathered to determine what their own stake in a campaign on racial equality might be, some came in believing that Jews must take a stand against systemic racism, while others were unsure. One person stood up to speak, trembling a bit as her story unfolded. She had recently adopted a young African American boy and had gone to a local African American pastor who was a friend of hers to talk about this new responsibility in her life. She sought advice for how, as a white woman, she should responsibly raise a black boy. The pastor told her, "It is dangerous to be perceived as an angry black man, so teach him to smile." She nodded. "But," he continued, "nobody trusts a black man who smiles too much, so teach him only to smile a little." She cried as she spoke to her fellow congregants. "How can I teach my beautiful son that he only gets to be half happy?" Those in the room were moved, transformed even. The story of their fellow congregant changed them and changed the course of Temple Emanuel's organizing work. We don't have to agree with another person's opinion about an issue. We can contest their analysis of a problem. We can even reject a person's political convictions. But a person's lived experience cannot be denied. A person's story, if we are willing to listen and be moved by it, is itself truth. This is why community organizing is built upon the practice of storytelling. We sit in paired conversation called "relational meetings" or small-group discussions called "house meetings," because stories have the power to change hearts and minds and can move us to want to cast our lots together in common cause. The trust built by sharing our real selves with one another can give us the courage to take action together, even on issues that may be controversial or complicated, for the sake of addressing real pain in our fellow members' lives and in our world.

Building Power

When many people are willing to share their stories, it is possible to see where our experiences and values overlap. And when we see that we face similar challenges, we might decide that we would like to address a certain shared issue of injustice or pain. In order to do that effectively, we need to have enough power to make the kind of change we want to see.

In Boston, Reform congregations, as part of the Greater Boston Interfaith Organization (GBIO), spent several years working first with Governor Mitt Romney and then with Governor Deval Patrick to develop and implement near-universal health care for the state's residents, creating a model that became a template for national reform. In doing so, GBIO built a base of thousands of people of faith who could speak personally about their own experiences, the prohibitive cost of health care, how they and their loved ones were suffering in the broken system, and how they would benefit from a victory on this issue. These thousands of people organized tens of thousands of fellow congregants, Massachusetts voters, who would show up and be counted when it mattered most. They convened meetings in their institutions in order that attendees would put pressure on state representatives and senators across the Commonwealth; it was so successful that thousands showed up to meetings with the governor and his staff, and they collected more than one hundred thousand signatures that would have forced the issue on a state ballot initiative. GBIO's role in the passage of near-universal health care signaled to then Governor Patrick that this was a base that could get things done. When. later, the state was being threatened by a ballot question that proposed to ban the state income tax and put in jeopardy state funding for seniors, children, people with disabilities, and critical infrastructure, Governor Patrick came to GBIO leaders and told them that to defeat this ballot question, he needed their help—would they stand with him and protect the Commonwealth? The ability to act powerfully and have an impact on a critical justice matter led to this public partnership with the governor, which gave people of faith an earned seat at the table when it came to questions about the laws and policies affecting the most vulnerable.

In community organizing, we define power as organized people or organized money. Organized people can be defined as at least two people who agree that there is a particular problem and agree upon a strategy by which to address that problem. The more people in that equation, the greater the power they have to make change. This is the process of raising up the people's voice in a way that allows us to determine what our society should look like and how to bring about greater justice and fairness for the most people possible. To build power effectively, we identify and cultivate leaders who will be able to weave together a community around its shared interests and prepare them for action.

Leadership

When Danny Ocean decides to break into a Las Vegas vault in the movie *Ocean's Eleven*, he first builds himself a team that has all the necessary talent to get the job done. Each member of the team has a unique set of skills that are needed for a successful heist. Sure, we are not breaking into vaults, but we do need a team of people who can work together to unlock an often stuck political system. To do so, we build teams of leaders who also have unique skills and who, together, are greater than the sum of their parts. A so-called leadership team is not composed of the foot soldiers of one top person, but rather are the discerning body who unearth their congregation's interests, help craft strategy, lead campaigns, and whose responsibility it is to open up meaningful opportunities for many others to engage in justice work and possibly become leaders themselves. This guiding body is built of individuals with certain salient traits—people who are team players, have or wish to have a network of relationships within the community, think strategically, have a sense of humor, are not too risk averse, have a good balance between ego and humility, and are deeply curious—about the world and about other people. The most effective leaders are committed to their own growth and learning and are invested in the leadership development of others in the congregation. Leaders take a community into action.

Action

You might hear an organizer say that "action is the oxygen of community organizing." We spend time in relational meetings, sharing stories, developing our leadership, and building our power so that we can make the world a better place. In order to do that, we must figure out which actions we can take in order to have a measurable impact on injustice. We ask ourselves: What is the reaction that we want? Do we need the governor to propose a different budget? A legislator to vote yes? A chief of police to commit to training officers differently? A national bank or a school or a corporation to change a policy? In order to take effective action, we must determine what action will result in the "reaction" we are seeking, as well as who has the power to enact the change we want. For the TRUST Act, for example, we needed to take action with regard to our legislators and our governor by demonstrating that a powerful base of leaders, who also were voters—something that was in the interest of our elected officials—were committed to addressing the suffering of immigrants in the state. So why is action like oxygen? Because when we take action successfully, and make the change we seek, it allows us and others to breathe more expansively, moving from the constricting stranglehold of oppression to the wide-open expanse of justice and freedom.

Acting Out of Our Self-interest

When Rabbi Jason Gwasdoff of Stockton, California, considered getting involved in the TRUST Act campaign, he wanted to know if and how issues related to undocumented immigrants mattered to his community. He brought together a house meeting to test the issue. One mother told the group that her husband had recently been deported to Mexico, and her children, who attended the congregation's religious school, were not sure when they would see their father again. Across the state, others shared stories about how domestic workers in their homes, people who were like family to them, were undocumented and at risk. And still others shared that their grandparents' generation, who had come to this country illegally, would never have been allowed in today. The issue was personal because it affected our lives as well.

A community's self-interest might also manifest as a question of values. New York City's Central Synagogue prepared to engage in issues facing the city and state, by first running a listening campaign to unearth congregants' stories and values. Congregants said: "We were taught by our parents that caring for the vulnerable is our responsibility and we want to model for our children what it looks like to be a good person." And: "We believe that equality is a Jewish value, that Judaism is and should be a force for good in the world, and we want to leave the world better than we found it." And: "We have experienced antisemitism and know that no one should be attacked for what they believe or who they are."

Whether our personal connections to an issue reflect our own experiences, the experiences of people we know and love, or our deeply held Jewish values, the model of organizing asks of us that we get clarity on our own "self-interest" on any issue we engage in. This does not mean we only take on issues that singularly affect ourselves, but it equally does not mean that we take on issues out of pity for another person or group of people. Self-interest means we have a horse in the race.

Why is this important? Understanding our own self-interest can give us the fortitude to keep on going when issues become complicated and tensions rise. And when we are partnering with people of different faiths and races, articulating our own self-interest in an issue can mean the difference between coming to the table as an outsider, or coming to the table with equal partnership and a shared commitment to victory. These qualities help us weather the challenges inherent in navigating relationships and politics.

Given the tensions in the political system, the controversy when it comes to certain issues, the different reasons why people join congregations, and the representation in our congregations of the entirety of the political spectrum, we can understand why there are challenges to congregation-based community organizing as well. In this model of change work, we are deeply committed to evaluation and reflection and, therefore, offer with transparency some of the challenges we face when applying the tools of organizing.

For one, it is important to discern whether an issue or campaign could be divisive in a community. Leaders must work hard to choose issues that will not tear a community apart, thereby destroying relationships and making a team even less powerful—two outcomes that are the opposite of the results we seek to achieve. This does not, however, mean that issues will not be controversial or that good people won't come to different conclusions about issues or the strategies for addressing them. As the heat rises on this challenge, it is critically important that we are in deep relationships of trust with our congregational boards, presidents, clergy, and other leaders, including those congregants who hold opposing viewpoints. It serves us well to remember that it is often a team of "unusual suspects" that can most creatively address the issues plaguing communities today. Critically, we value transparency in community organizing—this is work that should bring us closer and not drive us apart.

One of the greatest challenges we currently face is that of building deep relationships of accountability across lines of difference. This is not simply about clergy being in relationship with clergy of other faiths, but rather weaving together our communities who are working toward a common cause, but who come from different backgrounds. Many of us lead overscheduled lives, we live "inconvenient" distances from people of other backgrounds, and our different cultures and languages can make our interactions awkward and infrequent. Yet we know this is one of the most important and meaningful parts of our work to change the dynamics of our "every man for himself" culture. To rectify this, those in this work persist in the slow but steady effort toward building real relationships with our sisters and brothers outside our communities. We are always trying to learn how to do this better, with greater humility and enduring commitment.

A related challenge in our racial justice work is the need for us to do our own internal work as a community that is largely white, working on issues that are experienced most intensely by people of color, while understanding that we have people of color in our own communities who themselves have expressed feeling invisible and even unwelcome. We know that on issues of racial injustice, we must show up and listen hard, deepen our own understanding of white privilege, and humbly learn how to follow powerfully as allies or, as some of our partners prefer, as co-conspirators. In our commitment to participating in dismantling systemic racism, the Reform Movement has, in recent years, created a context for congregations to engage in deep and meaningful learning and reflection on race in this country. Many communities have taken part, even as we know we have a far way yet to go.

Finally, we face the challenge of partnering with people and organizations who may hold vastly different beliefs than we do on issues of great import to us. This can surface when a relationship with Israel becomes a barrier to engaging in other progressive issues, when certain partners on a campaign are opposed to LGBT rights, when elected officials stand with a community on one issue but vote in opposition on other deeply held beliefs, and myriad other challenging situations. Organizers and leaders grapple with this regularly. While it can be painful to appear to legitimize ideas anathema to our values, working on the issues that we are aligned on together means we will be in relationship with one another, come to know one another's stories, experience empathy through understanding each other's struggles, and, hopefully, develop a sense of trust with and responsibility to one another. Through such powerful interaction, we can come to see each other with greater humanity and talk about things we otherwise would never be able to talk about. So while partnering with those who hold different beliefs isn't easy, it is, perhaps, a pathway to greater understanding and possibility.

And yet, even with these real challenges, thousands of clergy members, staff, and lay leaders in our movement are committed to this work. Why? Because with the tools of organizing, we have healed suffering, strengthened our congregations, and transformed lives. Today, the Reform Movement is taking action in three different arenas—locally, statewide, and nationally. In their neighborhoods and cities, congregations are partnering across lines of difference to enact change both in their congregations and outside their walls. In California, Ohio, New York, Texas, Illinois, North Carolina, and many other states, congregations are coming together from urban, rural, red, blue, and purple regions to build statewide power that has been making a measurable difference on immigration, affordable housing, the environment, transgender rights, criminal justice reform, racial inequality, women's rights, voter suppression, and more. Nationally, our congregations are pledging to stand together as a movement committed to raising a prophetic voice and living our Jewish values in the public square so we can participate in the repair of our world. Our congregations in California have prevented government officials from cooperating with a federal registry based on religion, ended workplace discrimination based on reproductive choices, and protected environmental whistleblowers. In Ohio they have responded to the problem of mass incarceration by ensuring that those with low-level felony convictions receive community supervision and treatment as an alternative to prison. In New York we helped raise the age of criminal responsibility to eighteen years old, treating children like children in our criminal justice system. We are partnering with organizations around the country to stand together with our sisters and brothers of faith and no faith, to protect the most vulnerable and move the world closer to redemption.

We learn in the Book of Ecclesiastes, "Two are better than one . . . If either of them falls down, one can help the other up. But pity anyone who falls and has no one to help them up. . . . Though they may be overpowered, two can defend themselves. And a threefold cord is not quickly broken" (4:9–12). Navigating this sharp-edged world alone can be daunting and dangerous. The most vulnerable can be easily crushed under the weight of unjust laws and a system stacked against them. Today, we are witness to a world replete with systemic discrimination, fear, distrust, and hopelessness. But acting powerfully together, employing these tools and the many other models celebrated in the pages of this book, we can help one another up, we can live our Jewish values of compassion and justice, and we can make real a vision of the world as it should be.

TRAINING

The Key to Effective Action

Rabbi Karen R. Perolman

What prevents us from directly and regularly engaging in social justice work? So many of us want to make a difference and help to repair what is broken in our world, and yet, it can often feel overwhelming. Instead of doing anything, we feel paralyzed; we sit at home reading articles or watching other people's actions posted on social media. What can push us past thought toward action?

In my experience and opinion, the tipping point for action is training. Social justice classes, seminars, groups—all the different intentional experiences that fall under the category of "trainings"— are essential to move us from the mere desire to act to *actual* action. Through these trainings, participants gain community, confidence, and concrete knowledge in order to act with purpose and presence. Even more, these intentional types of preparation for the work of social justice can also function as their own type of justice work.

My first social justice training experience took place in the summer of 2010, shortly after I had been ordained as a rabbi and before I began at my first pulpit. I signed up for a weeklong community organizing training hosted by the Industrial Areas Foundation (IAF) at Drew University. Each morning as I drove early to beat the Brooklyn traffic across two rivers to New Jersey, I was transformed from recently ordained leader into once-again student. Though I had completed my rabbinic coursework and had received ordination, I was just starting out fresh that week at Drew.

Those five days were packed with power and helped me find my potential. During the training, I learned in-depth about a wide variety of subjects: the history of community organizing, the functioning of systemic oppression, the tools for speaking truth to power, and the power of sharing stories (for more on these subjects, see the chapters in this volume by Kolin and Asch). Looking back on the journal I kept at that time, I reflected on how humbled I felt in the presence of the master trainers who served as our faculty. They were unemotional and passionate, instructive and open to questions. They were not interested in holding the hands of their students; rather they empowered us to pay attention, learn, and internalize and then translate that knowledge into concrete action.

Much more happens at a five-day training than can or should be summarized in an article. Many of the specific points of instruction build not only upon each other, but also through the shared experience of dedicating time *with others* to become a better advocate and to advocate for the work of social justice. I recommend to every reader that they go and seek out a training opportunity in order to gain the concrete knowledge, help see themselves as part of a community, and gain the inner confidence needed to stand up to systemic oppression.

Community

Trainings are the perfect environment to create organic community. Instead of forcing a group of people to come together, trainings attract like-minded individuals who are both open to and interested in learning. Since trainings are often held in university, religious, or communal spaces, they will appeal to those who are already active in their community. A social justice training also often appeals to those with a curious and interested mind-set. These may be individuals who not only want to participate in civil and communal life, but also are seeking relationships with others like them. These may be those who are already active in their individual faith or area community or who are likely to go beyond their safe and comfortable circles.

One of the tremendous benefits of attending training is the interwoven circles of community to which each participant becomes immediately connected. One circle is those in the specific program, the individuals with whom you shared a precise and time-limited experience. A second circle is all of the people who have engaged in similar trainings in the same area, through the same organization; as one example, there is a special connection among the many people I know who have taken an IAF training. A third circle represents all those people who have been trained—even over a lengthy period of time—on the same subject and who therefore share a common knowledge and commitment. The largest, fourth circle connects an individual to all of those who have done any kind of social justice training, ever. Through the single act of attending one training, one can become linked in what I think of as a *shalshelet hatikkun*, a chain of repair that has the power to right the wrongs of our world through thoughtful and direct action.

Confidence

I mentioned earlier that trainings often attract those who are already involved and invested in various causes and their local communities. Despite this orientation, many who attend trainings are hoping to gain the sense of confidence essential for taking action. I can share a personal example of the lack of confidence I felt I faced before training. The first was connected to the building block of community organizing, the one-on-one conversation. Even though I was a rabbi and was invested by the community with a certain authority, I felt shy and anxious thinking about asking someone I didn't know to meet for a conversation. And my self-doubt ranged from the interpersonal to the pulpit. Before training, I felt worried that I wouldn't have the conviction to speak on issues of injustice with authority. Having never intentionally spoken truth to power, I wondered: If I did speak, would anyone listen?

Confidence is often tied to our own sense of self, and often our lack of confidence is connected to our having experienced powerlessness. Trainings create the opportunity for dedicated, passionate individuals to work through their own experiences of oppression, inequality, or trauma so that they might find their own inner strength. In order to speak truth to power, it is essential for those in positions of leadership in community organizations to have insight and reflection regarding their own feelings of power and powerlessness. Through multi-day trainings, one can first work through one's own personal experiences and then build the self-confidence that will be critical in the work of organizing and justice.

For some individuals, a single training can provide this wellspring of confidence; for others, ongoing training and learning remain a steady and important piece of their justice work. For all, a sense of authenticity and certainty is a benefit of training work.

Concrete Knowledge

More than ever, information on every subject is available almost immediately in the palms of our hands. Despite the relative ease by which we can access information on every facet of social justice, the dissemination of misinformation can be just as prevalent. In the age of googling experts, there is nothing that feels as authentic as going to an IRL training session with live professionals whose goal is not to pass on information about issues or policy, but to impart knowledge about how a group of dedicated individuals can effect constructive change.

In short, here are three reasons to attend a community organizing or social justice training:

1. To learn firsthand from experts and seasoned organizers.

2. To take the opportunity to rehearse, build confidence, and work through any personal baggage.

3. To meet like-minded individuals and build community.

In the years since I attended that first IAF training, I have found myself in many similar rooms focused on training as passing on the knowledge born of experience. Every time I walk out of those rooms—often at the end of a long day or days—I always have the same feelings: humility for all that I do not know, hunger to make a difference, and a sense of hurry to get to work. After all, the world isn't going to fix itself.

CUTTING AN ISSUE

Moving from the Big to the Doable

RABBI ERICA SEAGER ASCH

A woman walked into my office one day in February. She explained that she was feeling overwhelmed. There were an increasing number of worries that she was turning over and over in her mind, including climate change and the possibility that the United States would pull out of the Paris accords, and increasing antisemitism and anti-Muslim sentiment. She felt overwhelmed by possible changes in educational policy and worried about funding for local schools, and she wondered what would happen to her health care. She is not unique.

Faced with all these problems, any one of us would feel helpless. There is no way we can stop global warming or antisemitism. We can't change federal or even state education policy. We cannot figure out our own health care, let alone deal with the U.S. health-care system. These are problems—big, amorphous, and intractable—and we can't solve them on our own. They are the things that keep us up at night. They don't have an easy solution. They seem impossible to address.

Looking at all the problems in our world can make us feel hopeless. One way to help combat this hopelessness is to turn a problem into an issue. In organizing this is called "cutting an issue," that is, taking a piece ("cut") out of an amorphous, big, and seemingly intractable problem to turn it into a smaller, manageable goal toward which we can take action. There is no perfect blueprint for turning a problem into an issue; organizing is an art and not a science. But there are some principles that are helpful to keep in mind as you move from problem to issue.

The first step is really a "pre-step": hold a series of house meetings (small group meetings held at people's homes) to discuss what people care about. These meetings are a way to start hearing stories about what really matters to people in your community. After having many of these meetings, you will be left with a long list of problems that are of concern to the people in your congregation. In order to narrow those down to an issue, you are going to need to do research.

When researching, you will explore, through "research actions," a number of possible issues that are key to the problems of the community. However, unlike problems, issues are specific. No one can take individual responsibility for a problem, but a good issue has someone who can make a change, someone who is accountable.

As you do your research actions, you will want to keep in mind your criteria for selecting an issue. First, an issue should be winnable, but not too easy to win. If it is too easy, you will not need to gather a large group of people or partners. Building a bigger team is essential to taking on a bigger issue next time you organize. Second, the issue needs to be deeply felt (people care a lot about it) and broadly felt (many different people care). Third, it has to have a clear target—someone who can say yes or no. Finally, it should build power for your synagogue or local partners. The goal of good organizing is to be able to gather more people and more partners in order to be able to take on a bigger issue next time you organize. You might start with a local stoplight, but through building relationship with local partners, getting to know your city council members, and becoming known as a group that is able to organize consistently, you will be able to take on a bigger issue, say building a new community center, next.

We cannot do the work of cutting an issue in isolation. In order to organize successfully, we must work within our congregations and with partners in the community to identify problems, turn them into issues, and then act on those issues. A campaign in which Temple Rodef Shalom (TRS) took part, in concert with community organizing groups in Washington, DC, can serve as an example about how we turn problems into issues.

A series of house meetings we organized at TRS in Northern Virginia identified a problem: older members of the congregation felt isolated. Despite the active senior groups at the synagogue, there were many problems seniors faced, such as lack of transportation, finding affordable living options, and a lack of learning opportunities. Leaders at TRS knew they had to pick an issue that was winnable but not too easy. In doing research, it became clear that the issue of housing was not something that we could win. The congregation had already done substantial work on housing, including helping to found and fund an affordable senior living residence with a local church. We did not have enough power or energy to effect zoning changes, which our research showed would be a next step to alleviating the housing problem.

The lack of learning opportunities was a problem we chose to research in the hopes of finding an issue we could organize around. It was clear that seniors were not concerned about more social opportunities, as the temple had a number of social groups and seniors were actively involved in the local community as well. There was also not a lack of monthly lectures or trips. What seniors missed was access to high-quality, intellectual classes taught over a number of months. At a house meeting, one retired government worker explained that she had spent her whole professional life involved in the DC political scene, meeting interesting people and thinking deeply about major events that impacted our country. She had talked to ambassadors and helped to set government policy. Now that she was retired, she didn't want to have a monthly lunch group or trip to a play. She wanted intellectual stimulation and engagement—to learn with others who were interested in thinking critically about the world. We had turned an abstract problem—not enough for seniors to do—into an issue: lack of sustained, high-quality learning opportunities for seniors.

This issue fit our criteria. It was widely and deeply felt within the congregation. Many seniors spoke about the need for this program and felt strongly that it would improve not only their lives, but the lives of other seniors in the community. But we did not yet have a target—someone whom we could ask to implement such a program. Further research showed that there was a model for these types of programs already in existence. The Osher Lifelong Learning Program is a national program run by seniors that offers classes in conjunction with local universities. The nearest program was half an hour away, too far for participants to drive to in notoriously bad traffic. So we met with several local community centers and learned that while they offered a number of athletic and artistic classes for seniors, they did not currently offer any academic classes. Finally, we had a target. We could ask the director of the local community center, an easy five- to fifteen-minute drive on side streets, to offer space and publicity for a program where seniors would take high-quality classes.

Often when we tell stories about how we organize, it sounds like an easy, direct line from our house meetings to picking an issue to taking action on that issue. This is rarely the case. In this instance, it took quite a bit of research and several false starts to go from a problem to an issue. We had to do a second round of meetings with seniors in the congregation to gain clarity about their needs, meet with people who run the current Osher program to see if it would possibly work for our community, and meet with many people at several local community centers before we found a willing partner.

During our research actions, we kept in mind our core principles. First, we needed an issue that we could win but was not too easy. This was the first issue our temple had taken the lead in working on. Our synagogue leaders had been involved tangentially in much bigger campaigns as part of Virginians Organized for Interfaith Community Engagement (VOICE), our local community organizing group. Because we were just starting to take the lead in our own organizing, we picked a smaller issue that we thought we could win. Although it was smaller, it would still make a real difference in the lives of our members.

Second, this issue was deeply and widely felt. Even those who were not seniors were concerned about this issue. Those who were still working but nearing retirement age wanted opportunities available when they retired. Quite a few younger members of the congregation had parents who were also members of the community and would directly benefit from these classes. This issue also helped to build power within the congregation. Working on it gave the organizing group visibility and recognition and showed that we could get things done. It did not, however, build power outside the congregation. In order to do that, we had to pick a second issue.

The tree-lined streets of the Northern Virginia suburbs are beautiful. Lawns along the wide suburban streets are well maintained, and beautiful homes are set back from the streets. But once you leave the neighborhoods, you enter into a traffic nightmare. Even a "quick" trip to the grocery store can involve overcrowded streets, impatient drivers, and a lot of sitting in traffic. The danger and stress of driving made it difficult for many temple members to maintain their independence. Trips to the grocery store, to meet friends, or to go to the library were just too difficult with the traffic. Seniors needed transportation. This was an excellent example of a huge problem: amorphous, not clearly solvable, and with no one to ask for a solution. Again, we had to do some research to turn this problem into an issue.

First, we talked more with those who were affected. We learned that even seniors who lived in senior housing found that the shuttles already offered were not enough. Taxis were too expensive and often unreliable. Those who could not drive themselves relied on family and friends. This left their family members stretched. One man we talked with didn't ask his friends to drive him places because he felt like he was imposing on them. When a neighbor would call to offer, he would accept, but he would never initiate a call. He would occasionally take taxis, but they were expensive and drivers were often impatient with how much time it took him to get out to the curb. What he and other community members really needed was reliable, inexpensive transportation to be able to get to the grocery store and social outings.

In the course of our conversations, we saw that this issue was widely and deeply felt. Again, many congregants who were still able to drive knew that they would have to stop driving one day and worried about a future loss of independence. We also saw that the issue of transportation was felt deeply outside of the temple community. Other congregations in VOICE also had members who needed more reliable transportation. A year earlier, VOICE had run a successful campaign to add a bus line in a neighboring county. The Department of Health and Human Services had moved to a new location, which was too far for residents to access easily. They had to take two buses and transfer across a busy street, often with several young children and strollers, or pay over $20 for a taxi from their home. Residents organized, and county board members agreed to add $225,000 to the county budget to extend a bus line so that residents could take only one bus to reach the HHS department. In working with the county board, this campaign helped to build power for future actions.

In doing further research, we discovered that a nearby county had buses that would deviate off of a standard route to pick people up at their homes. This seemed like a possible issue for us to take on. Many of our seniors lived near a bus line, often only one or two blocks away, but walking to their houses with groceries or packages was too difficult. We met with the people who ran the bus service to see how this could be implemented and with the county board chair to discuss county support for this program. We had turned the problem of transportation into an issue: buses deviating from their planned routes to pick people up at their homes.

In this case, our research showed us that we could have cut the issue in a different way. We could have decided to address the lack of access to grocery stores and solved that issue by creating a cadre of volunteer drivers to take people to the grocery store. Assuming that we could have successfully implemented such a system, it also would have addressed the issue. Seniors would have gotten rides to where they needed to go. But leaders rejected this because it did not create long-lasting, systemic change. The system would have relied on volunteer drivers to keep it going. Furthermore, it would not have built any power for the organization. We would not have been in contact with elected officials or been able to show we could create or impact legislation. An all-volunteer effort did not engage with elected officials.

The issue of bus service was in many ways more difficult. It required a lot of education of seniors. They needed to understand how to call ahead to request a route deviation and how to take the bus (many were not regular riders of buses earlier in their lives). It also required retraining of drivers. The Department of Transportation would coordinate the program; we would just have to make sure that it was implemented successfully.

There is often more than one way to cut an issue. This way of cutting the issue built more power than the other option. By working with the county board, we continued to establish VOICE as a powerful organization in the county. This not only built power, but, if implemented, would create systemic change that did not require volunteer commitment. It is important to figure out which way of cutting an issue will help to build power, engage allies, and address something deeply and broadly felt.

Across the river at Temple Sinai in Washington, DC, one deeply felt problem was concern for the environment. Congregants at the synagogue were increasingly concerned about global warming and pollution of area waterways. The environment is a classic problem—amorphous, no target, not actionable. Also, while concern for the environment was deeply felt within the congregation, it was not a pressing concern for other congregations in the Washington Interfaith Network (WIN). In Ward 8, a primarily African American ward, jobs were the most pressing issue. The unemployment rate was almost 18 percent and higher for those without high school diplomas or who had been incarcerated. People in congregations in the southeast part of the city cared about jobs, not polluted waterways.

These two deeply felt problems overlapped in an interesting way. Washington, DC, was under a federal consent decree and was required to update the city's storm water system. For years, heavy rains had caused sewers to overflow, sending thousands of gallons of sewage into city streams and rivers. The city was proposing a "gray" solution—digging tunnels to capture extra rainwater and send it into rivers so sewers would not overflow. WIN proposed a solution that met both environmental and job concerns. In addition to building tunnels, the city should also invest in "green" solutions, capturing heavy rainfall in green infrastructure—newly created rooftop gardens, porous pavement, and rain barrels. Further, the city should train and hire DC residents for these new green jobs.

WIN leaders faced two problems: the environment and jobs. By looking at what the city was already doing, they were able to figure out two issues that overlapped and addressed the larger problems. Green infrastructure would not only solve the problem of polluted waterways, but mimic the natural water cycle. This would bring more greenery to the city, reduce the amount of nitrogen and carbon dioxide in the atmosphere, support natural habitats, and help to cool extreme summer temperatures. The project would also train and employ DC residents in high-paying jobs. DC Water had a track record of not hiring district residents. Giving priority to residents of the district would mean taxpayer money would create jobs for local citizens. Furthermore, the jobs would require green infrastructure certification, and that training would help residents to find other employment at a later date. These green solutions would also require ongoing maintenance and compliance, which would mean long-term jobs for residents.

The issues chosen were combined into a campaign called "Green City, Green Jobs." These two issues were winnable and had clear targets. The city council, the mayor, and the head of DC Water could commit to a green infrastructure plan and to training and hiring DC residents instead of out-of-state contractors. The city was already obligated to invest this money. With the right amount of organizing, WIN could get them to achieve the goals of reducing pollution in this different way.

This issue was widely and deeply felt. Members of Temple Sinai and other congregations cared deeply about the positive environmental impacts this would have on the city. As they developed relationships with DC residents who faced underemployment and heard their stories about the difficulty of finding living-wage jobs, temple members also came to care deeply about the jobs portion of the proposal. DC residents who needed jobs were frustrated by repeated attempts to work for DC Water and the barriers that were put in place. They needed good jobs. These concerns were shared widely—from the primarily white, wealthy neighborhoods in Northwest DC to the primarily black, struggling neighborhoods in Southeast DC. This issue would help to build WIN's power. It required strengthening relationships with the mayor and city council and developing a new relationship with DC Water. A victory on this issue would show that WIN could push the council to pass legislation that had a major impact on the city and that involved billions of dollars.

This example helps to show how powerful it can be to work in a group of congregations and what cutting an issue looks like when you are working with an effective broad-based organization. Many congregations do not have an existing local organization. Even so, it is still possible to turn a problem into an issue and figure out how to take action.

I am now at Temple Beth El in Augusta, Maine, a small community very different from the urban and suburban mix of the Washington, DC, region. Here, we do not have a broad-based organization to work with, but we do have tremendous faith and community partners. Through a series of house meetings, we identified several problems that we were passionate about: transportation, education, food insecurity, and housing. We realized that this list needed to be narrowed into one actionable issue. First, we brainstormed potential issues we could imagine coming out of each area. For example, our education brainstorming included Head Start funding, education funding from the state, helping children who suffer from trauma, protections for Muslim and Jewish students (e.g., putting holidays on the academic calendar, no tests on those days), shifting money from administration into the classroom, better and more ESL services, decreasing testing, and access to remedial services. We looked at each problem and potential issue areas and asked ourselves: What do we have the power to change? Which issues are deeply and widely felt not only in our congregation, but in the broader community? Which issues have a clear target? Where can we make an impact?

Using these criteria, we narrowed down two problems: education and food insecurity. We carefully examined the list of potential issues and picked areas for additional research based on the questions listed above. In our education group, we quickly decided that we did not have enough power to influence Head Start funding or other education funding from the state. We also had to acknowledge that shifting money from administration to the classroom was too large an issue for us to tackle. Our congregants live in multiple districts, and therefore the issue of testing, while potentially deeply and broadly felt, had too many targets for us to be able to make a real change. We also saw that schools were taking steps to provide more and better ESL services already, so our work there would not necessarily have a large impact. Access to remedial services did not have a clear target, and there was feeling among some in the group that this was an issue that was not broadly felt.

This left us with two potential issues. The first was helping children who suffer from trauma. This issue is deeply felt by families who had undergone trauma. It was also broadly felt by the wider community. The high rate of drug abuse and opioid addiction in our area is connected to effects of childhood trauma such as domestic violence and accidental deaths in the family. There are also a number of refugees in our community, and their children underwent traumatic experiences on their way to America. We also knew that a nearby school district had implemented a very successful trauma program for its students, so there was a strong possibility of collaboration and learning from their model. At this time, we think that the target will be the local school board, and possibly the superintendent, but we are still in the process of doing more research to see how the program was implemented in the nearby district. We think we have potential partners to work with in order to build enough power to make a change. These potential partners include other faith communities, the refugee community, the domestic violence shelter, the homeless shelter, and the local hospital. We must begin meeting with these diverse partners as well as with our own congregants who are mental health professionals, doctors, or social workers and have expertise in this area. Our research will let us know if this will be a good issue for us.

The second potential issue was initially thought of as protections for Muslim and Jewish students. Local districts have an increasing number of Muslim students who are refugees. The schools do not know when Muslim holidays occur, are unsure of the dietary needs of Muslim students, and communicate with their parents in English, which many of them do not speak. Muslim families care deeply about this issue, as do members of the faith community who are working closely with the Muslim community. Additionally, the Jewish community has long been frustrated by the school's lack of acknowledgment of Jewish holidays. Schools routinely schedule tests and sporting events on Rosh HaShanah and Yom Kippur, leading many students and parents to feel the schools do not respect their religious holidays. This issue is deeply felt among our members who currently deal with or have dealt with schools in the past. It is also broadly felt throughout the community. We also have a number of congregants working in the school system who are particularly invested in this issue. This issue has a clear target—the local school boards, which set policies. It has the advantage of being more easily done in the number of different districts where our members live, unlike the trauma program, which would be harder to implement in various districts. We feel that we have the power to make some smaller changes that would have a big impact on our communities: having schools not schedule tests on or around Jewish or Muslim holidays, publishing those holidays on official school calendars, not scheduling sports events on those holidays, and working with us to implement a series of faculty workshops to help staff better understand Judaism and Islam. We have more research to do on how these policies have been implemented in other districts and how to approach our local school boards to make this change.

We are also in the process of thinking about how to further broaden the appeal of this issue, perhaps by framing it as creating "welcoming schools," which could grow to include protections for LGBTQ students. While we know that many in our area might not deeply care about the rights of Jewish and Muslim students, we do think the broader community is disturbed by divisive and hateful rhetoric at a state and national level. We think we might have broader support if we talk about the issue as educating our students about differences and respecting those differences. More research will help us to answer these questions and to pick the right issue for our community.

As you can see from these examples, cutting an issue looks different in different communities. After you hold house meetings and start to research in order to turn problems into potential issues, keep in mind some basic principles. An issue should be winnable but not too easy. It should be deeply and widely felt both within your congregation and by your partners. An issue should have a clear target. Finally, an issue should build power both for your synagogue and for your partners. Do not be afraid to experiment and try something new. This process takes time. It is rarely a straight line from problem to issue, and you will take many twists and turns along the way. It is good to explore several possible options before settling on one issue that works for your group. With the right issue, you have the potential to build power and to make real and lasting change in the world.

THE POWER OF THE PULPIT

When Sermons Lead to Action

Rabbi Ken Chasen

We rabbis spend a lot of time writing and delivering sermons . . . and often wonder whether that time is ultimately well spent.

After all, a sermon—even one given to an extremely large gathering—is an inherently limited mechanism for changing lives. It can only be experienced in its ideal form once, for whoever happens to be present. And even then, the most focused listeners struggle to maintain attention throughout the entire presentation, for even a momentary mental drift can cause the argument to be derailed or the metaphor to be missed. Sometimes, hours of careful speech-craft are lost on a worshiper just because of sixty seconds spent distracted or exhausted. Social media might extend the reach and life span of a sermon, but the opportunities for distracted listening online can be even greater. And then there is the question of ultimate impact: Beyond some spirited conversation during the car ride home, how long does a good sermon endure? Will it be remembered a day later? A week? Will the actions urged by the rabbi actually be embraced? Or will the listener simply be satisfied having heard an inspiring message and return to life largely unchanged?

These are the realities and questions that have caused me throughout my career to wonder whether my hours spent on sermon writing were worthwhile . . . until Rosh HaShanah 2013, when I discovered the capacity of a sermon, under just the right conditions, to change millions of lives.

In 2012, under the leadership of Rabbi Stephanie Kolin, I was privileged to be a part of a small group of Los Angeles–area rabbis who launched Reform CA, a new community organizing initiative enabling Reform rabbis statewide to mobilize together for justice and to lead their congregations into collective action. By the time 2013 arrived, we had assembled a leadership team of twenty-five rabbis throughout the state and were preparing to embark upon our first campaign, immigration reform. This would be pursued by organizing in favor of the TRUST Act, a piece of legislation aimed at stopping the deportation of undocumented immigrants arrested for nonviolent and minor offenses. Written and introduced by Assemblyman Tom Ammiano, the TRUST Act was a risky choice for our first campaign, as a very similar version of the bill had already been vetoed by Governor Jerry Brown just months earlier. Many in our coalition feared that we were setting ourselves up for a certain defeat that might finish our fledgling organization before it could even get off the ground. However, this was the issue that kindled the passion of our member rabbis, who saw in it the brave experiences of their own American immigrant ancestors. Even if we were to lose in this maiden effort, we felt we would stand our best chance of developing a durable movement by fighting the fight that resonated most deeply in our souls.

During the next several months, Reform CA built its power, relationship by relationship. There were one-to-one meetings between rabbis and within our congregations. There were workshops at CCAR conventions. There were house meetings and community forums. There were Jewish holiday observances with special resources and rituals connected to our campaign. Reform CA also joined forces with a statewide interfaith coalition, attaching us to numerous organizations that had invested years in the battle for immigration reform. Quickly we confirmed that the challenge wasn't going to be moving the TRUST Act through the statehouse; the difficulty would be winning the governor's signature on a bill he had just vetoed in the previous legislative cycle. We turned our full attention, therefore, to bringing pressure upon the governor to sign the bill once it landed on his desk.

Governor Brown was not an easy man to engage on this topic. For years he had declined invitations for personal meetings with the leaders of our interfaith coalition. We knew we would need to build relationships with his staff. In May 2013, a group of thirty-five Reform CA activists traveled to Sacramento to meet with June Clark, the governor's lead staffer for the TRUST Act. Ms. Clark was courteous and engaged, but it was impossible to gauge from her comments whether the governor would ultimately sign the bill. We headed into the summer understanding that we would need to pull out all the stops if we were to sustain any hope of impacting the governor's decision. By September, the TRUST Act would be on his desk, and there would be only a few weeks left before he would either sign or veto.

This led the leadership team of Reform CA to adopt a "High Holy Days strategy." Our goal was to persuade as many California Reform rabbis as possible to give a Rosh HaShanah sermon on immigration reform and, in it, to ask their congregants to call the governor's office to demand his signature. If we could generate large numbers of phone calls during the critical weeks, we thought, perhaps we could prompt a different outcome than had occurred the previous year. We prepared texts and resources for our rabbis and led workshops helping them to construct their sermons and their appeals for phone calls. A large group of rabbis throughout the state agreed to join in the effort. Everything was proceeding perfectly—and then some unexpected eleventh-hour political negotiations threatened to make it all meaningless just days before the shofar's blast.

Our interfaith coalition partners informed us that Governor Brown had contacted Assemblyman Ammiano with a series of amendments he was requesting. Some of them seemed rather benign. Two of them, however, would impose severe limits on the impact of the TRUST Act. The governor told the assemblyman that if his amendments were made, he would commit in advance to signing the bill into law—and if not, he would make no commitment at all. Assemblyman Ammiano was given just twenty-four hours to decide.

The leaders of Reform CA were deeply concerned. Our rabbis were about to preach their TRUST Act sermons, and it seemed that the game might already be decided before they stepped onto the bimah. Moreover, both of the options available to us seemed unappealing. Either we would have to accept a victory that accomplished little or face what appeared to be an inevitable, looming defeat. What should we do?

A small group of us participated on a conference call with the interfaith coalition leaders. We argued for accepting the unobjectionable amendments that the governor had proposed and refusing the two problematic ones. We didn't want a Pyrrhic victory. We wanted to achieve meaningful change for the three million marginalized immigrants in our state, and if we had to risk defeat in order to keep that dream alive, we felt it was worth it. We urged our partners to tell Assemblyman Ammiano to stand his ground with the governor, and we promised we would support his actions publicly in the event that the TRUST Act went down to a veto once again.

This was the treacherous political backdrop against which I stood before my congregants on Erev Rosh HaShanah 2013 and said the following:

> For the past year, our Reform Movement in California has been organizing to achieve immigration reform in our state via the TRUST Act, a bill that will stop the deportations of thousands of immigrants with no criminal records. Right now, immigrant children in our state are ending up in foster care because their parent was jailed and then deported for something as minor as a traffic ticket. And when any discussion with the police can turn into an immigration arrest, we shouldn't be surprised that immigrants are now becoming unwilling to report crimes. Too many Latinos in our own state now see police protection as a luxury item that they cannot afford.
>
> As an immigrant people ourselves in America, we think of this country as a place that has always been a safe harbor from that sort

of fear, not a perpetrator of it. Fifty years ago, the Jewish community stood with the African American community because we as a people had lived some version of their plight. Can we, whose loved ones came to these shores dreaming of what our lives actually became, do any less for those attempting to complete the same journey today?

I knew only one of my great-grandparents personally—my *bubbe*, who suffered a stroke on the evening of my bar mitzvah party, but she's there in all the photographs that morning. To me, she was the little old lady with the Eastern European accent in our family, but when I learned her story after she had died, I discovered that she was a whole lot more than that. My *bubbe* was a mail-order bride—and when she got to this country and met the guy who brought her here, she didn't like him. Somehow, my *bubbe*, a powerless and penniless immigrant woman, mustered the courage to ask her "fiancé" if she could go to work in order to buy her way out of the arrangement—and incredibly, he allowed her to do it. And because she pulled it off, she ended up marrying my great-grandfather instead, which, of course, is what made my life possible.

Dig deeply enough, and almost every single one of us has in our family narrative a loved one who did something unbelievably brave for us. They stared down every challenge—language, employment, living conditions, antisemitism, you name it—all so we could sit here comfortably in Bel Air and greet the new year. The fight for immigrant justice is our fight.

The California State Senate will be receiving the final amended version of the TRUST Act within the next few days . . . before Yom Kippur will have come and gone, in fact. And it appears the votes are there to pass it—so all we'll need *then* is for Governor Brown to sign it into law . . . and that means all we need *now* is an avalanche of phone calls to the governor, insisting that he turn our state back in the right direction.

You know, one of the big reasons we often choose silence over action is that we don't like losing. And fighting for justice means a whole *lot* of losing—and somehow continuing to believe after every defeat, continuing to fight until victory is won. Governor Brown vetoed the last attempt at a law of this sort. The pressures of the status quo upon him were greater than the pressures from those demanding justice. We get to decide whether they will be again. We get to decide whether we'll fuel the national movement for immigration reform by creating success in our state. We get to decide how we want this episode in the American story to read to those who will stand in judgment of *us* fifty years from now.

So in the next few days, once the TRUST Act reaches its vote in the Senate, I am going to e-mail you and ask you to call the governor that day. I want his switchboard to break. My e-mail message to you will provide simple instructions for making the call. Just our congregation alone could produce many hundreds of calls, and hundreds of calls might just be the difference between a veto and a signature this time. Will you put yourself out?

Indeed, hundreds of our congregants did put themselves out—as did congregants from other Reform CA congregations throughout the state. We started to hear stories of their conversations with the governor's staff, who reported that their phones had been ringing off the hook with calls of support for the TRUST Act. Our strategy was working in congregations all over the state.

Just as Rosh HaShanah drew to its end, I also received an e-mail from the assistant to my congregant Ari Emanuel: "Rabbi Chasen, Ari would like to set up a time for you to speak with Governor Brown and himself."

As the CEO of the groundbreaking entertainment, sports, and fashion conglomerate Endeavor, Ari Emanuel is an enormous figure in American business life and popular culture. Actor Jeremy Piven's much-fabled character, agent Ari Gold in the award-winning HBO television series *Entourage*, is said to have been based upon Ari Emanuel. Moreover, Ari is a part of one of America's most influential families. His eldest brother Ezekiel, vice provost for global initiatives at the University of Pennsylvania, is one of the nation's most renowned bioethicists. Middle brother Rahm, a former U.S. congressman and chief of staff to President Obama, serves as the mayor of Chicago. As one of America's most powerful voices in the arts, social innovation, and culture, Ari is deeply respected by political leaders on the local, state, and national levels, where he is consistently engaged in advocacy activity.

At our congregation, Ari Emanuel has been a longtime participant, supporter, and friend. Our sons attended our temple preschool together many years ago, forging a warm bond between our families that has only grown during life-cycle celebrations, travel to Israel together, and many other memorable experiences we have shared. Usually, Ari and his family find me after Rosh HaShanah services to wish me a *shanah tovah*. In 2013, I did not notice them in the sanctuary or see them afterward, but when I received the e-mail message from him, I knew that he had surely been there.

For three years, leaders in our interfaith coalition had been attempting without success to gain an audience with Governor Brown to discuss the TRUST Act. Suddenly and unexpectedly, we had that opportunity. With the assistance of Rabbi David Saperstein, then still the director of the Religious Action Center of Reform Judaism in Washington, DC, I prepared to partner with Ari in making our case.

Governor Brown couldn't have been more gracious or respectful in hearing our argument. Ari opened the conversation with passion and purpose: "Mr. Governor," he said, "I was at synagogue with my family on Rosh HaShanah, praying for my soul. And my rabbi gave a sermon about a bill pertaining to immigrants being forced to leave the country and being separated from their families. This has been troubling me deeply ever since, so I wanted to invite him to join me in discussing this with you."

I followed by explaining to the governor why the TRUST Act had taken on a greater emotional significance for California's Jews than he could likely have imagined. Ari was hardly alone in his concern. The hundreds of phone calls to his office testified to that. As an immigrant people ourselves, Jews were seeing this issue through the lens of their own family stories. Poignantly remembering the opportunity afforded by America to their loved ones in previous generations, Jewish Californians were focused upon this particular piece of legislation with unusual zeal. This, I explained, was why the Rosh HaShanah sermons given by rabbis throughout our state had centered not on Israel or Iran, but on the TRUST Act. This was what our congregants were talking about—and what they wanted to hear us talking about.

Governor Brown, a man of deep religious conviction himself, acknowledged that he had been unaware that immigration reform was such an essential issue to his Jewish constituents. Ari quickly responded, "Jews *are* immigrants. We can't do this to immigrant families. This is a straight moral issue for our state. We need you to sign the TRUST Act." I added that I could promise a sweeping demonstration of appreciation from religious voters across the state—not only Jews, but the many other people of faith with whom we had been partnering on this campaign. The governor indicated that he couldn't make any firm commitments to sign a bill on a call of this sort, but he felt that the chances for a positive outcome were strong, and he would bear our words in mind as he continued to work on the matter. Most of all, he expressed his gladness that we had raised and framed this as a moral and religious issue and thanked us for sharing our views with him.

I hung up feeling guardedly optimistic—and then my phone rang just seconds later. It was Ari, calling to ask about the timeline that remained. I explained that the Senate was all but certain to pass the bill that night, and the concurrence vote that would bring the measure to the governor's desk would likely happen within the next two days. At that point, the governor would have approximately four weeks either to sign or veto. Ari stated that he would continue to call the governor every week until he signed the bill. I promised to keep him apprised of developments that could impact the focus of his calls. We also jointly sent a couple of personal letters to the governor during those remaining weeks, summarizing our case for the TRUST Act and reiterating our request for his signature.

On October 5, 2013, Governor Jerry Brown signed the TRUST Act into law. In announcing his decision, he declared, "While Washington waffles on immigration, California's forging ahead. I'm not waiting."[1] Ari and I wrote to the governor to thank him:

> As we indicated throughout this past month, we see your enactment of the TRUST Act as much more than just the fulfillment of a legislative priority. It required a true act of moral courage on your part

to confront the forces of resistance in our state and restore hope to California's three million immigrants. We promised you that California's religious community will long remember your leadership on the TRUST Act. Please know that we will always stand ready to honor that promise by demonstrating the depth and breadth of the support you have engendered from religious Californians with your bold and principled stand for our immigrant brothers and sisters. With tremendous gratitude, Ari Emanuel and Rabbi Ken Chasen.

A couple of weeks later, my family joined Ari and his family for dinner at their home, and we joyfully relived the steps we had taken together. The combination of Ari's access, his passion fueled by his soul-opening religious experience at our services, and my partnership with a state-wide network of activists had proved to be a powerful formula. When Ari enthusiastically said later that evening, "So what do we do next?" I was thrilled.

The last few years, blessedly, have provided us with numerous opportunities to collaborate on direct advocacy with Governor Brown in support of campaigns mobilizing Reform Jews across our state, and in each case, the governor has proceeded to take bold steps in support of some of our Jewish tradition's most cherished ideals. We met with him by phone in June 2014 in connection with Reform CA's successful campaign to ensure that more than $2 billion from the state's cap-and-trade funds would be dedicated to the construction of affordable housing near rail transit. In the fall of 2015, Ari and I spoke with the governor in support of AB 953, a bill he ultimately signed into law, to identify and prevent racial profiling in policing. But perhaps the clearest sign of the strong relationship we had built with Governor Brown came in April 2016, when the governor phoned me to seek my help in mobilizing the Jewish community to amass signatures to get Proposition 57, the Public Safety and Rehabilitation Act, onto the ballot.

What impressed me most in our phone conversation was how the governor framed sentencing reform as a matter of religious justice—Jewish justice, in fact. Said the governor, "There is no greater incentive than freedom." He spoke of *t'shuvah*, our Jewish process of turning toward self-change, and insisted that Proposition 57 would open the gates to that type of growth for countless young nonviolent offenders languishing in prison without any reason even to try to transcend their errant ways. He knew from past experience that California's Jewish voters would be hungry to move our state from the futility of mass incarceration to the humanity of rehabilitation, supervision, and education.

Once again, Ari Emanuel provided the platform for our collective voice to be heard. In the Endeavor conference room, I convened a meeting for Governor Brown with two dozen leading Los Angeles–area rabbis. Our Reform CA coalition adopted the governor's initiative as our 2016 campaign, which brought dozens of our activists to Sacramento to meet with the governor during the final weeks before the election. Proposition 57 passed at the ballot box, bringing fairer sentencing to young Californians needing rehabilitation, not hopelessness.

The growth of my bond with Ari Emanuel and the development of a relationship with Governor Jerry Brown have led to the most meaningful opportunities to achieve social justice I have ever experienced. It all began with a Rosh HaShanah sermon. I will never again wonder whether my hours spent on sermon writing are worthwhile, and neither should any rabbi. After all, our sermons are one of the most effective conduits of communication we have with our congregants, our congregations, and, at times, the broader community. They are a primary form of ongoing adult education for our congregants. They are an essential vehicle through which we bring to bear the perspectives and moral insights of our Jewish tradition to the personal challenges afflicting our congregants and to the great social justice challenges of our society and the world. And sometimes, when all the pieces fall into place, our sermons can literally lead to systemic change in our world. For every state has a governor. Every congregation is a potential phone bank to crash that governor's switchboard. Every community has congregants with relationships to government leaders. Our words from the bimah possess the power to activate them all.

NOTE

1. "Signing Trust Act Is Another Illegal-Immigration Milestone for Brown," *Los Angeles Times*, October 5, 2013.

TOOLS OF RESISTANCE

Interfaith Partnerships

RABBI JOSHUA M. Z. STANTON

I was a twenty-five-year-old rabbinical student when I first saw the power of interfaith partnerships as a tool of resistance. A group of far-right provocateurs were sensationalizing a proposed Muslim community center in Lower Manhattan. They maligned it as a "monster mosque," saying it was "sponsored by al-Qaida" or at best a "Ground Zero mosque" that dishonored Americans who had fallen in 9/11 and the war on terror by its very presence.

The community center's leaders, Imam Feisal Abdul Rauf and Daisy Khan, were progressive Muslims helping to create a truly American brand of Islam, and they served a community that had been a feature of Lower Manhattan for years. I had known this husband-and-wife team for several years and had worked with them periodically to improve interfaith collaboration in our city. They were close colleagues and people I could count on. Yet they were now being smeared as "terrorists" and traitors.

The worst part of these allegations was how hard it was for Imam Rauf and Ms. Khan to prove a negative. They were so far from being anything like terrorists that they did not seem to know where to begin in telling their stories; when they tried, they got little news coverage. The negative coverage was much more exciting to the public in the worst of ways. Saying "I am not a terrorist" is hardly a compelling narrative—and nearly impossible to show. The vicious news stories grew and spawned others; and the situation rapidly spiraled out of control, entering national discourse.

I had never seen anything like it and did not know what to do. Like a dismaying number of progressive religious leaders, I found myself watching in horror and hoping that the dust would settle on its own. I was too afraid to get involved. What would the right-wing fanatics say about me? Could they become violent? I wasn't even a rabbi yet; shouldn't someone else take this issue on?

Days went by, and I received a message from my mentor, Dr. Eboo Patel, executive director of the Interfaith Youth Core. He was in town and wanted to take my friend Frank Fredericks and me out to talk. Sitting together, he told us how incredibly disturbed he was by the situation, most of all because of the deafening silence from natural allies of the community center. Silence from allies was in many ways worse than hate from right-wing extremists. Where were the interfaith partnerships? Where were the leaders? Would the two of us stand up and do something, or would we stay on the sidelines? He said that he would remain in relationship with us either way, but that he thought we had an obligation to stand in solidarity with other people of faith, be they Muslim or of any other tradition.

He was right.

Within a couple of days, Frank and I met with Imam Rauf and Ms. Khan and began writing articles in support of their community center. People were surprised by our pieces, and especially that an evangelical Christian and a future rabbi would stand in support of Muslims—and no less do so together. It challenged the narrative of the Muslim community standing alone or somehow being worthy of suspicion and hate. If we would stand (and write and speak and meet and organize) with Imam Rauf and Ms. Khan, might they not be terrorists after all?

Our efforts grew over time. We had articles translated and published around the world and gave interviews to countless media outlets. We met, called, and cajoled religious leaders across faith communities to join their voices with ours, and we helped convene gatherings of them as well. We attended *iftar* dinners (break-the-fast meals during the Muslim holy month of Ramadan) to make clear that the Muslim community was not alone: and we organized rallies and demonstrations in support of the community center.

Our largest rally, on September 12, 2011, brought together close to one thousand people of faith to stand in support of the community center. One thousand people in a city like New York is not an especially impressive turnout, but for a shoestring operation like ours (literally, two unpaid activists with laptops), we thought it signified a real impact. People in yarmulkes and hijabs, people of all races and gender identities. People in groups and people alone. It was America at its best and felt like a success.

Looking back on it, Frank and I failed to change the story—and failed to significantly change the outcome for our friends. Feisal and Daisy were devastated by the months of being harangued. They saw their dreams dissolve in a wave of in-person and online hatred. The Muslim community felt more isolated than ever before, and many of their leaders felt cornered. As it turned out, the right-wing extremists were incredibly well funded and able to hire professional staff to create rancor with precision.[1] We were outmatched—but not ineffectual.

Our greatest impact was in rallying moderates from across religious traditions and pushing them to reexamine their roles during a moment of such crisis. We helped break the diffusion of responsibility and bolstered the growing ranks of people willing to respond actively and proactively in the future. In joining with other leaders to make clear that hate was not a religiously acceptable value, we conveyed that people who considered themselves religious had an obligation to stand against it, even if it meant personal risk.

Unfortunately, the kind of hate that we stared down with limited success has only grown and become more mainstream. Islamophobia has become a rallying cry for right-wing politicians, including President Trump, who tried in various incarnations and finally succeeded in instituting a partial "Muslim ban" on immigration from many majority-Muslim countries. Antisemitism has made a comeback in both extremes of the political spectrum, most terrifyingly with neo-Nazis marching by the hundreds in Charlottesville. Sikhs (often mistaken for Muslims) have been killed in hate crimes, most horrifyingly during the veritable massacre at the Sikh Temple of Oak Creek, Wisconsin. A white supremacist opened fire at the Emanuel African Methodist Episcopal Church, one of the oldest and most historic black churches in the country. Hate crimes have risen significantly across the board, especially in connection to the 2016 election cycle.[2] The hate focused on the nascent Muslim community center presaged the widespread hatred we hear today from politicians, civic leaders, and extremist media outlets. In spite of these paradigmatic changes, there are some helpful lessons to be gleaned from my first foray into interfaith partnerships as a tool of resistance.

First, we are living in uncharted territory, and that means new demands on lay and clergy leaders. According to Professor Diana Eck of Harvard University, the United States has the world's most religiously diverse society since the fall of the Roman Empire.[3] Historically, such diversity lends itself to friction and division, but that is far from inevitable. Instead, if religious leaders feel an obligation not only to their own religious communities, but also toward each other's, this diversity can foster genuine religious pluralism. If we recognize that when one is under duress, none are truly safe, we all become our brothers' keepers.

Since the civil rights movement (and in a surprising number of cases before it), religious diversity has led to meaningful partnerships around issues of shared concern. If our uniquely diverse society is to thrive, interfaith partnerships cannot merely be a tool of resistance, but need to become an intentional part of our day-to-day existence as religious communities.

Second, we too often wait until a moment of crisis to reach out to lay and clergy leaders from other religious communities. Had Frank and I not known Imam Rauf and Ms. Kahn (and for that matter, each other) personally, it would have been far more difficult to support them in their time of need. Further, the absence of more and deeper relationships between religious leaders contributed to the slow and spotty response time to such a public crisis. If we are not breaking bread, building bridges, or teaching text together, how can we work together effectively when so much more is at stake?

Third, we need not agree on all issues in order to stand in solidarity on some. At times, coalition building can become contentious. It is not always possible to include members of all groups in a given coalition. There are limits to whom we should be willing to join in coalition. Thankfully, we nearly always have choices. A decision not to work with a particular controversial Muslim leader, for example, has little to do with the broader question of whether Jews can actively build coalitions with other Muslim leaders on issues of shared concern. Further, remaining in coalition with challenging allies can sometimes yield positive outcomes and provide more direct ways to address grievances.

In many ways, differences are inherent in interfaith partnerships. We would all be the same religious tradition were it not for disparate worldviews, which in turn lead to disparate senses of need and calls to action. You can protest against each other about American aid to Israel and protest with each other about Islamophobia—and maintain relationships throughout. The growing assumption that we must agree on everything to work together on anything will undermine almost any coalition. Coalitions are inherently diverse but exist due to relationship and shared interests, needs, or beliefs about specific topics. Were I not collaborating with Frank, an evangelical Christian, we would not have been nearly as effective in our efforts to combat Islamophobia. If I agreed with him about everything, I would leave my synagogue and join his church—or vice versa. The key is knowing one's own boundaries, choosing coalition partners accordingly, and using those relationships not only to advance a shared cause, but also to navigate other issues more directly, and civilly.

Fourth, resisting together at moments of great personal or reputational risk can transform relationships. My relationships with Muslim leaders around New York (and beyond) were changed by my advocacy in support of the Muslim community center downtown. They trust me. They know that I will be there for them when it counts, and they know that I expect them to be there for me. In parallel, many other religious leaders (from Episcopalian to Hindu to Humanist) saw how I conducted myself at a time of urgency. The relationships I now have are likely to continue growing through active engagement and more modest forms of mutual support for years to come. Crisis is the testing ground of trust.

Finally, prepare for how you will continue your relationships after a specific set of actions by your coalition. Partnerships go through more active and passive phases. Setbacks or victories can disrupt a steady flow of collaborative engagement. Frank and I had to figure out how we could keep working together even after the controversy surrounding the Muslim community center had passed. Our relationship has continued through our writing, socializing, and working on our respective nonprofit endeavors. Although we have not again worked together on anything of the same magnitude, because of the ongoing mutual investment in our relationship we could get back into action easily if the circumstances called for it.

In this period of social upheaval, interfaith partnerships have gone from advisable to essential. No single religious community is in the majority (when looking at Catholics and mainline Protestants and evangelical Protestants separately), and the growth of the religiously unaffiliated continues to transform the religious landscape. It is difficult if not impossible to advance social causes in isolation, especially for a religious community as small as our own.[4] Whether or not these coalitions are easy to create or sustain, they are indispensable to our pursuit of justice.

NOTES

1. For more, read Wajahat Ali, Eli Clifton, Matthew Duss, Lee Fang, Scott Keyes, and Faiz Shakir, *Fear Inc.: The Roots of the Islamophobia Network in America*, a

report put out by the Center for American Progress, posted August 26, 2011, https://www.americanprogress.org/issues/religion/reports/2011/08/26/10165/fear-inc.

2. *Hate Crimes Statistics 2015*, U.S. Department of Justice—Federal Bureau of Investigation, Fall 2016, https://ucr.fbi.gov/hate-crime/2015/topic-pages/incidentsandoffenses_final.pdf.

3. Diana Eck, *A New Religious America: How a "Christian Country" Has Now Become the World's Most Religiously Diverse Nation* (San Francisco: HarperSanFrancisco, 2002).

4. Estimates vary, but there are probably fewer than six million Jews in the United States. "Jews," in *The Future of World Religions: Population Growth Projections, 2010–2050*, Pew Research Center, April 2, 2015, http://www.pewforum.org/2015/04/02/jews.

THE WORK OF REPAIRING THE WORLD

Resilience and Failing (in Order) to Succeed

Rabbi Sharon Kleinbaum

If you had told me forty years ago—when I was deep in the closet at Barnard—what the world would look like for LGBT people in 2018, I would have asked you just how gullible you thought I was. And yet in the twenty-five years in which I've served as the senior rabbi at Congregation Beit Simchat Torah (CBST), the world's largest LGBT synagogue, and in the years I spent before that as director of congregational relations at the Religious Action Center of Reform Judaism, I've seen our community make tremendous strides toward social justice and equality for LGBT people, strides that my college-age self would have found incredible, in all senses of the word. We've seen the downfall of DOMA. Marriage equality. Trans people in the military. Workplace protections. Housing protections. Friends in all corners.

And how did we do it?

We did it by failing.

Over and over, we failed. We lost in the courts, we lost in the streets and at rallies, we lost in the media, we took what felt like ten steps back for every step forward. And yet, in the end, justice prevailed. We won allies and friends, we changed hearts and minds, and we changed policy.

330 · Moral Resistance and Spiritual Authority

One of the most significant political changes in the American landscape in my lifetime has been the often frustratingly stop-and-start move toward justice and equality for LGBT people—both within American society and within synagogue and Jewish life. These extraordinary changes did not happen by osmosis or because millions of people watched Will kiss Jack on NBC. They happened because LGBT people thoughtfully, passionately, and persistently advocated for change—within Jewish institutions, within the legislatures, and in the courts.

The LGBT world argued endlessly about strategy. We divided, we shouted, we came together again. Should we fight for employment protections, so that LGBT people could no longer be fired simply for being LGBT? Should we focus on marriage equality, which some saw as a basic civil right and some as damaging assimilation? Should we try to ensure that our LGBT siblings in uniform could serve openly? Many argued for support for gays in the military as the biggest bang for our legislative buck; the military is the largest employer in the United States, we could push through change with a single policy, and no one could argue that a serviceman would be threatened by working with a gay person (or so we thought). And so the Campaign for Military Service was formed. Passionate advocates and allies descended on Capitol Hill, lobbied, wrote papers, gave speeches, shouted and persuaded and convinced.

And we got "Don't Ask, Don't Tell."

The perpetual soundtrack of advocacy work is the WHOOMPH of a door slamming in your face. The key to opening those doors—to creating powerful social change—is developing a thick skin and a long view, in resisting the (very human) urge to give in to despair. Defeat and disappointment are not signs that your cause is doomed—they are an integral part of the process. The struggle for marriage equality ultimately triumphed, and I believe that success was the result of an approach both social and political: because we told the stories of our queer lives over and over again, insistently and urgently, and because we formulated a thoughtful and clear strategy to promote change in each state, one at a time. Through internal debates and battles, and opposition from a political climate that worked to convince the world we were second-class citizens and not worth defending, we fought. Each state was encouraged to form its own local organization and focus on local legislatures. Evan Wolfson formed Freedom to Marry, which took a broad, nationally targeted strategy.

In New York, local LGBT rights groups organized days of lobbying in Albany. At CBST, we organized people to join with the larger coalition; advocacy requires numbers, and boy, did we have them. Our community had the passion, but not always the experience, or the language, or the skills. We created training sessions and briefings so that each person felt confident in their knowledge of the issues. We practiced speeches. We wrote talking points.

On June 20, 2011, I went to Albany with Rabbi Ayelet Cohen and others from CBST. We wanted to make sure that "religious" did not become synonymous with "anti-equality," as so many of the loudest voices arguing against marriage at the time claimed to be speaking for God. We visited our elected officials and made our case, telling the deeply personal stories of how inequality had affected our lives.

As we left one building, we found ourselves surrounded by a large group of Chasidic teenage boys and their rabbis. They had bused into Albany to try to convince their representatives that they spoke for all of Judaism and that every Jew opposed LGBT rights and marriage equality. They were out to frighten politicians into believing that they would be alienating an entire bloc of voters if they supported marriage equality.

We were prepared. We had brought signs that made clear that our Judaism, our faith, did support marriage rights. We let them know that all Jews do not speak with one voice and that we as progressive Jews believed strongly that civil marriage should not be determined by religious values—ours or anyone else's. We supported any religious leader's right not to perform a religious ceremony for a same-sex couple but made clear our view that no one has the right to determine civil law based on their religious practice. The legislators needed to hear what we had to say. They were concerned about insulting a major religious group, and our message—that rabbis and observant religious Jews and people of faith supported civil marriage equality—came through loud and clear.

On June 24, 2011, as CBST worshiped at *Kabbalat Shabbat* services, the New York State Legislature voted to make marriage legal in New York State.

Bringing the Tactics of Advocacy to Your Own Community

Advocating for justice is more than a societal imperative. It is a moral requirement, an essential component of Jewish life. *Tzedek, tzedek, tirdof,* "Justice, justice shall you pursue" (Deuteronomy 16:20), is the rallying cry of Judaism everywhere. If we are not working tirelessly to improve the world around us, if we are not raising our voices to call for help in these important causes, if we do not provide both spiritual encouragement and practical direction to those in our community who want to make a difference, we might as well cast off our *kippot* and go home. Justice is not optional.

CBST's location in the center of New York City means that we can never look away from the injustice and poverty that surrounds us. When our congregation assembles for Friday night services, they have passed, just on the way from the subway, people who are homeless, people who are ill, people who are abused, undocumented, underrepresented. Opportunities to serve the cause of justice surround us but can feel endless and insurmountable. If we give the homeless man on the corner the last bill in our pocket, he is still homeless the next day. If we hoist a sign at a rally for paid sick leave for all workers, we may see our efforts blocked by a deep-pocketed politician the next week. We don't always know where to start or how to find a corner to grab. It's easy to feel defeated.

As Jews, called to *tikkun olam,* the repair of the world, we struggle to bring about real, substantive change in a world that was not built for it, that relies on institutional structures that are racist, misogynist, classist, and unconcerned with the needs of our poorest citizens. We may be dedicated, we may keep showing up, but we can't do this alone. Institutional change calls for legislation, the support of powerful and influential players, strategy, and knowledge. It is our job as clergy, lay leaders, organizers, and community members to bridge the gap between the sometimes insular world of the synagogue and the wider world of advocacy outside. We need advocacy to make structural changes and bring about institutional shifts and to bring action to speech. We will fail to solve the global hunger crisis, over and over, but we can help pass laws and policies that begin to gnaw away at it. We can be the beginning.

Kim Bobo, the brilliant Christian social justice activist and former executive director of Interfaith Worker Justice, describes a three-pronged approach to social justice in a faith community setting: educational/liturgical, direct social services, and advocacy. These three essential efforts together make up the basis of our most effective plan for pushing through real change, and it is the job of clergy and congregation together to create and drive programming that speaks to all three. Speakers, classes, and days of learning can be focused toward education on the issues, deepening intellectual understanding; *d'rashot* and prayers can increase awareness and socialize concerns that may not always be obvious to more privileged populations. A social justice coordinator—staff or volunteer—can rally congregants to events and assist those who want to help but don't know how to find the right service project. Clergy can use their voices and their reach to advocate for active change in policies that created the problems in the first place.

Rabbis and their communities may be afraid of "dragging politics" into their synagogues. They may have their plates full, whether with pastoral care and spiritual leadership or with the cares of the world. They may wonder how to marry the needs of the world outside the synagogues with the very pressing and visible needs within them. Rabbis and congregants may be overwhelmed by the needs they see on their doorsteps and not know where to start.

That's fine. As *Pirkei Avot* says, we are not obligated to complete the work of repairing the world, but neither may we desist from beginning it (2:21). It is the role and calling of Jews to find a corner—any corner—within our grasp, and to seize the work before us, undeterred by failure, and to bring their communities with them.

How can you get started?

- **Reach out and deputize.** Rabbis need to be the ignition but need not be the only one driving the bus. Congregational social justice leaders should find those congregants who have experience in influence and in politics, whether that's the White House, the city planner's office, or the PTA. Likely they are already aware of these issues. Work together to get your synagogue invested in the fight.
- **Rally the cavalry.** Many people who would never dream of joining a delegation to the senator's office or making fundraising calls will happily show up for a letter-writing campaign or hold a sign at a rally, if someone who is comfortable being the loud voice will recruit them and lead them there. (Bring pizza. And doughnuts. Praying with your feet is hungry work.)
- **Empower, empower, empower.** In 2015, I joined CBST's delegation, a fleet of CBST regulars, to attend the Religious Action Center's Consultation on Conscience in Washington, DC. Most of them thought of advocacy as something done by well-heeled lobbyists and quick-talking politicians, far outside the reach of ordinary people. We joined other attendees for on-the-spot training, learned context and talking points on a selected list of issues, and split up into teams for a Day of Advocacy, speaking to New York State's representatives about these issues that meant so much to us. The group came away aflame with the power of being taken seriously by their elected representatives and brought that passion into synagogue life.
- **Strengthen and unify the theme.** It takes multiple exposures to an issue before it sinks in. If your passion is hunger abatement, ask your rabbi to include the hungry in your prayers at *Kabbalat*

Shabbat, ask the office manager to post brochures for national food access advocacy groups prominently in synagogue spaces, work with educational leadership to offer programming on the state of hunger in your city by speakers as prominent as you can manage, and volunteer to help the social justice coordinator—staff or volunteer—make calls to organize a monthly group to staff a local soup kitchen. Social justice work should be inseparable from the life of the synagogue and inextricable from the day-to-day conversation. You may fail many times at keeping this theme prominent in your congregation. Keep going.

- **Don't be afraid of the language of morality.** Too many strong, important phrases have been co-opted by political causes with a knack for clever framing. Phrases like "right to life," "right to work," "the moral majority," and so forth have made progressive leaders and organizers shy about using the language of ethics and morality to rally their troops, relying instead on self-conscious language that can neither offend nor convince. Don't hold back from calling out what is right—and what is not right. Forty percent of New York City's homeless youth are LGBTQ, and many have engaged in survival sex. Sixteen million American children have inadequate nutrition. This is wrong. This is unjust. Don't be afraid to say so.

- **Call upon your influential contacts.** You may have a reach beyond your shul. Don't be afraid to call on contacts in the secular world to help advance your cause.

- **Don't give up.** Failure is part of the process. Learn from it and move on.

The roots of poverty and inequality are deep, but the roots of our obligation to pursue justice are deeper. If we act strategically and thoughtfully, if we are committed, we can work with and alongside our elected lawmakers, like-minded lobbyists, and allies to change the world. If we take failure in stride and view our defeats as just one more step in the long march toward justice, who can stop us?

CREATING YOUNG STAKEHOLDERS IN THE PURSUIT OF SOCIAL JUSTICE

Rabbi Michael Namath

The recent decision to rename the Program Department of the Religious Action Center of Reform Judaism to "Leadership Development" was far more than a semantic change. It reflects the evolution of how we engage Reform Jews and the broader world in our work—including teens, lay leadership, cantors, and rabbis—to create a world in which all people feel wholeness, justice, and compassion. Our goal is to create leaders within the Reform Movement who can work within their communities and with outside partners to create the world we want. Through programs that match the age and interest level of individuals, we work to infuse Jewish values with tools for making systemic change. This chapter will explore just a few of these programs as examples and will offer ideas about what makes these effective methods of training future Jewish leaders, in particular our teens and young adults.

Kesef, Koach, Politica: Creating Teen Stakeholders in the Political Process

At the heart of the RAC's approach to education is a combination of experiential learning alongside more traditional transmission of information by experts. The exemplar of this model is the "Kesef, Koach, Politika" program, which has long been the centerpiece of the Bernard and Audre Rappaport L'Taken Social Justice Seminar for teens. L'Taken is a weekend social justice and Jewish values program that brings over two thousand people a year to Washington, DC, for an intensive educational experience. Kesef, Koach, Politika—known as KKP—focuses on how people and companies with huge sums of money distort the political process.

KKP attempts to blend Jewish values, learning about the role of money in politics, and timely policy issues into a two-hour program that engages as many as five hundred students in each weekend. Students are divided into two teams that represent the two major sides on a given policy issue; past topics have included gun rights, climate change, energy production, the minimum wage, and conflict minerals. Climate change, for example, pitted environmental advocates against the coal industry; the minimum wage topic had businesses and low-wage workers face off. The two sides are responsible for advocating either for or against a real piece of legislation—using various advocacy tools to convince three chaperones who act as "senators" to vote their side's desired way.

After the students split into two teams, they are then divided into various task forces that represent different methods of political engagement. Students work on lobbying, letter writing, social media, phone calls, fundraising, TV advertising, and demonstration task forces, each group representing the many forms of political engagement that people in the real world utilize to achieve positive social change. Each of the two teams receives a certain amount of money—as well as a maximum amount of money they can raise—to fund their operations. They work to persuade the chaperones who act as senators, and by the end of the program, students have learned some of the tools they can use in advocating for a social justice cause or even for just a change in their school's policy. Though the medium might be a phone call, an acted-out TV ad, or raising money from a "wealthy donor," the students begin to understand the basic tools of creating and presenting an effective advocacy ask.

What makes KKP a unique experience involves not only the skills students develop as part of the program, but also the lesson about the larger system. The two teams in the program return to the main ballroom, where the "senators" sit to consider the two sides' advocacy efforts. Students perform their "TV" ads, get critiqued on their letter writing, social media, and lobbying efforts, and break out into cheers supporting their respective sides. Just before the senators vote, a "surprise" TV ad plays on the screen—funded by a shadowy, outside Super PAC—that advocates for the side favored by major corporations and businesses. Soon after, the senators vote—and the "big money" side wins every time.

The students cheer and boo loudly after the senators announce their decision. The students chant "kill the bill," "coal, coal, coal—it's good for the soul," "JRA [Jewish Rifle Association]—don't take our guns away," and more. The RAC legislative assistants running the program then make another major announcement: the entire program was rigged. The team that represented the "big business" interest had more and very well organized money—not only making it easier for their team to support the senators' PAC, but also allowing them to pay for more TV ads, social media posts, and phone calls. The students from the small-money side groan in disappointment, upset that the system was rigged against them from the beginning, making it almost impossible for their side to prevail. Students then listen to brief explanations from RAC legislative assistants about the role of money in politics, as well as about how it affects the issue their simulation addressed.

One student, Sarah, arrived at L'Taken already passionate about gun violence prevention. One of her classmates, a fifteen-year-old freshman, was shot and killed after being mistaken for someone else during his second week of high school. Sarah understood gun violence viscerally and personally. During the KKP program, she and other participants crafted clever slogans and made phone calls to their "senators" to advocate for legislation to prevent gun violence. But once she learned at the end of the program that the "pro-gun group" was given more money from the beginning of the program, she began to understand why her opponents were able to air more commercials, buy more posters, and conduct more lobby visits. And she also began to understand why it was so hard to advocate for gun law changes, with groups like the NRA using money to influence politicians.

Sarah used this anger to fuel a passionate speech when she went to Capitol Hill on Monday. Sarah did not have the money to offer politicians a contribution; instead she knew her power emanated from her personal connection to gun violence. While writing her speech, Sarah discussed her friend's death and how it impacted her. She had the opportunity to speak directly with Representative Jan Schakowsky, who affirmed her position and told her that it was stories like her own that helped her advocate tirelessly for gun violence prevention legislation. Sarah left her lobby visit knowing that while she had not solved the problem, she had made a step in the right direction.

Sarah's story demonstrates how the L'Taken experience often feels like a swinging pendulum for our participants. Sarah came to L'Taken excited to learn more about gun-related legislation and to advocate for change. She soon learned that the issue was far more complex than she imagined and that special interest groups have an outsized influence on legislation. But that did not deter her from speaking out and using the power she did have to make a difference.

KKP is at the heart of the L'Taken experience largely because of the intended response it inevitably provokes. Students are upset because they put in two hours of hard work to convince the senators of their position, only to be told that the game was rigged and their hard work did little to change the outcome. Perhaps this is counterintuitive, but the sense of failure students feel is much more powerful than an illusion of success. While it would be nice for students to feel that the "good" side always wins, they feel far more motivated to act for justice when they see just how difficult it can be to compete with monied special-interest lobbies. It underscores the importance of organized people when going up against organized money.

KKP is also unique because of the larger context in which L'Taken takes place. KKP takes place on the Saturday of a four-day weekend. On Monday, students ascend Capitol Hill, meeting with members of Congress and their staff to deliver prepared speeches on policy issues of their choosing. The sense of failure they feel during KKP is often mirrored by the disappointments they feel on the Hill. Students complain that at times the Hill staffers weren't listening to them, that they were unable to convince their member of Congress to support their chosen legislation, or that they were disregarded because of their age. Many of the same students, at the exact same moment, are still struck by the awesome power of walking through the halls of Congress. They are excited that they were able to walk into their senator's or representative's office and are treated like they belong. Students are able to use their personal passion and transform it into action.

Teens are able to sniff out the phoniness in programs that offer simple solutions or quick fixes. L'Taken forces students to wrestle with the political process as a tension between power and helplessness, success and failure. Without the reality of failure, students would have no compulsion to continue to work for justice. The desire to overcome the challenges of being a teen advocating for social change, of special interests distorting democratic ideals, and of a deeply partisan Congress makes students want to continue to engage with the issues we discuss.

In other words, L'Taken is about transforming students into stakeholders in the world they wish to create. It is important that they develop skills of lobbying and learn about major public policy issues of the day. But the overriding value that L'Taken provides is a value that can be re-created by any program that makes students feel a sense of ownership in the larger structures that impact their lives. That begins with the sense of helplessness they may feel at the end of KKP. It is reinforced when they learn about the policy details of major issues of the day—whether gun violence prevention, health care, or reproductive rights. And it is strongest when they exit Capitol Hill, imbued with the skills to make a difference and a zeal for overcoming the challenges that stand in justice's way.

Machon Kaplan: The Daily Challenges of Justice

If L'Taken is about helping students feel like owners of the political process, Machon Kaplan offers a sense of the daily challenges that come with pursuing justice. Machon Kaplan offers college students the chance to come to Washington, DC, for six weeks during the summer and be placed in an internship at one of the RAC's coalition partners. Students who are accepted into the program live with other participants in a college residence hall and attend professional and leadership development classes at the RAC and around the city.

The students' internship experiences vary widely in terms of the type of work they do, the organization in which they are placed, and the people they work with. Students intern with labor unions, research institutes, Jewish and secular groups, and many more. The placements include the National Council of Jewish Women, the NAACP Washington office, and the Food Research and Action Center. Despite the variety of internship locations, the students are united by the lessons they learn about the difficulty of pursuing justice as a profession. For some, this includes an understanding that justice-seeking groups also need people who scan documents and stuff folders. Others begin to accept that even the most prominent and well-connected organizations have difficulty persuading decision-makers to do what they want.

One student learned firsthand that even working in her field of interest would involve setbacks and disappointments. Part of her responsibility included organizing documents and catering for summer events. However, she understood the importance of doing so: "This helped my bosses focus on issues that were less menial. I focused on the details, so they didn't have to." Some students would think of the experience as a reason to pursue a different path or work at a different organization. However, because her internship also included opportunities to attend interesting events and rallies, she saw firsthand how being responsible for "menial" tasks worked within the larger picture of making change:

> The key learnings on leadership I learned are that you don't make change alone. A lot of the time we hear about these prominent civil rights leaders and we only hear one name. We forget they had an army of people behind them, supporting them, working with them, doing the hard work in order to create change.

Internship programs like Machon Kaplan are common—especially in DC—but the opportunity to learn about Jewish values and tradition, live with other Jewish students interested in social justice, and live in the center of American political life makes Machon Kaplan unique. Students cannot help but think about how Jewish values relate to the issue they are working on, because they talked about it with their fellow participants the night before. The students also feel deeply connected to the political process when they are living within a mile of the White House.

Some students did not conceive that Judaism could include the type of social justice work the RAC undertakes. Sam, a recent Machon Kaplan alumna, had grown up in a community that volunteered frequently at a soup kitchen. Sam was inspired by these efforts but believed this was the extent to which Jewish communal institutions created changed. Sam observed:

> I had no way of seeing how Jewish organizers and activists doing the big-picture work fit into the puzzle until I came to the RAC and met Jewish professionals sitting on the boards of major organizations, not to mention directing them. I had known Jewish professionals . . . but I had never met a Jewish professional fighting for reproductive rights or racial justice. Now I have, and my ideas about what I can do with my Judaism as I enter the workforce have expanded. My religion doesn't have to be a part of my life that I keep separate from everything else, reserved only for Friday nights and special occasions. I can infuse it into whatever career path I end up going down. And that's exactly what I intend to do.

The RAC's infrastructure gives the students opportunities to visit the White House, meet with members of Congress, and have regular lunches with RAC staff. These exciting pieces of the program help the students feel reenergized even as many of them are adjusting to a nine-to-five work schedule for the first time in their lives. The students also benefit from professional development sessions with guest speakers who discuss networking, the tools of community organizing, and leadership development.

In this sense, Machon Kaplan fuses together elements of Jewish summer camp, professional social justice training, and academic learning. Each of these aspects is critical for developing future Jewish social justice leaders. Following the program, some students go into the Jewish professional world, others pursue careers in nonprofits, while many students opt for something entirely unrelated. While we are delighted that some students choose Jewish or social justice paths, the beauty of Machon Kaplan is that it is a training for how to balance Jewish, professional, and social justice interests. Students begin to understand how these aspects of life need to be in balance with their personal interests, and these new experiences help them as they develop that understanding. The fact that they can do so in a relatively controlled and safe environment is a necessary bridge for the even more challenging decisions they will have to make later in life. Like L'Taken, much of what makes Machon Kaplan successful is students realizing the amount of work that is necessary for living the lives and creating the world they desire. As a spouse of another hard-working rabbi and parent of three, I can empathize.

Eisendrath Legislative Assistant Fellowship

No RAC program better trains young Jewish leaders than the Eisendrath Legislative Assistant Fellowship. The fellowship brings recent college graduates to Washington, DC, to participate in every aspect of the RAC's work—from policy research, coalition building, community organizing, programming for youth seminars, and more. RAC legislative assistants (LAs) are well known across the Reform Movement. They are the first point of contact for rabbis across North America seeking assistance with policy issues or looking for useful resources. Many graduates of the program have also gone on to serve in important roles in the movement as rabbis, cantors, and lay leaders, and far beyond in government, policy making, law, and nonprofits.

As discussed with L'Taken and Machon Kaplan, the Eisendrath Fellowship owes much of its effectiveness to giving young people the agency to make the change they seek. L'Taken students are given the sense of being a stakeholder necessary to make change and are introduced to the knowledge and skills they need to make a difference. Machon Kaplan students learn many of these skills but have only a short period of time to utilize them. The LA program allows young people to put these skills to test.

The LA program is unique in a city full of worthwhile internships and fellowships because of the level of autonomy the fellows have in their daily work. As in other programs, LAs write policy memos, draft speeches, and assist in our programming. But RAC LAs serve as the face of the organization during their interactions with partner groups. They represent the RAC at coalition meetings, routinely lobby members of Congress and their staff, recruit Reform Jews to participate in campaigns, and educate L'Taken and Machon Kaplan students. Many LAs reflect that it is not until many years after the program that they are given the same power to determine their schedule, priorities, and strategies.

Being an LA at the RAC gives a very small group of people a true sense of the challenges and excitement of working for social justice in DC and within the Jewish community. And the LAs give the RAC a set of fresh eyes and a deeper understanding of the interests and priorities of young Jewish leaders. It is because of these young people that the Reform Movement became the first major religious denomination to publicly proclaim its support for transgender people when the CCAR passed the resolution "The Rights of Transgender and Gender Non-Conforming Individuals" in March 2015, followed by a resolution at the 2015 URJ Biennial Convention. The LAs not only helped shape the policy, but also put this resolution into practice through a campaign

346 · Moral Resistance and Spiritual Authority

that is focused on protecting the rights of transgender students in public schools.

All of these programs involving teens and young adults carry with them risks. Not surprisingly, high school students who participate in L'Taken sometimes make statements that we would rather they not share. With Machon Kaplan, asking our coalition partners to take college students into their organizations as interns carries some uncertainty as well. And the LA program is a risk for the RAC as well—allowing recent college graduates to represent the organization after only a two-week orientation sets up many potential challenges. But these risks are taken because the rewards far outweigh the challenges, and in the end, the young people feel a sense of ownership that is critical for their continuing to be part of the broader social justice mission.

The objectives of these programs are not only short-term. The RAC's mission is determined by centuries of Jewish values and traditions that inform our desire to create a more just world. This cannot be accomplished in one weekend of a L'Taken seminar, or six weeks of a Machon Kaplan experience, or even a year of an LA fellowship. But the thousands of students who have gone through L'Taken, Machon Kaplan, and the Eisendrath Fellowship are trained with the real-world experience of learning how difficult it is to achieve social justice. The alumni of these programs are now serving in leadership roles in their communities, congregations, and the Reform Movement as a whole. They are the members of the Commission on Social Action. They are rabbis who use the skills and experiences the RAC gave them to better bring social justice to the center of their congregations. They work for non-Jewish nonprofits and bring the knowledge of the importance of coalition building to their work. They devote their time and resources to the work the RAC does because of their desire to be part of Reform Judaism's movement to make a more compassionate world.

The most exciting part of the RAC's work today is the strong engagement of young people and congregants in states across the country to work toward social justice. Many of the RAC's youth programs are focused on bringing students to Washington, DC, to allow them to experience the excitement the city has to offer. This sense of ownership that is at the heart of our youth leadership development can be cultivated anywhere regardless of geography.

What is needed is an opportunity in which students can make positive change if they work hard. Visiting a state capitol can do this, as can attending a city council meeting or school board meeting and speaking out in favor of a new policy. It can also happen when students make changes in their temple youth groups or synagogue to better reflect Jewish social justice values. While the RAC's youth leadership development opportunities have often focused on the federal level, the lessons learned can easily be transferred to any level of government or even non-government institutions.

On the first day the legislative assistants arrive every year, they study the Talmudic text that asks, "Which is greater—study or action?" (*Kiddushin* 40b). Those who are familiar with the text know that the Talmudic rabbis conclude that the answer is study, because it can lead to action. When discussing the passage with the LAs, they provide a variety of responses. One year an LA argued that action was greater, because it leads to study. Others have argued that they see study and action as constantly working to inform one another. Study does indeed lead to action, but so too action leads to study. Action can be a laboratory for how to best work for the justice we are pursuing. Each year, the various interpretations of the texts provide a reminder of the most important lesson of all: that allowing the students to take the reins will make their work better, will enhance the Reform Movement's work, and will, one day, repair our world.

AFTERWORD

A Note on Shabbat:
Reflection, Evaluation, and Celebration

RABBI SETH M. LIMMER, DHL AND
RABBI JONAH DOV PESNER

Sister Judy Donovan is a supremely talented community organizer based in California. She has devoted her life to teaching faith leaders to build relationships across lines of difference, organize their communities, and build power to make concrete political change for the common good. Among the many lessons she taught us is how important it is, while we are organizing our faith communities to pursue justice, to pause on a regular basis to reflect, evaluate, and celebrate. The work can be exhausting. Campaigns can seem endless, the setbacks insurmountable. Sister Judy understands that by reflecting regularly and in community, we are able to learn from one another and to continue to grow. She also understands that by evaluating, we hold ourselves accountable to our shared goal. There is too much at stake to be self-satisfied because we are busy and exhausted. We will win only when we step back and assess what we accomplished and how we achieved our accomplishments. Perhaps even more importantly, such reflection can help us learn from our failures and ensure we will be successful in the future. Finally, Sister Judy understands that without joy we will starve. Though we may be in part motivated by outrage of all that which is broken and all those who suffer, we can only sustain ourselves and one another when we rejoice together. That is why when we pursue justice, we must sing. And dance. And celebrate.

Years ago, Jonah expressed his frustration to Sister Judy: his synagogue does not spend enough time reflecting, evaluating, and celebrating, because everybody always seems to rush from program to program and activity to activity. At that moment, Sister Judy reacted in a very surprising way. She shared that one of the many aspects she loves about Judaism is the way in which the elements of reflection, evaluation, and celebration are built into the very liturgical rhythm of Jewish life. Six days we work, she reminded us; on the Seventh Day, we rest. We reflect. We evaluate. And we rejoice. In the opening verses of Genesis, God models behavior for us human beings, created in the divine image: by stepping back from labor, observing that which is created, and reflecting on its goodness.

These pages do not mark the end of a campaign for justice, but of a book about justice and Judaism.

Let us pause for a Sabbath of sorts and spare a few words of reflection, evaluation, and celebration.

Reflecting back on this book, the overwhelming sense we editors share is pride mingled with amazement. Our colleagues—leaders of the Jewish people—are tremendous resources, teachers, leaders, and human beings. Even as we remain amazed at all we have read, we still wish we could have included countless others. And we lament in much pain that between the inception of this book and its seeing the light of print, we needed to add the words *zichronam liv'rachah* next to the names of two cherished colleagues: Rabbi Lynne F. Landsberg was an inspirational teacher to both of us. In her later years, she taught incredible lessons of perseverance, and in all of her years she modeled how to be an advocate for justice. Rabbi Aaron Panken was a friend, mentor, jokester, lunch date, dinner guest, and a national partner to both of us from our teenage years. We miss them both more than words can capture.

The evaluation of this book is not about the countless collaborative hours contributed to writing, editing, proofing, introducing, preparing, and pre-selling, although those were wonderful and benefited from the generosity of so many, foremost among all the professional staff of CCAR Press. In fact, the evaluation of this book cannot be printed in this book at all: the ultimate value of the words on these pages are *what you, the reader, do with them. If you, in your own way, go out and change our world for the better because of the lessons encountered between these covers, that would be the highest evaluation it could ever receive.*

Evaluation incomplete, we nonetheless turn to celebration. The voices collected in this book unite in a collective call to divine service. They remind us of the Jewish obligation to pursue justice. They ground that obligation in Jewish texts, values, and experiences. They offer practical lessons, tools, and guidelines for a generation who takes its place in this moment. But let us not forget the importance of pausing to reflect, even as we redouble our efforts. Let us not forget every seventh day we rejoice and call it a delight . . . Let us pause, at this moment, to celebrate. Refreshed and with new spirit, we will then go change our world.

CONTRIBUTORS

Rabbi Seth M. Limmer, DHL, serves as senior rabbi of Chicago Sinai Congregation. During his rabbinate he has served as chair of the Justice, Peace, and Civil Liberties Committee of the Central Conference of American Rabbis, as vice chair of the Union for Reform Judaism's Commission on Social Action, as dean of faculty for Eisner and Crane Lake Camps, and as a member of the Board of Trustees of the CCAR. On behalf of Chicago Sinai Congregation's lead role in organizing the Reform Movement's participation in the NAACP's 2015 America's Journey for Justice, Rabbi Limmer accepted the Rabbi Maurice Eisendrath Bearer of Light Award, the highest honor of the URJ. He is the author of many articles, and 2016 saw the publication of his first full-length book, *Medieval Midrash: The House for Inspired Innovation*.

Rabbi Jonah Dov Pesner serves as the director of the Religious Action Center of Reform Judaism, in Washington, DC. He has led the Religious Action Center since 2015 and also serves as senior vice president of the Union for Reform Judaism, a position to which he was appointed to in 2011. Named one of the most influential rabbis in America by *Newsweek* magazine, he is an inspirational leader and tireless advocate for social justice. Rabbi Pesner serves as a board member of the National Association for the Advancement of Colored People (NAACP), the Leadership Conference on Civil and Human Rights, JOIN for Justice, the National Religious Partnership for the Environment, and the New England Center for Children. He is a member of the Leadership Team for the Jewish Social Justice Round-table and has served as a scholar for the Wexner Foundation, American Jewish World Service, the Nexus USA Summit, and Combined Jewish Philanthropies, among others.

Rabbi David Saperstein currently serves as the senior advisor for Strategy and Policy for the Union for Reform Judaism. For decades, Rabbi Saperstein directed the Religious Action Center of Reform Judaism, representing the Reform Jewish Movement to Congress and the Administration. For over two years, Rabbi Saperstein served our nation as the U.S. Ambassador at Large for International Religious Freedom, carrying out his responsibilities as the country's chief diplomat on religious freedom issues. He is also an attorney and has taught seminars on church-state law and Jewish law for thirty-five years at Georgetown University Law Center and currently serves as a senior fellow at both the Georgetown University's Berkley Center for Religion, Peace and World Affairs and its School of Foreign Service's Center for Jewish Civilization.

Reverend Cornell William Brooks is the visiting professor of ethics, law, and justice movements at Boston University School of Theology and Boston University School of Law; a senior fellow at the Brennan Center of Justice at New York University Law School; a visiting fellow and director of the Campaigns and Advocacy Program at the Institute of Politics at Harvard Kennedy School; a visiting research scholar at Yale Law School; a regular contributor to CNN; and a former president and CEO of the NAACP.

***

Rabbi Mona Alfi is the spiritual leader for Congregation B'nai Israel in Sacramento, California. Concurrent with her work at B'nai Israel, she has served as the chaplain of the California State Assembly and the California State Senate, was a member of the Bioethics Committee at Sutter General Hospital, was on the Commission on Social Action (CSA) as a representative of the Central Conference of American Rabbis, and is on the leadership team for the California Religious Action Center of Reform Judaism (RAC-CA). She received Truah's Rabbinic Human Rights Hero Award in 2017 for her work on marriage equality and immigrant justice.

Rabbi Erica Seager Asch worked as a community organizer with the Industrial Areas Foundation after ordination. She currently serves as the rabbi of Temple Beth El in Augusta, Maine, and assistant director of the Center for Small Town Jewish Life. She is active in the local community, most recently working with the Capital Area New Mainers Project to welcome immigrants and refugees to the Capital Area. Rabbi Asch serves on the Board of Trustees of the Central Conference of American Rabbis.

Rabbi Ken Chasen is senior rabbi of Leo Baeck Temple in Los Angeles. He is a leading activist and prolific author on a wide variety of social justice matters in the United States and in Israel, with writings appearing in numerous books and print and digital media publications. Rabbi Chasen is also the co-author of two books that guide Jewish families in the creation of meaningful Jewish rituals in the home. In addition, he is a nationally recognized composer whose original liturgical and educational works are regularly heard in synagogues, religious schools, Jewish camps, and sanctuaries across North America, in Israel, and in Europe.

Rabbi Jonathan Cohen, PhD, an Israeli-born scholar, is the senior rabbi at The Temple-Tifereth Israel in Beachwood, Ohio, having served previously as associate professor in Talmud and halachic literature at Hebrew Union College–Jewish Institute of Religion and as dean of the Cincinnati campus. He was appointed assistant professor in Talmud and halachic literature in July 1998 and as director of the Hebrew Union College–University of Cincinnati Center for the Study of Ethics and Contemporary Moral Problems in January 2000. In November 2003, he was awarded the Rabbi Michael Matuson Professorship for Emerging Scholars, and he was named affiliate member of the Laboratoire Des etudes sur les Monothéismes of the French CNRS (National Center for Scientific Research) in August 2005. He was appointed dean of the Cincinnati campus in September 2011 and ordained a rabbi in 2012.

Rabbi Shoshanah Conover is an associate rabbi at Temple Sholom of Chicago. She is a senior rabbinic fellow of the Shalom Hartman Institute and serves on the Executive Committee of the Chicago Board of Rabbis as well as the Rabbinic, Educator, Cantorial Advisory Committee (RECC) of Olin Sang Ruby Union Institute (OSRUI). Rabbi Conover enjoys co-hosting a podcast on Jewish and Israeli film called *The Chosen Films* and is grateful to work in and for a community in which she is proud to raise her two sons, Eli and Ben, with her husband, Damien.

Rabbi Marla J. Feldman, a Reform rabbi and a lawyer, is the executive director of Women of Reform Judaism (WRJ). Working in the headquarters of the Reform Movement for over fifteen years, she served previously as the director of development and the director of the Commission on Social Action of Reform Judaism. Prior to that, Rabbi Feldman worked in the Jewish community relations field, serving the Detroit and Delaware communities, where she also taught as adjunct faculty at the University of Detroit–Mercy and the Widener University College of Law in Wilmington, Delaware. She has authored Reform Movement action manuals, published modern midrash in several collections, and written articles and Op-Eds for numerous publications and newspapers.

Rabbi Edwin Goldberg, DHL, is the senior rabbi of Temple Sholom of Chicago. He has published numerous articles and books and served as coordinating editor of the new Reform High Holy Day prayer book, *Mishkan HaNefesh*.

Rabbi Lisa D. Grant, PhD, is director of the Rabbinical Program and professor of Jewish education at Hebrew Union College–Jewish Institute of Religion in New York. Her research and teaching interests focus on adult Jewish learning, Jewish leadership development, and the place of Israel in American Jewish life. In addition to numerous articles, book chapters, and curriculum guides, Rabbi Grant is co-author with Ezra Kopelowitz of *Israel Education Matters: A 21st Century Paradigm for Jewish Education*. She is also co-editor of *The International Handbook of Jewish Education* with Helena Miller and Alex Pomson, and with Diane T. Schuster, Meredith Woocher, and Steven M. Cohen, *A Journey of Heart and Mind: Transformative Jewish Learning in Adulthood*.

Rabbi Rachel Greengrass, MARR, RJE, MAHL, believes Judaism nourishes and gives life meaning. She is deeply committed to *tikkun olam* and has brought this holy work to her congregation, Temple Beth Am, in Miami, as well as to the URJ. Rabbi Greengrass is a Rabbis Without Borders Fellow, Balfour/Brickner fellow, VP of the Miami board of Rabbis, and serves on the CCAR responsa committee.

Hilly Haber is a fifth-year rabbinical student at Hebrew Union College–Institute of Jewish Religion in New York City. She holds a master of theological studies from Harvard Divinity School and a BA from Mount Holyoke College. She recently got married to Rabbi Rachel Marder.

Rabbi Rick Jacobs is the president of the Union for Reform Judaism (URJ), the largest Jewish movement in North America, with almost 900 congregations and nearly 1.5 million members. An innovative thought leader, dynamic visionary, and representative of progressive

Judaism, he spent 20 years as the spiritual leader of Westchester Reform Temple in Scarsdale, New York. Prior to his tenure at WRT, Rabbi Jacobs served the Brooklyn Heights Synagogue, where he founded and co-directed the first synagogue-based homeless shelter in New York City. Deeply dedicated to global social justice issues and the State of Israel, he has led disaster response efforts in Haiti and Darfur, and has studied for two decades at Jerusalem's Shalom Hartman Institute, where he is a senior rabbinic fellow.

Ilana Kaufman is the director of the Jews of Color Field Building Initiative, a national effort focused on building and advancing the professional, organizational, and communal field for Jews of Color. Framed by the concepts of Racial Justice and Equity as well as centering the voices and experiences of Jews of Color, the Initiative is dedicated to grant making, research and field building, and community education. As a guest on NPR's *Code Switch*, with pieces featured in eJewish Philanthropy and *The Foundation Review*, and an Eli Talk titled "Who Counts? Race and the Jewish Future" with more than 16,000 views, Ilana is passionate about all things at the intersection of Jewish Community/Racial Justice/Jews of Color/Education/Philanthropy. Kaufman, a Schusterman Fellow who is always searching Jewish text for discussion of equity and justice, received her BA in Sociology from California State University-Humboldt and her MA in Educational Pedagogy from Mills College.

Rabbi Sharon Kleinbaum serves as spiritual leader of Congregation Beit Simchat Torah in Manhattan. She was installed as CBST's first rabbi in 1992, arriving at the height of the AIDS crisis when the synagogue was in desperate need of pastoral care and spiritual leadership. She guided the congregation through a period of loss and change, while addressing social issues of the day and building a strong and deeply spiritual community. Under her leadership as senior rabbi, CBST has become a powerful voice in the movement for equality and justice for people of all sexual orientations, gender identities, and expressions and a significant force challenging the radical right's dominance over religious and political life in the United States and around the world. *Newsweek* ranked Rabbi Kleinbaum among the fifty most influential rabbis in America. She has been honored by dozens of religious and secular institutions for her social justice work. Recently Rabbi Kleinbaum has led her community to be a bold spiritual community of resistance and love. Rabbi Kleinbaum's synagogue is a member of the New Sanctuary Coalition working daily to support immigrants, Muslims, and other targeted communities.

Rabbi Stephanie Kolin is a rabbi at Central Synagogue in Manhattan and an Auburn Seminary senior fellow. Her rabbinic journey began at Temple Israel in Boston and continued as she served as co-director of the Union for Reform Judaism's Just Congregations, formerly the community organizing arm of the Reform Movement, and lead organizer and a founder of Reform CA, a statewide campaign for a more just and compassionate California. Stephanie was named as a "Game Changer" by the *Los Angeles Jewish Journal*, one of *Newsweek*'s "Rabbis to Watch," and one of the *Forward*'s "America's Influential Women Rabbis." Stephanie now lives in New York City with her wife and their daughter.

Rabbi Lynne F. Landsberg, *z"l,* was one of the American Jewish community's best-known, most eloquent, and beloved social justice advocates. As associate director of the Religious Action Center, and then a regional director for the Union for Reform Judaism, she was a respected and influential leader in civil rights, reproductive rights, and interfaith relations. Following a long recovery from a traumatic brain injury, Rabbi Landsberg refocused her efforts on disability rights, serving as senior advisor on disability rights for the Reform Movement and playing a key role in mobilizing the religious community generally and the Jewish community more particularly to address issues of accessibility in religious life, including co-founding the Jewish Disability Network and playing a key role in establishing Jewish Disability Awareness and Inclusion Month. The first graduate degree student from Harvard Divinity School to become a rabbi, Lynne worked under the renowned theologian Harvey Cox, who said of her, "Of the hundreds, maybe thousands, of students I have taught over more than four decades at Harvard, she stands out and is in a class of her own."

Rabbi Emily Langowitz joined the clergy staff at Temple Solel in Paradise Valley, Arizona, in July 2017. A native of Wellesley, Massachusetts, Rabbi Langowitz received a master of Hebrew letters and was ordained by Hebrew Union College–Jewish Institute of Religion in New York in 2017. She completed a bachelor's degree in Modern Hebrew at Yale University in 2012. Rabbi Langowitz is driven in her rabbinic work by a commitment to Jewish learning, building community, and the pursuit of interfaith partnerships and social justice.

Rabbi John A. Linder was ordained by Hebrew Union College–Jewish Institute of Religion in 2003 and has served as senior rabbi of Temple Solel in Paradise Valley, Arizona, since 2008. Among other leadership roles, John is active in the Valley Interfaith Project and serves on the board of the Southwest Industrial Area Foundation's Interfaith Education Fund. Rabbi Linder sees his role as spiritual leader to inspire and engage his community to serve as messengers of peace and justice through the enduring wisdom of Torah.

Rabbi Jill L. Maderer has served Congregation Rodeph Shalom in Philadelphia since her ordination from Hebrew Union College–Jewish Institute of Religion in 2001 and since 2017 has served as its senior rabbi, the first woman to hold that position. A graduate of Brandeis University, she grew up in New Jersey, where her Jewish life was shaped by her family and her hometown congregation, Temple Emanu-El of Westfield. She lives in Philadelphia with her husband, Len, and their children, Moshe and Pria.

Rabbi Edythe (Edie) Held Mencher, LCSW, serves as Union for Reform Judaism faculty for Sacred Caring Community and is director of the URJ Presidential Initiative for Disabilities Inclusion. In her role as director of the URJ Ruderman Disabilities Inclusion Initiative, she helped to create the online learning site www.disabilitiesinclusion.org. She writes and consults regularly on disability rights and inclusion, on mental health, and on helping children and adults to find support and resilience when confronting difficult personal and communal events.

Ruth W. Messinger is currently the inaugural global ambassador for American Jewish World Service (AJWS), the international human rights organization that she led for eighteen years. She is also the inaugural Finkelstein Institute social justice fellow at the Jewish Theological Seminary of America and the social justice activist in residence at the Marlene Meyerson Jewish Community Center in Manhattan. In these positions Messinger is engaging rabbis, interfaith leaders, and lay activists to take action on behalf of oppressed and persecuted communities domestically and globally. She previously spent twenty years in public service in New York City, and she is married to an educator and has three children, eight grandchildren, and two great-grandchildren.

Rabbi Adam F. Miller currently serves as the senior rabbi at Temple Shalom in Naples, Florida, having previously served Temple Beth Am in Framingham, Massachusetts, and Temple Beth El of Northern Westchester in Chappaqua, New York. A graduate of the University of Kansas, Rabbi Miller was ordained by Hebrew Union College–Jewish Institute of Religion in 2003. A passionate advocate for social justice, Rabbi Miller is a board member at Meals of Hope, is a Brickner Fellow, and spent more than ten years on both the Commission for Social Action of the Union for Reform Judaism and the Central Conference of American Rabbi's Justice, Peace, and Liberties Committee. Rabbi Miller and his wife, Jennifer Siegal-Miller, live in Naples with their three sons.

Rabbi Joel Mosbacher serves as the senior rabbi of Temple Shaaray Tefila in Manhattan, New York. He is the national co-chair of the Metro Industrial Areas Foundation's "Do Not Stand Idly By" campaign, which seeks to use the gun purchasing power of public officials and the leverage of major institutional investors to press gun manufacturers to play their part in reducing gun violence. Rabbi Mosbacher is the lucky husband of Elyssa and the proud father of Ari and Lev.

Rabbi Michael Namath is the director of Leadership Development at the Religious Action Center of Reform Judaism in Washington, DC. He received his rabbinic ordination from Hebrew Union College–Jewish Institute of Religion. Rabbi Namath regularly serves on the faculty of URJ Camp Harlam in Kunkletown, Pennsylvania, and as a member of the board of directors of Planned Parenthood of Metropolitan Washington. He was a member of the Faith and Reproductive Justice Leadership Institute at the Center for American Progress as well as a Beyond the Call: Entrepreneurial Ministry Fellow.

Rabbi Aaron D. Panken, PhD, *z"l,* was the twelfth president of Hebrew Union College–Jewish Institute of Religion (2014–18). Ordained by HUC-JIR in New York in 1991, Rabbi Panken served as a member of the faculty teaching Rabbinic and Second Temple literature since 1995, as dean of students (1996–98), as dean of the New York campus (1998–2007), and as vice president for Strategic Initiatives (2007–10). An alumnus of the Wexner Graduate Fellowship, Dr. Panken earned his doctorate in Hebrew and Judaic studies at New York University. His publications include *The Rhetoric of Innovation,* as well as articles in leading academic journals and scholarly volumes. He served on faculty for the Wexner Foundation, on the Editorial Board of *Reform Judaism* magazine, on the Rabbinical Placement Commission, on the Birthright Education Committee, on the CCAR Ethics Committee, and in a variety of other leadership roles within the Reform Movement and greater Jewish community. Prior to teaching at HUC-JIR, he served as a congregational rabbi at Congregation Rodeph Sholom in New York City and as a rabbinical intern at Westchester Reform Temple in Scarsdale, New York. A native of New York City who graduated from Johns Hopkins University's Electrical Engineering Program, Rabbi Panken was also a certificated commercial pilot and sailor.

Rabbi Karen R. Perolman has been serving Congregation B'nai Jeshurun in Short Hills, New Jersey, since 2008, as a rabbinic intern, assistant rabbi, and now associate rabbi. She was ordained by Hebrew Union College–Jewish Institute of Religion in New York in 2010, where she also received her master's degree in Hebrew literature. She credits her involvement with NFTY, URJ Camp Harlam, and the Maryland Hillel community for her desire to pursue the rabbinate, including a pivotal summer traveling with the NFTY in Israel program. Rabbi Perolman is a voracious reader, which fuels her passion to understand the intersections between food, politics, Judaism, feminism, and social justice. She is on all things social: @rabbikrp.

Rabbi S. David Sperling, PhD, is the Julian Morgenstern Professor of Bible at the New York school of Hebrew Union College–Jewish Institute of Religion.

Rabbi Joshua M. Z. Stanton is spiritual leader of East End Temple in Manhattan and a senior fellow at CLAL—The National Jewish Center for Learning and Leadership. He serves on the Board of Governors of the International Jewish Committee for Interreligious Consultations, which liaises on behalf of Jewish communities worldwide with the Vatican and other international religious bodies. Rabbi Stanton was in the 2015–16 cohort of Germanacos Fellows and part of the inaugural group of Sinai and Synapses Fellows from 2013 to 2015. He is a founding editor emeritus of the *Journal of Interreligious Studies*, a publication that has enabled interreligious studies to grow into an academic field of its own.

Rabbi Rebekah P. Stern has served as the associate rabbi at Congregation Beth El in Berkeley, California, where she also grew up, since 2014. She was ordained by Hebrew Union College–Jewish Institute of Religion in 2011. Her "first awakening" to issues of race and to her own privilege came in high school, learning from an extraordinary teacher, Lisa Arrastia. Today she strives to be an ally as she continues to learn from many teachers about her privilege and place in the world as an Ashkenazi Jew, a married straight person, a woman, a rabbi, and a mother of two young children.

Rabbi Rachel Timoner is the senior rabbi of Congregation Beth Elohim in Brooklyn, New York, where she facilitates vibrant Jewish life at the meeting place between spiritual practice, learning, and social justice. Her community has become an active center for resistance and a hub for community organizing for democracy, human rights, and human dignity.

Rabbi Eric H. Yoffie served as President of the Union for Reform Judaism from 1996 to 2012. He lectures and writes on Israel and the Middle East, Reform Judaism, and American religious life, and contributes a regular opinion column to the Israeli daily *Haaretz*. His writings may be found at ericyoffie.com.

Rabbi Mary L. Zamore was ordained by Hebrew Union College–Jewish Institute of Religion (New York, 1997) and is the executive director of the Women's Rabbinic Network. As part of her work supporting and advocating for Reform women rabbis, she is co-leading the Reform Pay Equity Initiative, to narrow the wage gap for all female employees of the Reform Movement. She is also the editor of *The Sacred Table: Creating a Jewish Food Ethic* (CCAR Press, 2011), designated a finalist by the National Jewish Book Awards. She is currently editing her second anthology (CCAR Press) on the topic of Jewish ethics and money.